COMPARATIVE
PUBLIC MANAGEMENT

COMPARATIVE PUBLIC MANAGEMENT

Putting U.S. Public Policy and Implementation in Context

Edited by
Randall Baker

Foreword by Alfred M. Zuck

 PRAEGER

Westport, Connecticut
London

Library of Congress Cataloging-in-Publication Data

Comparative public management : putting U.S. public policy and
    implementation in context / edited by Randall Baker ; foreword by Alfred M. Zuck.
        p. cm.
    Includes bibliographical references and index.
        ISBN 0-275-94347-X (alk. paper).—ISBN 0-275-94348-8 (pbk. : alk. paper)
        1. Public administration.   2. Comparative government.   I. Baker,
    Randall.
    JF1351.C587   1994
    353—dc20   93-43438

British Library Cataloguing in Publication Data is available.

Library of Congress Catalog Card Number: 93-43438
ISBN: 0-275-94347-X
        0-275-94348-8 (pbk.)

First published in 1994

Praeger Publishers, 88 Post Road West, Westport, CT 06881
An imprint of Greenwood Publishing Group, Inc.

Printed in the United States of America

The paper used in this book complies with the
Permanent Paper Standard issued by the National
Information Standards Organization (Z39.48-1984).

10 9 8 7 6 5 4 3 2 1

This book is dedicated to
William J. Siffin
1922–1993
Wit, Mentor, and Seminal Figure
in Comparative Affairs

Contents

Foreword

The context and content of American public administration is undergoing a fundamental change. Technology and economies are transcending the historical boundaries of the nation states, thereby creating global economies and information societies. In the political context, a search for new institutions of governance has begun as the old structures disintegrate, in areas such as Eastern and Central Europe, the former Soviet Union, and South Africa. In the United States the search for more effective government has attracted efforts to "reinvent" government, and the private sector is initiating business process re-engineering. In the administrative context, the bureaucratic paradigm is being challenged by new theories of organization and human interaction, while the focus is being placed on program outcomes rather than administrative processes. In the policy context, there is a new recognition that policy issues are amazingly similar among countries, and there is substantial benefit in considering other countries' experiences before designing policy options for the United States.

All of these changes point to a need to reintroduce a newly defined comparative public administration to the field, and particularly to the public managers and executives for whom an understanding of the international context enhances performance and mission accomplishment. Since the 1950s, comparative public administration declined as descriptive model comparisons lost their relevance. The objective of *Comparative Public Management: Putting U.S. Public Policy and Implementation in Context* is to enhance the capacity of American students to understand the international context in which they operate and to act based upon the knowledge gained from comparative study. The international context and dimension is every bit as much a part of the public administration environmental scan (or, to use John Gaus' phrase, "the ecology of administration") as the domestic political, social, and economic environment. Moreover, as we search for solutions to particular policy issues or management challenges, the experiences of other countries can be of great assistance, since they provide not only a better understanding of our own environmental context but also examples of possible policy options for us to explore as we fashion our own solutions.

The public administration community in the United States has been slow to recognize the extent to which the international perspective is an important ingredient in the life of the American public administrator. Unlike business administration, public administration, in general, has not introduced the international dimension to the public policy and public management curriculum. *Comparative Public Management: Putting U.S. Public Policy and Implementation in Context* provides a useful and timely resource in filling this void. Its major purpose is not to introduce comparative study as a field or concentration but to explore the international context and dimension in all elements of the public policy and public administration curriculum. In so doing, it will enhance the capacity of the U.S. public administrator to perform more effectively for the American public in an interdependent world community.

Alfred M. Zuck
Executive Director
National Association of Schools of Public Affairs and Administration

Preface

This book was produced in response to fast-changing times, but more slowly changing curricula. It is our hope that we have provided a useful vehicle for the introduction of a comparative perspective into the teaching of public policy, public affairs, and public administration.

During the course of the book's preparation, on June 18, 1993, one of its principal contributors died suddenly. William "Bill" Siffin was not an expert, but a scholar, with a scholar's true love of knowledge and compassion for humanity. Eloquent, witty, amusing, and brilliant, in the truest sparkling sense of that word, Bill Siffin was a central figure in the comparative movement. Like his good friend Fred Riggs, Bill Siffin came increasingly to appreciate the relevance of such study to interpreting American public policy and administration—rather than just "making us better informed about faraway places." First and last he was a distinguished scholar of the American policy and administration field. Sadly, he lived to see official interest in his perspective diminish before the unscholarly advance of parochialism. Partly that was due to the overemphasis given to "developing" countries by the comparative movement to which many in the profession in the United States could not relate. This was a time of great sadness to Bill because he saw the baby and the bathwater flying out of the window simultaneously. If this book achieves nothing else, it is hoped that it will restore serious interest in the comparative approach, the crossing of geographical and intellectual boundaries, and the restoration of scholarship in ascendancy over narrow expertise.

On the computer disk Bill Siffin left, as part of his uncompleted chapter for this book, the following conclusion was found. It may well be the last thing he wrote in a long and creative career:

The study of moral philosophy often becomes an end in itself, rather than a source of solutions to particular problems. Even "middle range" ethical theory, which aims to describe, explain, or perhaps prescribe proper human arrangements in the real world, is often confounded by the diverse and elusive qualities of empirical reality. Yet empirical reality constantly confronts us with ethical questions. . . . They present us with our most profound issues, for the manner in which we deal with ethics determines how we answer the question of meaning, which is what life is all about.

Bill's wife Cathy captured the essence of his spirit when, after reading this final paragraph, she wrote, "Isn't it moving to think of searching unto the very end of life for its meaning? As one of my friends wrote to me, Bill is probably having a wonderful time probing the mind of God."

Acknowledgments

I would like to give my sincere thanks to my assistant Maggie Pearson for doing sterling work on reconciling everyone's computer quirks and for making corrections on disk; to Cynthia Mahigian Moorhead for skillful typesetting of the manuscript; and to my wife Susan for attempting to impose order on intellectual chaos.

Randall Baker
Bloomington, December 1993

COMPARATIVE
PUBLIC MANAGEMENT

1

Comparative Public Management: Coming in From the Cold

Randall Baker

As the examples drawn from our own comparative studies of bureaucrats and politicians in Western countries democracies demonstrate, the U.S. administrative system is best understood in a comparative context. . . . We not only understand our own systems better when we compare, we gain a better understanding of the methods, concepts, and theories we employ. . . . The muddle of comparative administration may well be a hell, but one whose suggested motto is "abandon hope all ye who do not enter here!" (Aberbach and Rockman 1988)

WHY THIS BOOK?

If only to appease the spirits of those departed trees sacrificed to produce a given book or article, authors and editors should be duty-bound to justify their addition to *Books in Print*. The origins of this volume begin with attempts by a small group of persons in the National Association of Schools of Public Affairs and Administration (NASPAA), the professional accrediting body for public administration programs, to bring the winds of international change into the curricula of the 230-plus member institutions. That was, sad to say, a depressing experience since the indifference of so many organizations to the geographical realities of the late-twentieth century context of public life was, as the late Bill Siffin would have said, almost palpable. Indeed, the international group quietly died from this lack of generalized support, though NASPAA itself was always strongly supportive.

The reality is that it is not only President Clinton who has an agenda for change—the world itself seems to be working with that agenda, and its impact on U.S. public life is both comprehensive and accelerating dramatically. Public administration as a subject has long had a parochial cast, but even the most avowed parochialist must be aware of some fairly radical forces at work in the local parish. In Indiana, the economic mainstays and the revenue generators for public programs include automobiles and automobile accessories, agriculture, steel, and pharmaceuticals. Not one of these operates in a state, or even a U.S., context. The talk is about European agricultural subsidies, Japanese penetration of the auto market, the impending employment nemesis accompanying the North American Free Trade Agreement NAFTA that includes Mexico, the dumping of East European steel on the American market, wholesale illegal copying of patented drugs, and so on. At the same time, even mid-sized communities are actively trying to promote foreign investment—some say by giving away the store through intrastate and interstate competition.

It has long been recognized by political scientists and pundits, from Washington's farewell address onward, that foreign affairs feature last in the public ranking of the top ten policy issues of the day. President Clinton, indeed, asserted that he would return the country to a domestic agenda and won many votes on that score. The political history of the United States is one of exceptionalism, a deep suspicion of international entanglements and organizations (unless there was a veto possibility involved), periodic retreats into isolation, and an increasingly pervasive ignorance of geography.

The Orthodox Approach to Teaching Public Administration

A glance at almost any major text book in the field of public administration reveals a conspicuous absence of the word "American" (or, more strictly, the words "United States"). The connotation is that the contents are somehow *generic*, perhaps perpetuating the ideas of Woodrow Wilson. Quite possibly this is not the intention. The authors are, after all, writing for the U.S. market, and this assumption is understood. On the other hand, after the last world war there was quite an industry exporting public management to developing countries as though it really was a generic commodity (Baker 1991).

Of course, U.S. public administration and public management are *distinctly* a product of the culture and history of this country and no other. Furthermore, the U.S. system is dramatically different from almost all others in developed democracies. Rowat (1990) has shown this difference admirably relative to the overall size of the bureaucracy in terms of the working population (18 percent in the United States, 33 percent in France, and 38 percent in Sweden), the differences in the size and importance of different levels of government, the degree of decentralization (70 percent local and regional in the United States, 13 percent in Italy), relative growth in the size of the public service (1.3 percent in the United States versus 23 percent in Sweden 1951–1981), the relative importance of public corporations (50 percent of public employment in the United Kingdom, and 8 percent in the United States), and the nature and composition of the upper echelons. These differences in themselves are interesting and should be an explicit part of the consideration of U.S. public administration. Some writers have, however, pointed to this gulf between the

U.S. public administration system and those in other developed democracies as a reason for the lack of interest in comparative study:

I continue to think that the underlying reason for this decline [of comparative public administration since the 1950s and 1960s] has been our own ethnocentrism in continuing to view American public administration, and the truly exceptional solutions we have found for coping with our peculiarly presidentialist problems, as a general paradigm for the field as a whole. (Riggs 1991, 475)

Comparative study has never achieved center-stage status in the profession. In contrast to the requirements of the business schools' professional organization, there is no professional *requirement* to feature anything comparative, or international for that matter, in the core teaching of a professional master's degree. Where this material has been offered at all, it has usually been within the context of a concentration, optional courses, or some sort of minor. Its status is somewhat akin to that of the environmental dimension in engineering degree programs some years ago, until that profession finally woke up to the fact that the public would not tolerate constructions that polluted and the fact that there was money in clean technology.

Apart from its peripheral, specialist status, comparative study is also generally acknowledged, as Riggs observed above, to have been in decline for some time, which is unfortunate now that the international and global pressures of the environment, trade blocs, terrorism, AIDS, tourism, finance, communications, and almost every other aspect of life have changed so dramatically. Later in this book, two of the contributors, Ventriss and Ryan, show conclusively how international the agenda has become, even at the state level, and some of the wrong-headed things we are doing to react to this.

Herein lies the purpose, and we hope the value, of this book. We should not be reacting, we should be anticipating, and we need to understand that the people graduating from public administration education programs are going to have their greatest impact, perhaps, ten years from now. This means that we should be equipping them for that world, not this year's or last. In other words the comparative component, and an exposure to an international agenda, are something that *every* public official emerging from a public administration program should have—not some favored few headed for the State Department or the Peace Corps. One of the missions of this book is to make it undeniably clear just how far into the global context we have moved, even if our curricula still owe allegiance to Harry Truman and Ike.

A New and Revitalized Approach

The approach to comparative study should now be an *integrative* one. Ferrel Heady (1984, 48) has written, "It is neither necessary nor feasible to strive for restoration of the degree of autonomy and separatism once characteristic of the burgeoning comparative public administration movement." Looking at the earlier attempts to broaden the scope of our teaching, van Wart and Cayer (1990, 238) observed that "the major criticisms were that the field was too involved in the quest for a comprehensive paradigm or metatheory, that it was not empirical enough, and that it was too self-absorbed in academic concerns and insufficiently relevant."

The same pair of authors, reviewing the evidence presented in the leading journals for a recent change of attitude and approach toward the comparative context, observed the following characteristics:

[They] include a significant practitioner component, a substantial orientation toward policy recommendations, a relative paucity of theory-testing studies, wide and mature coverage of a range of studies, and methodological studies that seem slightly better than in the past, but still far from ideal. The field as a whole, however, lacks features that give it clear identity (e.g., state-of-the-art critiques, methodological pieces, and broader, middle-range theorizing), and thus the overall status of comparative public administration remains ambiguous. (Ibid. 238)

Another issue that lurks beneath the surface, closely related to the startling pedagogical indifference to comparative and international material in the approved core of degree programs, is the issue of tenure and promotion. A study conducted by professor Larry Schroeder of the Maxwell School for NASPAA's now dormant international activities section indicated clearly that younger faculty perceived, rightly or wrongly, serious dangers in "fooling" with comparative fields before their tenure was affirmed. Many thought that this was some sort of luxury reserved for older, more secure faculty members. The general impression was that since this material received no official recognition in accreditation or core course construction, then it must be peripheral. In many cases they may well be wise to so believe. It is not so long ago that a faculty member at Indiana University's School of Public and Environmental Affairs—one of the most international schools in the country—was advised not to "mess around" with this international study until the serious matter of tenure was completed. The peripheral role is still the one that seems to prevail in most institutions, forcing younger faculty to fit into the mold of the orthodoxy. Heady stated the matter this way: " . . . parochialism is a persistent dominant feature of American public administration, evidenced in the curricula of institutions of higher education and in the conduct of public administration by practicing professionals" (Heady 1987, 480).

THE APPROACH OF THIS BOOK

One of the principal concerns voiced at discussions about "internationalizing" the curriculum for public administration at NASPAA was that there was "no one to teach this," especially in the smaller departments, and that there were "no useful books." The intention behind this book is that *everyone* can and should teach comparative material. It is neither exotic, nor is it peripheral. As Bekke and others stated, "Comparative analysis is integral to theory development and testing. It is necessary for identification of key concepts, relations among concepts, and the underlying logic or dynamic of the associations" (Bekke et al. 1991, 28).

This book is intended as a vehicle that will allow all teachers to integrate some comparative material into most of the major fields of public administration, or at least understand why and how they should. The main purpose is to equip all public servants with a new perspective on their own country—not to make them authorities on Sweden, Singapore, or some other place. For many years the business literature ran article after article trying to discover the "secret" of the Japanese miracle, much as they had done with the German miracle years earlier. The most accurate conclusion from all this is that the secret of the Japanese miracle may be that they are Japanese, and facile attempts at copying deny the reality of a U.S. cultural context. We should, instead, be clear about what we do well, value, and feel we should preserve. One of the best ways of understanding this is to examine how others approach the same problem, not that we may copy it, but that by making comparisons, all sorts of *implicit* and *underpinning* cultural assumptions come out of the shadows. This is as it should be. The secret of the American miracle may be revealed when we finally realize that we are Americans, and ask what we do well and why that works *here*. The main value of comparative study is *to understand ourselves*. Riggs makes this point clearly in his chapter in this book, and presents this as a radical revision in the thinking behind comparative study. It is also a profound reason why comparative study should now be integral to all elements of the syllabus, finance, management, policy, whatever.

What Comparative Study is Not

It is not
- the search for universal truths, generic culture-neutral models.
- a vehicle to help us to copy.
- descriptive; instead it is analytical. Articles about other places do not necessarily qualify as comparative. We look instead for the analytical underpinnings of comparison, and the utility of transferring policy and practice across cultures.
- a country "a"- and country "b"-type study that simply describes approaches and practices from place to place apropos of nothing in particular.

The Structure and Purpose of the Book

The underlying purpose of this book is to provide, in one volume, the following elements:
- the international context of public service in the United States.
- an overview of the comparative approach.
- comparative studies of different components of public administration as taught in programs in the United States—in effect: comparative "modules."

The International Context. In this section two authors demonstrate, in concrete terms, the pervasive significance of the international context in all areas of public administration. In one study, Ventriss uses the medium of international trade to illustrate the profound degree to which this has a decisive impact on both national and subnational levels, demonstrating a need for awareness at all levels. Ryan explores the practical importance of a comparative agenda in the training of future public servants by looking at the realities of what practitioners do—which is frequently distinctly international. Riggs, emphasizing his belief that comparative study is a major tool for understanding the American system, presents a study of why the bureaucracy has not assumed the smothering political role it has in other presidential systems and highlights the unique historical and cultural qualities of this country's bureaucratic institutions and traditions. A concluding article by Baker illustrates the malaise of public service in a developed state that has, until recently, been denied democratic rights. This study is used to illustrate the crucial role of democratic principles embodied, but possibly well hidden, in the operation of our national bureaucracy.

The Comparative Approach. The strengths and pitfalls of the comparative method over time are explored in this section by two authors approaching the subject from a different perspective. Though this book is not devoted to theories of government, it is necessary to present the state-of-the-art on the methods and utility of the comparative approach. Making comparisons is fraught with problems of definition, overlapping terminology, different roles for the state in a democracy, and so forth. All too often the conceptual framework for comparative study has been woolly or indefinable. Peters provides an exhaustive insight into the comparative tradition and provides useful guidelines for the application of this dimension. He examines many of the worrisome questions about how far we are looking at "universal" management principles and practices, and how far at culture-specific aspects such as the role of the state, acceptable levels of taxation, the role of the family, etc. Carrying these ideas forward, McGregor outlines a research agenda to give comparative study of the public service more relevance and methodological integrity in the future.

The Component Elements. In this final section authorities from different recognized fields of public administration provide an examination of the comparative element in each field. Each study provides a module that may be used to broaden the dimensions of the course material taught within any conventional MPA or related public administration degree in this country. We hope this takes care of the questions, "Who teaches this?" and "Where are the books?"

Insinuating the comparative approach into the broad spectrum of the public administration curriculum is but one element. Institutions may also pursue exchange programs, the utilization of visiting overseas professionals and academics (to talk about the United States and not just their home country), creative use of international students, and other avenues. But until full recognition of the value of comparative study shows up in the baseline requirements for the professional degree, and as a fully recognized *legitimate* area of study for tenure purposes, I fear we are dealing with little more than lip service.

This book was deliberately called *Comparative Public Management* to stress its applied and practical nature. *Management* is also a word that carries with it connotations of dynamism and the need to anticipate and respond to change. Ours is a world in which change is the order of the day, and sometimes it appears that the pace of change is itself moving along an exponential curve. On the other hand, the use of the term *management* must not be taken to imply any crude idea that government is a business—for it is not.

The authors of this book are concerned with the way in which problems are tackled, rights defended, society advanced, and the earth protected around the globe. Consider, for instance, what is happening in the health field. In Britain the "nanny state" is finding itself financially unable to bear the burden of supporting a universal health system. In the United States the concern is about the state's inaction since more than 30 million people, supposedly, are without health insurance. Are these two nations facing different crises, or are they converging toward some practical "middle ground" of state involvement in health-care delivery? Most developed democracies are facing tax revolts and are coping with AIDS, privatization, footloose capital, aging populations, and many other common phenomena. All too often these are perceived as national issues amenable only to national solutions.

Deliberately we have held our frame of reference to the developed democracies, for once we move outside it, many other variables start to assume critical importance, and these modules will be much harder to teach. For many students the move to a radically different (*"National Geographic* class," as one student put it) cultural context may result in all comparisons being rendered inoperative because there is no way for the student to relate to the society involved—at least without deeper instruction than the typical Master of Public Administration program could provide. Again, this should not be taken as saying that developing democracies require fundamentally different principles, concepts, and methods. It is just that the preoccupation of the earlier comparative movement with *development* left many in the teaching profession out of the picture. At one astonishing annual meeting of the American Society of Public Administration held in Miami not too long ago, there was a two-day development jamboree held before the conference. On the other hand there was almost *nothing* to reflect the multiethnic workforce, or the culture of public administration in the subsequent main program, even though the whole event was in *Miami!* In the face of such cultural insensitivity, what hope has comparative awareness?

Our focus, as we have stated, is to put the United States center stage, for it is there that the vast majority of the students will inevitably work. Incidentally the predominance of the U.S. job market was often used in the past as a reason for not "messing" with the international dimension. While we are so wrapped up right now in the need to "reinvent government," it is sad to note that the principal work on this subject, and most of the political rhetoric since, continues to be stalwartly parochial.

We seem to be on the eve of a true millennium—a world in which new territorial polities emerge for which there is no precedent, such as the European Community. It is also a world in which global phenomena, such as ozone depletion or the possibility of global warming, produce consequences that are *global*. This stretches our comfortable concepts of national sovereignty to the limits, and perhaps beyond. Future public administrators may live not only in an increasingly international and global context, but in a world in which shared sovereignty becomes a reality in some fields.

The comparative element is a *context*. Rather than thinking of it as a field, or subfield, it should be thought of as an essential dimension of all parts of the basic curriculum. It is true that some of the larger schools and programs may also support a specialized concentration, but that should be in addition to the first line of attack. In fact anything that creates the illusion that comparative and international study is "different" can be misleading because it goes against the contextual approach. In 1947 Dahl stated, "As long as public administration is not comparative, claims for a science of public administration sound rather hollow." Nothing has changed the relevance of this remark in the intervening 45 or so years.

REFERENCES

Aberbach, J. D., and B. A. Rockman. 1988. "Problems of Cross-National Comparison." In *Public Administration in Developed Democracies: A Comparative Study*, ed. D. C. Rowat. New York: Marcel Dekker, 419–440.

Baker, R. 1991. "The Role of the State and the Bureaucracy in Developing Countries Since the War." In *Handbook of Comparative and Development Administration*, ed. A. Farazmand. New York: Marcel Dekker, 353–367.

Bekke, H., J. L. Perry, and Th. A. J. Toonen. 1991. *The Need for Comparative Research on Civil Service Systems*. Conference on comparative civil service systems, Leiden/ Rotterdam, October (unpublished).

Dahl, R. A. 1947. "The Science of Public Administration." *Public Administration Review* 7:1–11.

Heady, F. 1984. *Public Administration: A Comparative Perspective*. New York: Marcel Dekker.

_____. 1987. "Comparative Public Administration in the United States." In *A Centennial History of the American Administrative State*, ed. R. Candler. New York: Free Press.

Riggs, F. W. 1991. "Public Administration: A Comparativist Framework." *Public Administration Review* 51(6).

Rowat, D. C. 1990. "Comparing Bureaucracies in Developed and Developing Countries: A Statistical Analysis." *International Review of Administrative Sciences* 56:211–236.

van Wart, M., and N. J. Cayer. 1990. "Public Administration: Defunct, Dispersed, or Redefined?" *Public Administration Review* 50.

2

The Impact of International Trade and Direct Foreign Investment on the National and Subnational Levels: An Overview

Curtis Ventriss

Bayless Manning (1977), writing in *Foreign Affairs*, introduced a new term which immediately attracted the attention of many scholars. Manning's new term was "intermestic politics" to indicate a new (and growing) political and economic relationship that would have far reaching implications: the dynamic interrelationships between domestic economies and international economic factors. In the next breath, he went on to argue that the salient issue of international economic relationships are concomitantly "inter-local," meaning that international economic factors can have a direct impact on particular trade flows in certain geographical areas, and conversely, can have an impact on a variety of groups. Not surprisingly, intermestic politics has become especially important to governors and mayors who find their economies vulnerable to changes in the global economy.

This new involvement in international affairs by governors and mayors alike has been aptly called by Ivo Duchacek (1984), a part of "global microdiplomacy" which, among other things, refers to state and local public officials going overseas to promote subnational interests and appearing at trade and investment shows. Yet, it was Governor Luther H. Hodges of North Carolina who is often (and correctly) credited with providing the first impetus for gubernatorial involvement in international affairs when he traveled to Europe in 1959 to generate foreign investment for his state. By 1990, nearly all the states had conducted export seminars for small and medium-size businesses; 35 states have overseas offices in 17 countries; and all 50 states had sister-state relationships with governments around the world. John Kline (1987, 9), in his summary of state involvement in international economic affairs, put it this way:

Looking backward, the growth of state activities in international trade has been impressive. In slightly more than a decade, and particularly since the beginnings of 1980s, state governments have recognized and defined an increasingly important role in promoting beneficial international trade. As interests and activities in this area expand further, state officials will face new responsibilities in terms of national policy formulation and coordination.

It is important to note that it was local governments, not state governments, that first recognized the critical importance of forging international contacts. For example, in 1956 President Eisenhower started the U.S. Sister Cities program that promoted exchanges between American cities and foreign cities. "Presently, 750 American cities have trade developments with over 1,200 cities in 86 countries" (Luke, Ventriss, and Reed 1988, 113). In fact, many major metropolitan cities like Seattle, Los Angeles, San Francisco, Dallas, Atlanta, New York, and Des Moines have major trade centers and are so active in international affairs that they employ protocol officers and international affairs specialists.

In sum, state and local officials have been drawn into the international arena as a result of changing economic realities. For instance, in a U.S. economy where one out of eight jobs in manufacturing are now linked to exports, one out of three acres of farm land is for export production, and about one-third of U.S. corporate profits comes from international business activities, it is not surprising that states and localities are attempting to respond appropriately to the internationalization of their economies (Kline 1984).

As way of summary, Robert Ebel and Laurence Marks (1990, 6) have outlined the following changes as key factors of the nation's economic profile:

- In terms of GNP per capita, the United States led the world's economies throughout the 1960s and the early 1970s. Since 1973, however, the United States has fallen from first to ninth place.
- Each year since 1982, the United States has run a current account deficit—basically, the difference between exports and imports plus payments, such as interest and dividends.
- Beginning in 1985, the United States shifted from net foreign creditor, a status that was typical of the United States since about 1920, to net foreign debtor.
- The national savings has declined by nearly one-third since 1981, generating the need for a net capital inflow from foreigners well in excess of $100 billion a year for each year since 1984.
- Between 1981 and 1987, the productivity of American businesses has grown only 1.5 percent a year. Although this is an improvement over the 1973-1981 period, it represents a rate well below that of the rest of the post-World War II period.

Given these economic trends, state and local governments nationwide are enacting new economic development approaches to bolster state exports and attract foreign investment or tourism. Put bluntly, state and local communities have learned that they cannot wait for the federal government to help them with their economic conditions. By and large, their attempt to deal with changing economic realities now rest in their own political hands. Alice Rivlin (1990, 15–16) has spoken to this very point: "The federal government probably would not be very good at industrial policy, but there has been quite a lot of success with state and local industrial policy. Local [and state] governments working with local industry to improve conditions for competitiveness of that industry or that area seems appropriate."

This chapter will outline the various strategies and involvements of state and local officials who have tried to stimulate trade linkages and direct foreign investment. There will also be a discussion of whether states and localities need to develop a strategic approach that "fits" the unique and differing needs of their economies.

STATE AND LOCAL INVOLVEMENT IN INTERNATIONAL TRADE AND DIRECT FOREIGN INVESTMENT

It is not difficult to understand the saliency of international trade to a state, or country, and its relationship to economic growth, when it is estimated that exports account for about 20 percent to 50 percent of the GNP of most industrialized countries (McIntyre 1983). Or, more importantly, that about 70 percent of American industries are now exposed to foreign competition. The litany of vexing trade issues, and how they are wreaking havoc on certain parts of the economy have become increasingly commonplace. For example, the U.S. Commerce Department has calculated that for every $1 billion increase in the trade deficit, this translates into a loss of about 25,000 U.S. jobs. While figures vary depending on how one reads (and interprets) the data, an estimated 4 million jobs had been lost by 1990 due to the trade deficit. On the other hand, as many state and local economic development experts quickly point out, $40,000 dollars in exports creates one new job. One researcher has calculated that three-quarters of the total growth of the real GNP from 1978 to 1982 can be attributed to the improvement of the U.S. net export position (Ventriss 1986). For purposes of analysis, let us first discuss the role of the state in trade promotion.

State activities in trade promotion, to a large degree, have been directed at existing firms within the state, particularly small and medium-sized businesses. Yet, state governments are confronting a serious dilemma: small and medium-sized businesses have not been as successful in exporting their products. It is estimated, for example, that 250 to 300 firms account for 85 percent of all U.S. exports (Sylvester 1988). In dealing with this reality, Kathleen Sylvester (1988, 38) has outlined the following trend being pursued by most state (and local) governments: "To overcome the traditionally passive attitudes of U.S. businesses and lure them into the international arena, cities, counties and states are offering . . . a smorgasbord with a lot of little hors d'oeuvres. The staple of most of these smorgasbords is plain old-fashioned hand-holding, meaning that trade experts counsel businesses willing to try exporting. These experts help businesses find markets for their products, assess potential clients, market their products, negotiate contracts, obtain financing, ship the products, and collect payments."

As of 1991, 15 states have passed export promotion financing legislation, with several other states in the process of passing similar legislation some time soon. According to the National Association of State Development Agencies (NASDA) data for 1990, 42 states are members of a multi-state trade group; 17 states have how-to-export guidebooks; all 50 states have some kind of in-house counseling for export promotion; 45 states have trade lead programs; 30 states have state matchmaker programs to ensure that products are going to the appropriate overseas market; 42 states have trade development training programs; and finally, all 50 states have conducted trade shows and missions (NASDA 1990).

This wide range of international activity, primarily by state governments, can be classified into three broad categories: technical support, export finance, and information brokering (Clarke 1986). By far, most states have been the most aggressive in information brokering. This role pertains, by and large, to states holding seminars or conferences or the distribution of an export handbook or newsletters to foster more state exports. Recently, some states have developed an extensive comprehensive database that links firms with specific export opportunities. While 15 states have such programs, often these programs offer potential exporters with nothing more than a general product description used by the federal government. California's computerized system has been regarded as the most extensive inasmuch as California uses a tariff code classification that can both identify products and then match these products overseas. In general, information brokering by states involves two basic approaches: (1) providing export information as related to a specific company that hopes to export products, and (2) providing critical information that can alert certain firms to the realities of international trade (Luke, Ventriss, and Reed 1988).

Export financing programs are designed primarily to assist small and medium-sized businesses. The majority of states, in dealing with export financing, have implemented loan guarantees, and only occasionally, direct loans. Moreover, many states now offer export credit insurance usually in conjunction with the Foreign Credit Insurance Association, an association which works with the U.S. Export-Import Bank. Clearly, it is the Minnesota Export Finance Authority which has become the model for other states to emulate. The Minnesota Export Finance Authority was created in 1984 to provide both pre- and post-export loan guarantees to help firms get the financing necessary to export. In general, "Pre-shipment guarantees provide money to pay for labor, material and other expenses leading to an export sale. A post-export loan guarantee helps an exporter provide more flexible terms for a foreign buyer so that payments can be extended. The loans are guaranteed by a fund that is permitted to use up to four times its capital of $1.2 million for back-up conventional lenders" (Sylvester 1988, 38). Also noteworthy in this regard is California which has two export finance offices that make loan guarantees as well as provide counseling and coordination between federal and private financing. Considering the states that have already passed export financing programs, we find such programs usually involve the following approaches:

- providing guarantees to banks for working capital loans made to firms before an export shipment is made;
- providing postshipment guarantees to banks for short- and medium-term loans to foreign buyers;
- helping arrange insurance for the banks from federal or private sources against the risk of default by a foreign buyer (the state usually purchases reinsurance to protect itself from loss);
- acting as a delivery mechanism for some programs of the U.S. Export-Import Bank; and
- advising businesses and banks of federal and state export finance programs. (Pilcher 1985, 14)

The final category of state involvement in export promotion deals with the important function of what can loosely be considered technical support. This is, of course, a broad category that encompasses such roles as giving state exporters assistance with complex licensing procedures and providing critical documentation detailing such things as potential market demand, economic data dealing with particular markets abroad, financing issues, and political factors of other countries that can have an impact on the success of a specific product overseas. Coupled with this technical assistance from the state, universities have also played a salient role in offering potential exporters technical help as it relates to international business, foreign languages, and international law. Two noteworthy examples include Oregon's Portland State University Institute on International Trade and Commerce which helps small businesses prepare for export opportunities and Washington State University's trade center that is specifically designed to assist state exporters dealing with forest products (Pilcher 1985). In all, state assistance incorporates the following programs: "(1) identification of products sought; (2) specific information on manufacturer's products; and (3) personal contacts with individuals interested in, or becoming involved in, international business" (Ventriss 1991, 14).

Even given these activities, according to James Crupi (1988, 59), America's small businesses lack what he refers to as an "international mind-set." This results from the fact that:

- The strength and diversity of our economy has protected our business community from the realities of foreign competition and interdependence, thereby stimulating apathy to export investment and language development.
- Small businessmen who dominate Midwestern and Southern regions particularly have had little international exposure and have not had to pursue actively any specific objectives regarding world conditions.

- College business curriculums have not emphasized international trade and therefore have seldom been adequate in concept, scope, or technique.

No discussion of state involvement in international economic affairs, however, would be complete without an analysis of how states are encouraging foreign direct investment (FDI) as an economic development strategy to bolster job creation. In part, this emphasis on FDI by states can be seen in the proliferation of overseas offices and representatives abroad. In 1990, the total number of state offices and representatives stood at 163 (NASDA 1990). Presently, 43 states have state offices in 26 countries, with a large percentage of such offices residing in Asia. Illinois and Minnesota each have two state offices in Japan alone. In total, seven states (Illinois, Kansas, Minnesota, New York, Indiana, Michigan, and Mississippi) have more than five state offices and representatives abroad. While it is empirically difficult to gather data on what portion of the states' international budget is divided between export promotion and attracting foreign investment concerning these overseas offices, it is often very expensive for states to maintain these offices. For example, it is estimated that it costs a little more than $1 million to have a state office in Tokyo (presently, there are 18 state offices in Tokyo, excluding a number of state representatives) (Glickman and Woodward 1989). Or put in slightly different terms, states have steadily increased their international state appropriation from $590,142 in 1984 climbing to $980,125 in 1986, and in 1988 rising slowly to $1,295,785 and in 1990 jumping to $1,998,733.

Saying this, it is not surprising that states have increased their budget appropriation to international affairs, particularly in regard to FDI. Of particular importance to states, is FDI as it relates to building manufacturing plants or what has been called in the literature, "greenfield plants." Although states and localities yearn for such greenfield plants, the overwhelming majority of FDI goes to acquisition of existing American businesses. According to Fahim-Nader's (1991) figures for 1990, nearly 90 percent of FDI involved acquisitions. The country that has been active in building greenfield plants, until very recently, was Japan. For instance, in 1986 about 220,000 Americans worked for Japanese firms in the United States. Two leading experts of FDI have calculated that by the year 2000 this trend will continue and employment will grow to over 1 million (Glickman and Woodward 1989).

Insofar as most states have attempted to attract FDI through an array of different incentives, the pertinent question is where precisely is this FDI going regionally in the United States?:

In 1989, six states accounted for 51 percent of the total foreign direct investment. In terms of number of investments, California led the others with 213 investments, followed by New York (129). The others were Texas (81), New Jersey (52), Florida (50), and Massachusetts (42). However, if foreign investment is based on dollar values, New York was ahead of the others (in 1989) with $13.9 billion. Behind New York were the states of Pennsylvania ($10.4 billion), California ($9.5 billion), Minnesota ($6.6 billion), Tennessee ($3.3 billion), Illinois ($3.1 billion), and Ohio ($2.6 billion). (Ventriss, forthcoming, 16)

Given this regional distribution, what have states specifically put together in the form of incentive packages to attract FDI into their state? These economic incentives, for the most part, have involved providing such approaches as exemptions or deferrals from property taxes; exemption of business purchases from sales tax; repeal of unitary tax; enterprise zones; foreign trade zones; exemption of state taxes (e.g., corporate income tax); offering of industrial development bonds, low-interest loans, infrastructural improvements; job training; land acquisition assistance; tax credits on investment; and research and development facilities at a local or regional university (Poniache 1986). Understandably, governors have been in the forefront in attracting FDI into their respective state economies. As reported by the National Governor's Association (NGA), the microdiplomacy that governors now commonly partake in is reflected in the number of trips they have taken overseas for the specific purpose of enticing FDI into their state—82 trips alone in 1989 (Janesch 1990). Some of these tax incentive programs, however, have been rather expensive. The Isuzu/Fuji plant, for instance, in Lafayette, Indiana, offered more that $86 million in tax incentives which included infrastructural improvements like roads, highways, and sewer improvements, a job training program, and a $1 million cultural fund account to assist Japanese families. Yet, when you compare the cost of such incentives to the estimated employment of this plant, it equates into an incentive cost per job of $50,588! This cost is similarly echoed in the Toyota plant located in Kentucky where the state offered an incentive package totaling more than $324 million (with an employment base of 3,000 to 5,000) for an incentive cost per job of $108,333 (Calautone et al. 1986). Such cost experiences have also been reported in automotive plant incentive packages in Tennessee (Saturn and Nissan plants), Illinois (Diamond-Star plant), Michigan (Mazda/Ford Motor), and Pennsylvania (Volkswagen).

Although foreign firms employ somewhere between 3 to 5 percent of the total workforce, states will most likely continue to design programs to encourage foreign business activity within their states. Some states like Delaware have developed programs to enhance their strategic advantage in attracting certain foreign firms, particularly foreign banks. In 1986, Delaware enacted the Foreign Bank Development Act that allows foreign banks to strategically position themselves to take advantage of the state's regressive bank franchise tax. This legislation was built upon the previous domestic tax incentives passed by Delaware in 1983 (the International Banking Development Act) eliminating reserve requirements for foreign banking facilities. In other words, Delaware's policymakers tried to design policies strategically linked to the state's inherent advantage compared to other states. "The pivotal question for states," as asked by two researchers of economic development, "is how much states are willing to up the 'incentive ante' in what has been aptly called the great 'War Between the States'" (Luke, Ventriss, and Reed 1988, 120).

On the other side of the coin, is the role of American cities who have been looking overseas for assistance in creating new jobs and for generating economic growth. After all, trade and investment activities directly affect local communities.

For the most part, mayors have focused their attention more on foreign investments than on export promotion. As early as 1983, in a report entitled *International Trade: A New City Economic Development Strategy*, the National League of Cities concluded that mayors can no longer afford to ignore international economic affairs. The reason, according to this report, is simple: local economies are, more than ever, interdependent in an international economy, and this reality is ignored at the city's own economic peril. The report is noteworthy because it was one of the first reports to emphasize the city's role in promoting international business development and strengthening strong ties with the private sector that operate globally.

In 1991, the International City Management Association (ICMA) conducted a survey of American cities—small and large—to monitor the marketing activities of cities in soliciting foreign businesses. Approximately, 22.2 percent of American cities were actively marketing to recruit new foreign businesses, followed closely by 21.3 percent to bolster industrial development. Surprisingly, only 5.1 percent of cities were marketing to expand or retain businesses dealing with international affairs. The ICMA study also reported that of those cities attempting to attract new foreign businesses, the overwhelming majority of such cities had populations over 250,000. If we disaggregate this data by region, the Mountain Region (33.6 percent), the East South Central (31 percent), and the West South Central (29 percent) are the most impressive in marketing policies to attract foreign businesses. Conversely, among those cities, the most active in trying to attract FDI for industrial development purposes were the East South Central Region (35.7 percent), followed closely by West South Central (31 percent), and South Atlantic (29.2 percent).

An example of how cities have become major actors in international economic affairs, especially as it relates to FDI, can be seen in the stretch between Greenville and Spartanburg, South Carolina on Interstate 85. Spartanburg's public officials, along with private sector representatives, have long pursued strategies to bring FDI into their local economy. European firms, in particular, have flocked to this region—primarily representing foreign firms from Germany, France, and Switzerland. One researcher concluded that "over sixty foreign manufacturers and service companies from over 12 countries have settled in the area, accounting for over 7,000 jobs" (Glickman and Woodward 1989, 193). While Tennessee has received the most media attention in regard to FDI, with a majority of such investment residing in cities like Memphis, Nashville, Knoxville, and Chattanooga, the metropolitan area of Charlotte/Mecklenburg in North Carolina holds the distinction of possessing the largest concentration of foreign firms in the south. These southern (and western) American cities have been successful in attracting FDI, in part, because of their market accessibility. As Nashville's Economic Development Office openly boasts, the metropolitan area of Nashville is only 500 miles away from three-quarters of America's population. Although many Japanese auto-transplant firms have settled in the Midwest, the majority of Japanese investors have tended "to congregate on the West Coast because it is easier to arrange Pacific Basin transportation and the time zone facilitates communication" (Liou 1992, 8).

On the other hand, French, British, and Swiss firms have historically invested in the Southeast, while Canadian firms tend to favor the mid-Atlantic and Midwest regions of the United States.

Whatever the reasons for certain foreign firms locating where they do—and the different theories that are proposed to understand these location decisions—American cities have responded to capture this new influx of foreign monies that can possibly lead to job creation and increase tax revenues. This is evident in how many American cities have created foreign-trade zones (zones where imported goods can be distributed under reduced U.S. tariffs). There are presently over 65 foreign trade zones that have generated over 12 billion dollars in business and created over 115,000 U.S. jobs (Luke, Ventriss, and Reed 1988). These jobs are important to local communities (and states) because generally they are high-paying jobs. In a study conducted by the Bureau of Economic Analysis of the U.S. Department of Commerce, "the average American employee of a foreign-owned manufacturing firm earned $32,887, while the average American employee of an American-owned manufacturer earned $28,945" (Reich 1991, 147). Japanese-owned firms, in fact, invest $1,000 more on training than the American-owned counterpart (Lawrence 1989).

The information discussed so far, while important in giving a description of the scope of state and local involvement in global economic affairs, does not address the salient issue of the effectiveness of these state and local policies in trying to facilitate state exports or generate foreign investment. Let us now turn our attention to this issue.

THE EFFICACY OF TAX INCENTIVES AND
STATE EXPORT PROGRAMS

Evaluating the effectiveness of international state programs and tax incentive policies is somewhat difficult to do because most of these activities have only recently been implemented. This problem is made even more complex as a result of a myriad of different international approaches found among the states (Ventriss 1991). However, there have been studies completed that can provide strong indications of the effectiveness of these new programs. For example, Cletus Coughlin and Phillip Cartwright (1987) conducted an extensive research project quantifying the relationship between state exports and employment in all the states. They concluded, using a time series model, that state government policies dealing with state export promotion directly affect state employment. A caveat to this study should be noted: Coughlin and Cartwright used aggregate data to reach their conclusion; they did not individually determine the effectiveness of particular programs such as export finance, technical support, and so forth. In other words, we cannot say with certainty that an export finance program versus a technical seminar on foreign markets (or some combination of different export program policies) is the most efficacious approach that a particular state should pursue.

On the other hand, the empirical evidence concerning tax concessions is more persuasive. For instance, in 1989, the Council of State Governments did an exhaustive literature review of the cost effectiveness of business incentives. This review found, not surprisingly, that the vast majority of empirical studies on tax incentives regarded such tax concessions as not being a critical factor in a business location decision, and, more important, these incentives have little, if any, impact on state employment growth (Wilson 1989). A similar conclusion was reached by Riad Ajami and David Ricks (1988) when they analyzed the major motives for FDI into the United States and found that business incentives ranked low as a critical factor in any location decision. Following a related theme, Barry Rubin and Kurt Zorn (1985) have argued that there are three key cost factors which are crucial to a business deciding to make a location change: labor, energy, and transportation costs. Concomitantly, other crucial variables include such issues as the size of the market, market accessibility, quality of the workforce, and education (Beaumont and Hovey 1985).

If tax incentives are not, generally speaking, cost-efficient in drawing in domestic and foreign business, why do so many states still offer them? In examining this question, Dennis Grady (1987) asserted that states offer incentives not so much as a way to bolster state employment growth (although this may account for some of the rationale), but as a policy reaction against what competing states are doing. To some degree, this policy reaction can be seen in the proliferation of overseas offices since 1979. Interestingly, there is no empirical evidence yet that verifies the relationship of overseas offices and the state's effectiveness in generating reverse investment or state exports. Ironically, Tennessee, which has a reputation for being aggressive in pursuing FDI, has never had a state overseas office. Recently, many states have downsized their overseas offices, particularly in Japan. Some states such as California, Louisiana, Maryland, Nevada, North Dakota, Oregon, Pennsylvania, Texas, and Utah have closed down their Japanese overseas offices because of tight budget constraints as well as the uncertainty concerning the efficacy of these offices abroad. Even Michigan and Illinois, two states known for their aggressive international programs, have dramatically trimmed their operating budgets for state offices in Japan and elsewhere.

What states (and localities) need to do, considering the available empirical evidence, is to ask themselves the following questions as a means of determining the scope and appropriateness of international state and local economic policies:

- Do state and local governments have the necessary financial resources to effectively engage in international affairs, and, equally important, do they possess the important support of public and private leadership to ensure a successful program?
- Are state and local economic approaches strategically tied to policies dealing with education, infrastructural investments, and job retraining?

- When competing with other states or localities, do tax incentives really provide the best means to attract or retain international businesses in comparison to policies that emphasize human capital and infrastructural investments?
- Are international, state, or local policies designed for the strategic long-term needs and strengths of the state or local economy?
- Have state and local governments carefully assessed the global economic forces outside their control and how their economic development policies could be undermined by such forces?
- And, have local and state public leaders designed programs as merely a reaction to what other states are doing to create jobs or to increase tax revenues? (Luke, Ventriss, and Reed 1988, 133)

These policy questions are critical because many scholars maintain that policies specifically dealing with export-related activities and investment strategies are not as effective as policies trying to improve the quality of education or the infrastructure of the state. Following this line of logic, Edward Whitelaw (1986) has contended that for states like Oregon, which suffered enormously in the 1981–1982 recession, the export model (in spite of its political attraction) does not adequately exploit the inherent strengths of the economy. Whitelaw (1986, 2) convincingly argues his point can be applied to any state or locality:

The argument structuring runs this way: Income means today's pay, adjusted for living costs and amenities; adjusted income determines the location of households, household location determines the location of nonmanufacturing jobs; and households and nonmanufacturing jobs together determine the location and success of manufacturing jobs. If we want higher incomes in Oregon, we must begin with what we have—our amenities, households, and nonmanufacturing activities—and grow from them instead of hoping beyond hope that someone will give us what we lack. Hope may sell lottery tickets. It's not enough to build an economy on.

Whitelaw's idea can be recast to make another point: that it is not whether every state should be involved in international economic affairs, given global interdependency, but rather whether the extent and scope of state and local involvement has been strategically linked to the unique potential and strengths of their economies. This implies, among other things, a careful examination by state and local governments of the imports and exports of their economy, an analysis to identify appropriate international markets for small- and medium-sized businesses and what export businesses can compete in a particular market niche, and finally, a systematic analysis of the weaknesses and strengths of the state or local economy.

Thus, before a state starts experimenting with, for instance, an export trading company, which was created by the Export Trading Company Act of 1982, it has to determine whether it is wise to initiate such an approach when it has been demonstrated that there is a paucity of public sector expertise to successfully operate it, or when there may already exist experienced freight forwarding companies that can do the job equally well, if not, better than an export trading company. The critical issue is how a state or locality can design international programs that "strategically fit" other economic development policies such as job retraining programs, business expansion and retention, regulatory reforms, and educational programs, to name just a few. International programs, in other words, must not be exclusive but rather inclusive of a variety of economic development strategies to enter the local or state economy. These strategic linkages are crucial to make because without such linkages, "states and localities will find their international approaches, regardless of how well-conceived, divorced from the interdependency of issues that policymakers must face in designing an economic development program congruent to their specific needs and abilities" (Luke, Ventriss, and Reed 1988, 142).

CONCLUSION

The trend toward globalization and its impact on U.S. local and state governments is now self-evident. R. Scott Fosler (1988, 4) put it this way:

This growing global interdependence has been facilitated by rapid advances in transportation and communication technology, making the international movement of goods, people, and information fast, reliable, and inexpensive. For example: although California boasts a huge orange-growing industry, residents of San Francisco are just as likely to start their morning with orange juice from Newark, New Jersey, processed from oranges shipped through the Port of New York and New Jersey from Brazil.

Fosler maintains that the forces of globalization, along with other economic changes, will put greater importance on the roles of state and local governments in terms of designing programs that add to economic vitality and competitiveness. This will include the following factors:

    (1) a capable and motivated workforce;
    (2) a sound physical infrastructure;
    (3) well-managed natural resources;
    (4) knowledge and technology;
    (5) enterprise development;
    (6) quality of life; and,
    (7) fiscal soundness. (Fosler 1988, 77–78)

In the 1990s and beyond, state and local governments will continue to face, as they must, the challenges posed by a more competitive and global economy. When all is said and done, the real issue confronting states and localities is how effectively they can coordinate their international policies with a flexible strategic approach that can prepare them for future economic changes that globalization will inevitably bring. It will not be easy. But as states take on more responsibility for their own economic viability, their ability to meet this new challenge will, to a large extent, increase their chances to better adapt to new economic realities posed by globalization.

REFERENCES

Ajami, R. A., and D. A. Ricks. 1988. "Motives of Non-American Firms Investing in the United States." *Journal of International Business Studies* 12:25–34.

Beaumont, E. F., and H. A. Hovey. 1985. "State and Local and Federal Development Policies: New Federal Patterns, Chaos, or What?" *Public Administration Review* 45:327–332.

Calautone, R. 1986. *The Estimated Impact of Toyota on the State's Economy.* Lexington, Ky.: College of Business and Economics, University of Kentucky.

Clarke, M. K. 1986. *Revitalizing State Economics: A Review of State Economic Development Policies and Programs.* Washington, D.C.: National Governor's Association.

Coughlin, E. C., and P. A. Cartwright. 1987. "An Examination of State Foreign Exports and Manufacturing Employment." *Economic Development Quarterly* 3:257–267.

Crupi, J. A. 1988. "Changes Affecting the Economic Developer." *Economic Development Review* 15:57–60.

Duchacek, I. D. 1984. "The International Dimension of Subnational Self-Government." *Publius* 14:5–31.

Ebel, R. D., and L. Marks. 1990. "American Competitiveness in the World Economy." *Intergovernmental Perspective* 16:5–9.

Fahim-Nader, M. 1991. "U.S. Business Enterprises Acquired or Established by Foreign Direct Investors in 1990." *Survey of Current Business* 71:30–39.

Fosler, R. S. 1988. "State Economic Development Strategies." *Economic Development Review* 6:45–49.

Glickman, N. J., and D. P. Woodward. 1989. *The New Competitors.* New York: Basic Books.

Grady, D. O. 1987. "State Economic Development Strategies: Why Do States Compete?" *State and Local Government Review* 19:86–94.

International City Management Association. 1991. *Foreign Direct Investment in U.S. Local Governments.* Washington, D.C.: ICMA.

Janesch, A. 1990. "U.S. Governors' Travel Abroad Opens the Doors To Increased Exports and Jobs for their States." *Business America* 111:7–11.

Kline, J. M. 1984. "The International Economies of U.S. States." *Publius* 14: 81–94.

———. 1987. "State Programs, Policies Tap Global Markets." *State Government News* 30: 8–9.

Lawrence, R. Z. 1989. *Japanese-Affiliated Automakers in the United States: An Appraisal.* Washington, D.C.: Brookings Institution.

Liou, K.-T. 1992. *Foreign Direct Investment in the United States: The State Experience.* Chicago, Ill.: 53rd National Conference of American Society for Public Administration.

Luke, J., C. Ventriss, and B. J. Reed. 1988. *Managing Economic Development.* San Francisco: Jossey-Bass.

McIntyre, J. R. 1983. "The Role of State Governments as International Economic Actors." *Southern Review of Public Administration* 7:466–488.

Manning, B. 1977. "The Congress, the Executive, and the Intermestic Affairs: Three Proposals." *Foreign Affairs* 55: 306–324.

National Association of State Development Agencies. 1990. *The NASDA Database.* Washington, D.C.: NASDA.

National League of Cities, International Economic Development Task Force. 1984. *International Trade: A New City Economic Development Strategy.* Washington, D.C.: National League of Cities.

Pilcher, D. 1985. "Economic Development: Old Term Has New Meaning." *State Legislatures* 12:18–21.

Poniachek, H. A. 1986. *Direct Foreign Investment in the United States.* Lexington, Mass.: D. C. Heath and Company.

Reich, R. B. 1991. *The Work of Nations.* New York: Alfred Knopf.

Rivlin, A. 1990. "The Challenge of Competition to Fiscal and Functional Responsibilities." *Intergovernmental Perspectives* 16:15–16.

Rubin, B. M., and C. K. Zorn. 1985. "Sensible State and Local Economic Development." *Public Administration Review* 45:330–340.

Sylvester, K. 1988. "Exporting Made Easy (Or How States and Cities Are Selling Products Overseas)." *Governing* (January):36–42.

Ventriss, C. 1986. "American Federal Deficit and Its International Economic Effects." *International Journal of Public Administration* 8:103–123.

_____. 1991. "The Internationalization of Public Administration and Public Policy." Paper presented at the NASPAA Conference, October 1991, Salt Lake City, Utah.

_____. Forthcoming. "The Impact of Foreign Direct Investment on State Governments: An Examination of Japan and Pacific Rim Countries." In *The United States and the Pacific Rim,* ed. J. Jung. New York: Greenwood Press.

Whitelaw, E. 1986. "The Once and Future Northwest." *Pacific Northwest Executive* (July):2–4.

Wilson, R. 1989. *State Business Incentives and Economic Growth: Are They Effective? A Review of the Literature.* Washington, D.C.: Council of State Governments.

3

The Importance of Comparative Study in Educating the U.S. Public Service

Richard W. Ryan

THE NEW COMPARATIVE PUBLIC ADMINISTRATION

In a context of increasing economic, environmental, and demographic inter-dependence, U.S. public affairs/administration (PA) education is being reassessed by those who find its vision curtailed. Domestic administrative practice is changing in ways that are not yet fully clear. Simply stated, the premise of this chapter is that practice is becoming internationalized, however, not in the traditional sense of the term. "International" no longer denotes foreign or exotic; it simply indicates that domestic administrative functions and planning must increasingly take into account policies and opportunities in other nations (Rivlin 1992, 316). Further, the impetus for internationalization, I argue, is being supplied by state and local practitioners whose functional boundaries can no longer be restricted by municipal or state jurisdictions. PA education, by contrast, continues, with a few exceptions, to isolate international curricula in courses labeled "comparative" or "development adminis-tration" tailored for a select few. There is no integration of the new, domestically originated interest in international linkages into the PA core curriculum.

Administrators are coming to view the world as a vast organizational matrix which can be tapped for solutions to economic development or environmental problems. Likewise, unwanted situations may be generated by organizations far outside the administrator's immediate influence and jurisdiction. Internationalization is not always desirable; it is often thrust upon local administrators who do not welcome or understand the dynamics at work that are complicating the domestic administrative environment. The Mexicans say that when the United States sneezes Mexico catches a cold; this is only half the story. City managers in the border areas of California, Texas, New Mexico, and Arizona are no more immune from official Mexican policies regarding air quality or immigration than administrators in the state of Baja. As the North American Free Trade Agreement (NAFTA) makes clear, states and municipalities on both sides of the border will share the environmental, transportation, and urban sprawl impacts of unfettered trade.

The emphasis of this chapter will be the internationalization of a domestic-oriented U.S. administrative environment and the assessment of the potential impact on PA education. The former will be explored through examples of comparative policy opportunities and the recognition of increasing interdependence leading to transboundary agreements. Sketching the evolution of PA education is, however, more hypothetical and lacks the empirical base that is found in practice. This is a major reason for this book—to link evolving practice with a new pedagogy of internationalized PA concepts. What can be accomplished here is to outline a new set of expectations for PA education derived from the demands of current practice.

Practical and Educational Dilemmas of a Global Environment

The call to internationalize practice and curriculum is more often than not confusing on two counts. First, international interdependency is not something that can be chosen for participation or rejection. It is this feature of contemporary internationalization that is distinct from postwar foreign policy involvement or Third World development efforts. The agendas of state and local administrators now include economic development items, environmental agreements, and immigration issues that are partially created and solved by administrative actors in other countries. To cope, U.S. bureaucrats have adopted global perspectives for assessing their environments. Thus, it can be said that the new comparative public administration (CPA) is not foreign but is an inside-out perspective placing the United States in a global context.

Since it is an "inside-out" phenomenon, present-day internationalized administration is not something to be "chosen," it is simply an extended dimension of the functional domestic environment.

Second, internationalized environments present dilemmas particularly when local goals are compared with those of larger units. Civil servants and the public are exposed to sharply conflicting messages. These range from supporting international free trade agreements to buying American to save manufacturing jobs, and being made aware that environmental responsibility is shared by all while simultaneously being urged to establish community goals. For instance, local needs may place economic development over environmental protection. The reconciliation of these conflicts is then thrashed out in state and local political forums and agencies.

The potential for conflict between a limited domestic, and an expanded, internationalized view of administration presents a challenge to public administration education. On the one hand, U.S. public administration has since its inception extolled the virtues of American politics and administration. The dichotomy between politics and administration has been debatable, but what we teach about public administration's roots in the U.S. political and economic system is certain. In terms of organization theory, the institutional environment was delimited, the legal culture was understood, implicitly or explicitly, and the hierarchy of federalism created order.

On the other hand, the public administration community is being told that its locus is much less bounded by the 50 states. Civil servants at the state and local levels must be prepared to function with Canadian, Mexican, Japanese, and European counterparts in fashioning intergovernmental and public-private agreements. The focus is increasingly on governments' economic development role as well as with the attendant issues of immigration and environmental protection. This new organizational environment is a random, crowded, and highly complex one in which even small public organizations must negotiate their way.

TYPES OF INTERDEPENDENCE
AMONG ADMINISTRATIVE ENTITIES

Edward Rimer (1992) describes three "rationales" of comparative public administration (CPA): (1) imperialist-missionary; (2) anti-ethnocentric, anti-parochial; and (3) interdependence. The first wave of CPA followed World War II when most of U.S. foreign aid was intended to counter the spread of communism while expanding market economies throughout former colonies. The anti-parochial school has been articulated by Fred Riggs (1991) and Robert Dahl (1947) who contend that there cannot be a science of administration, or sound practice, without comparison among administrative systems worldwide. The emphasis on inter-dependence is more recent (Ryan 1990, Tucker 1990) and results from a recognition that the world can no longer be understood as a bipolar struggle between two major powers and alliances. Rather, the spread of democracy and economic well-being has increased egalitarianism at the expense of international hierarchical relationships. Now even (subnational) states, provinces, and cities are recognized as actors in international policy-making.

It is this third perspective on CPA that warrants examination in this chapter. It becomes necessary to examine types of interaction involved in a world marked by interdependence in order to expand understanding of the evolving roles of public administrators.

First, interdependence can be understood as *mutual vulnerability*: a recognition that the earth's resources are finite and that nations' physical and social environments are interrelated. This vulnerability is manifested in events such as transboundary pollution, the social-welfare impacts of legal and illegal immigration, and trade in illicit drugs. To cite a widely discussed example, it is feared that the North American Free Trade Agreement (NAFTA) will increase the incidence of pollution along the Mexico-U.S. border as more industrial firms relocate to Mexico taking advantage of cheap labor and lax environmental regulation. Thus, the U.S. border states are pressing for assurances from the Environmental Protection Agency (EPA) that environmental cleanup of existing problems will take place along with safeguards that anticipate further industrialization and urban growth. Even without NAFTA, Mexico's economic success and urbanization would have continuing impact on the air and water quality and water supply of cities that share air basins and aquifers along the almost 2,000-mile-long border.

Second, *cooperative policy response* indicates administrative arrangements designed to deal with mutual vulnerability. This is illustrated by informal bi-city pacts on the southern border of the United States, as well as increasingly formal cooperation among EPA and the Mexican environmental agency, SEDUE. Along the northern tier, Great Lakes United, an alliance of Canadian and American public and nongovernmental agencies, plays a watchdog role in improving the water quality of the Great Lakes shared ecosystem. It often represents alliances of smaller entities, for example, water districts, in forcing states to comply with federal standards. In these examples, local initiatives for solving mutual policy problems are generated even when the issues are transboundary in nature. International policy response is no longer the exclusive domain of federal agencies, although they continue to play coordinating roles (Ryan 1992).

Third, *random, localized economic agreements* detail another type of interdependence. With the free flow of capital among nations, states and cities have positioned themselves to attract investors from abroad. In 1989, 44 states reported having 158 economic development offices in 27 countries (Nothdurft 1992), and representatives of even small cities travel to Taiwan and Europe to arrange investment agreements.

Fourth, *planned trade alliances* seize upon interdependence as a strength with the purpose of establishing vast, shared markets. Unlike localized economic agreements, trade alliances are negotiated at the bi-national level. At the same time, however, domestic approval for planned trade agreements involves considerable bargaining between state and local jurisdictions and the federal government (i.e., to reconcile conflicting goals as noted above).

Fifth is the example provided by *global human rights enforcement* within the so-called New World Order. The role of the United Nations when intervening in cases of famine or human rights abuses of minority peoples will be an important institutional development to watch. However, it is not a focus of this paper.

In the next section, the first two types of interdependence—mutual vulnerability and cooperative policy response—will be explored further because these connect with those functions of domestic public administrators that are less examined than economic development. The expanding functional environment of administrators provides the bedrock of the new CPA.

PRACTITIONER CHALLENGES
AND INSIDE-OUT INTERNATIONALIZATION

In a 1991 editorial in *Public Administration Review*, Fred Riggs outlines a new comparativist framework that avoids isolating the American experience from "the study of 'foreign' governments." Riggs (1991, 473) is interested in a focus "on explanatory theories that account for the continuously changing properties and problems faced by governments as they seek to implement public policies." With such a perspective, Riggs believes, use of the comparative method will assist practitioners in a better understanding of domestic public administration and open policy deliberation to experiences of public entities worldwide. U.S. public administration would take its place in a global framework where the search for policy solutions would be enriched by international comparison.

How does public affairs/administration get there and what will be used to build the comparativist framework? Since the postwar era, academic internationalists have taken a normative approach, that is, attempting to convince the PA community of the conceptual benefits of comparativism, and they have failed. A more promising course is the inside-out, functional route: explore the international connections now being made by domestic administrators and ask why there is an incentive to do so. The chapters in this book can at best alert academics and practitioners to examples of international comparison and integration presently occurring in this country.

Increasingly, successful examples from abroad are being presented to U.S. policymakers as alternatives to their inadequate array of choices (Werlin 1992). The following example of drug policy is from Amsterdam.

Mutual Vulnerability: Treating Drug Abuse and AIDS

The Amsterdam model informs U.S. policymakers in two ways: (1) it emphasizes the mutual vulnerability of cities and nations when confronting the AIDS epidemic and trade in illicit drugs, and (2) it presents a model that can lead to a cooperative policy response. Amsterdam's approach separates lower risk, cannabis-based drugs from high-risk, hard drugs such as heroin and cocaine. In addition, drug policy has been closely connected with AIDS prevention. The model provides data on an alternative to the U.S. war on *all* drugs which has been costly ($12 billion annually). The focus in Amsterdam is on the suppression of high-risk drugs while low-risk drugs are legal in certain zones. This presents a policy alternative favoring detoxification treatment for hard drug addicts over the criminal justice system approach favored in this country. Amsterdam, however, is reputed to be more culturally liberal than most American cities. This model's appeal remains that it successfully addresses a major source of AIDS transference, addicts sharing syringes, while U.S. cities and counties separate criminal prosecution and drug treatment into rival police and health departments.

Amsterdam's approach is to link drug abuse and medical care both to treat hard drug withdrawal and to disseminate information on AIDS transference. Doctors visit police stations twice daily treating drug withdrawal and informing drug users of methadone and needle exchange programs (Hillenius 1990).

Of additional interest in the examination of comparative policy is a sidebar to the article describing "AIDS and drug related study visits" organized by the

Amsterdam Municipal Health Service. The explicit purpose of the visits is to "facilitate an exchange of information" presumably between city administrators and elected officials because the article appeared in a magazine directed at this audience. The itinerary includes a structured half day with an overview of Amsterdam's AIDS and drug policies, plus a visit to the methadone bus, and one and a half days tailored to the special interests of the visitor (Hillenius 1990, 10).

As interest in comparative policy grows, opportunities for obtaining information will increase. Amsterdam's study visits for administrators are not an isolated example. In Washington, D.C. the International Center of the Academy for State and Local Government monitors innovations abroad that may be useful to state governments. It also conducts exchanges of technical experts in support of the Council of State Governments and publishes *Public Innovation Abroad* (Wynne 1992).

This section has presented an example of comparative policy of use to individual U.S. jurisdictions. Next, a collaborative administrative structure created in response to a transboundary issue is reviewed. U.S. federal agencies continue to play coordinating and funding roles; however, the lead in creating transboundary pacts is shifting to the states and cities as their financial and personnel resources grow. Individual jurisdictions are finding that regional problems require a pooling of administrative expertise and resources, and that they cannot wait for federal agencies to make their specific issue a priority.

Cooperative Policy Response:
Transnational Management of Environmental Pollution:
The Gulf of Maine Council on the Marine Environment

The states of Maine, Massachusetts, New Hampshire, and the provinces of Nova Scotia and New Brunswick form the Gulf of Maine Council on the Marine Environment. Alarmed by the growing incidences of contaminated shellfish and potential harm to the public, the five states and provinces signed the Agreement on the Conservation of the Marine Environment in 1989. The catalyst that brought the parties together was a realization that information had to be shared and that neither the Canadian nor U.S. national governments had enough knowledge or regulatory power to solve the problem without the states and provinces forming a regional pact. The outcome was a pooling of policy strategies along with monitoring and enforcement resources. In addition, the Gulf Council staff continues to study the intergovernmental Great Lakes water quality agreements of the 1980s and 1990s in the development of Gulf policies.

Untreated waste water flowing into the Gulf is the major threat to marine life. In July 1991 the council adopted the Marine Action Plan which established four priorities for 1992: "compilation of regional data and information, control of point source pollution to the Gulf, protection and enhancement of regionally significant habitats, and initiation of Gulf education activities" (Gulf of Maine Council 1991, 7).

Included in these broad goals are specific recommendations for the Gulf's management that illustrate the degree of intergovernmental cooperation involved in this pact. They are: the creation of a Gulf of Maine coastal management personnel exchange program for the purpose of sharing technical expertise on water pollution; cooperative efforts with the U.S. Fish and Wildlife Service to map fish and wildlife habitats; meetings among state, provincial, and federal fish and wildlife agencies to propose joint regulatory programs; and joint efforts by the Gulf Council, the U.S. Food and Drug Administration, the Canadian Health Protection Branch, and the Interstate Shellfish Sanitation Commission to promote alternative standards for measuring shellfish contamination. Additionally, the Action Plan calls for a comparative evaluation of all U.S. and Canadian laws affecting the Gulf of Maine natural resource area (Waterman 1990).

The Gulf Council is an example of a cooperative policy response which contains at its core intergovernmental management and comparative administration. Each party reviewed what the others had been doing to solve gulf pollution and concluded that no one jurisdiction could succeed. The rationale for state and provincial water governance is that intervention by the national governments alone would be insufficient since they have neither the proximity to the gulf nor the responsibility for it.

LINKING PUBLIC ADMINISTRATION EDUCATION
TO THE NEW CPA

"American news commentators reporting from Europe have recently noted with surprise and indignation the comparative success of Germany and other European states in meeting basic human needs such as universal health services (and) housing ... which continue to baffle the American government" (Riggs 1991, 474). Riggs goes on to suggest that the difference in success rests in government structure—parliamentary for the Europeans—that provides a unitary framework for administrative and political response. This insight is a caution to those who would transfer entire health care or other policy models. Yet, this does not prevent borrowing select features of other systems as long as their applicability to the U.S. context can be ascertained.

The issue of what is transferable underlines the importance of the comparative study of political and administrative systems so theoretical frameworks can be developed for practitioners who are looking worldwide for policy alternatives. It is anticipated that for U.S. PA programs the decision to include comparative policy management models across the curriculum must be preceded by practitioners' interest in empirical policy examples. Within comparative policy analysis, the process of determining what parts of service delivery systems to borrow is complex. Not only does a foreign political-administrative ecology need to be understood, analysts must appreciate the subtle dynamics that make the domestic environment unique.

International Elements in Public Affairs Programs

A 1989 survey of the masters programs affiliated with the National Association of Schools of Public Affairs and Administration (NASPAA) revealed little about the integration of Americanized international issues into the MPA curriculum. Neither the Cleary (1990) study nor a critique of it by Roeder and Whitaker (1993) had much to say about international curriculum. Of the interviewees who answered Cleary's inquiry about "perceived gaps" in public affairs/administration masters programs, seven out of 85 programs mentioned the need for international affairs (Cleary 1990, 665). There is no explanation of the type of international affairs to which these programs were referring. Yet, it can safely be assumed that respondents were indicating curricula involving other countries in the sense of the old comparative administration, the outside-in perspective of internationalism, which insulates most of U.S. public affairs/administration from global dynamics.

In a 1963 address to the Graduate School of Business Administration at Harvard, Dwight Waldo held up comparative public administration as a favorable alternative to business administration's "root biases" and preoccupation with the "variables . . . within the organization." Business administration, according to Waldo's academic nose-thumbing, ignored the "possible significance of cultural differences" in the larger world and sought one best (Western) way to manage. CPA, in contrast, was committed to diversity (read: global comparisons) (Waldo 1968, 21).

How the tables have turned! One must now look to business and industrial vocational training to find curriculum models oriented toward a global environment. Some might counter that PA offers a selection of study abroad options from Bristol, England, to San Jose, Costa Rica. The limitation of these programs is that they depend on foreign travel which is financially prohibitive for most full-time students. For practitioners in MPA programs, such programs are difficult to schedule amidst busy work and study routines. Additionally, study abroad generally provides a type of raw empiricism which depends on the individual and lacks a conceptual framework for the transfer of ideas.

South Carolina's Technical Colleges

South Carolina has experienced remarkable growth in industrial jobs, and it claims that it has the highest level of foreign investments of any state in the union. From its creation in 1961 through the present, the State Board for Technical and Comprehensive Education has administered a system of 16 technical colleges with 56,000 students geared toward worker training programs. Graduating skilled workers custom-trained for specific, globally competitive industries has been a key element in South Carolina's efforts to attract diversified manufacturing jobs. Under the leadership of recent governors, including the Clinton administration's Secretary of Education, Richard W. Riley, the technical colleges have turned their attention toward Europe and entered into agreements with Bosch, Michelin, and BMW to prepare a workforce tailored to the needs of international manufacturers. The state has achieved what economists label the "virtuous cycle"—economic development through the provision of a skilled labor force to attract international investors. This in turn supports public services and infrastructure. Realizing that traditional domestic occupations could not absorb South Carolina's graduates, the state has tapped into the global economy.

A Special Schools program of the Technical Colleges provides pre-employment training through a curriculum jointly planned by the company and the college. The rationale behind the Special Schools is that the best way to attract industries is to guarantee "a first-rate worker training program and a willing workforce ready to begin when the doors of the plant open" (Brooks 1990). At no cost to the company, Special Schools will (1) assess, recruit, and train a workforce according to the company's specifications; (2) provide a continuing supply of skilled craftsmen; and (3) provide continuing education for up-skilling plant workers (Garrison 1993). The companies served by the Technical Colleges do, however, make in-kind payments to college foundations and purchase technical equipment for classroom training.

Tri-County Technical College has created a particularly strong global perspective. Its president reports that the college is adopting ISO certification for its student competencies in technical work (Garrison 1993). The ISO standard is the European technical measure of manufacturing skills, and its adoption is in support of the goal to make the institution a world-class college. Another step is the opening of the World Class Training Center in 1990 designed to make locally based manufacturing companies more competitive by teaching business concepts in a global context.

MPA program directors will question the relevance of a technical college system to their graduate, academic programs. The message is simple: get out and take a look at what types of personnel public agencies must recruit to operate in a global environment, and ask why the PA curriculum has failed, unlike the business curriculum, to convey the shrinking importance of organization and system boundaries.

More specifically, public affairs/administration programs should ask the following: (1) What level of international competency do NASPAA schools require to equip graduates to function in an internationalized environment? For example, what degree of knowledge about NAFTA, the EEC, and the ramifications of foreign investment in the United States should PA graduates possess? (2) What administrative system comparisons should PA students be exposed to (an administrative version of the ISO) so they have a working knowledge of how other influential nations process policy decisions and implementation? (3) What curricula innovation is already taking place in PA programs to provide a globally interdependent administrative perspective to generalist, domestic civil servants? (4) What types of policy management issues are more transferable from one political-administrative ecology to another? Which are not expected to be moveable? (Something can be learned here from the U.S. experiences of providing technical and administrative assistance around the globe during the last four and a half decades. The transfer, however, is now pointed in the opposite direction.)

Business programs nationwide, albeit reluctantly, are enriching their curricula to reflect employers' expanding needs. It is now fairly common to find degree programs in international business which include a business core complemented by area studies, for example, Asia or Latin America, and courses leading to competency in a second language. These are aimed at clientele who plan to seek employment with domestically based corporations that require international skills. Further, the national accrediting agency for business schools, the American Assembly of Collegiate Schools of Business, now requires at least one international course be compulsory in member programs. A popular approach in New England business schools has been to use international modules that can be integrated into numerous courses instead of finding experts to teach one or two specialty classes. This tack avoids the tendency found in public affairs and administration of limiting international subjects to select courses and regarding the internationalist as a specialist outside the realm of domestic administrative issues. The "de-specialization" of the international perspective in PA is the very goal of this book.

THE SHAPE OF THINGS TO COME?
PA PROGRAMS BY THE YEAR 2000

This chapter contends that there is a widening gap between U.S. PA curricula and the practitioner's environment. This is especially the case in policy issue assessment. The new CPA posits that U.S. practitioners can learn from solutions posed by their counterparts in other nations and can, at times, solve problems by forging pacts with public managers outside national boundaries. Indeed, traditional conceptions of jurisdictional boundaries are often misleading and force managers to ignore the reality of highly permeable borders and state and local lines.

A problem faced by U.S. PA is that signals about globalism are contradictory. Administrators and scholars are simultaneously directed to isolate from, to compete with, and to cooperate with, international actors in response to global interdependence. It is no wonder the United States lacks industrial policy regarding its strategy in global commerce; it cannot choose a direction.

To summarize the alternatives facing U.S. PA education, three scenarios can be posed. Each can find sufficient support to become the mode in which PA recognizes international factors in the next ten years.

First, the U.S. strategy would be to become better at dictating terms of international penetration of U.S. markets and administrative environments. Returning to Rimer's categories, this is akin to the imperialist strategy but with a New World Order twist. If the United States is the only remaining armed forces superpower, why cannot U.S. resources be shifted to the commercial sector so the country can regain dominance of international markets? The assumption is that military prowess can be traded-in for an equal measure of global economic control, and it views the world in bi-polar terms with one side or power dominating. The ramification for PA education is the preparation of public affairs specialists capable of supporting major U.S.-owned corporations able to battle for American market share. An us-against-them ethic will prevail.

Second, prepare a limited number of U.S. experts to deal with that part of the domestic environment that interfaces with the rest of the world. This response acknowledges a limited amount of interdependence but conceptualizes it in a highly rational way. That is, the U.S. interface with global forces is still seen as outside-in, creating occasional points of interaction which can be addressed by an internationally trained cadre. This in many ways reflects a business-as-usual attitude. It ensures that each governmental agency has its international operations division much as the Department of Agriculture maintains an Undersecretary for International Affairs. This also fits with current academic structuring of specialty tracks for those who are interested in the exotic study of other countries.

Third, recognize that national, state, and local boundaries have become so permeable that internationalization is an inside-out phenomenon where activities by all levels of government have global content. This response recognizes the United States as fully interdependent with the global environment and unable to seal off selected functions from international forces. Implicitly it rejects the superpower self-image and casts the United States as one of numerous, powerful, and sophisticated actors on the world scene. This, of course, is one of the several mixed messages U.S. policy managers have been receiving since the mid-1980s. Its acceptance is limited since it requires a lessening of hubris, a staple of the United States' image as a military super power. The academic impact would be in introducing globalism across the curriculum, and, as Riggs has argued, placing American PA within an international context, not vice versa.

CONCLUDING RECOMMENDATIONS

Only empirical testing and experience can answer the questions raised in this chapter about the potential role of the new CPA in PA programs. To reiterate an essential point made throughout this chapter, the shape of a new CPA will be defined by practitioners who find their domestic environment transformed by international factors. Thus, the first recommendation that follows is key, and all the other suggestions hinge on the response to it.

1. Academics in public affairs/administration need to conduct a dialogue with practitioners on the importance of "comparative" in contemporary PA. The conceptualization of CPA must be in terms significant to administrators, that is, the inside-out proposition about internationalization. Past "rationales"

concerning CPA have to be suspended if practitioners are to have input defining or rejecting the notion of a new CPA.

2. If there is a demand to include international elements in PA curricula, NASPAA should be in the forefront of establishing criteria for a global curriculum. NASPAA is in a position to link-up a national effort by faculty interested in internationalized domestic issues. It is preferable, too, that faculty not strongly identified with prior rationales of CPA, for example, overseas development assistance, lead the effort.

3. There is much to be learned from business management on going global. Encourage PA journals to emulate *Harvard Business Review*'s "Four Corners—Business Insights that cross borders" in order to provide readers with perspectives on administrative systems, personnel administration, and policy choices in other developed countries. Also, allow as PA electives business management courses that include cross-cultural management and international networking.

4. Invite PA practitioners who find their task environments increasingly globalized to teach PA students.

5. Write articles and textbooks that place the United States in a global context.

6. Develop mid-range theories that enable assessment of transferability of policy solutions from other countries. Assessing political systems is a key part of building such theories. It cannot be done solely from an administrative vantage. The political context for developing and implementing policy is key to understanding if that policy process is replicable in this country.

Several of these suggestions will rankle many of my colleagues because they urge PA to suspend disciplinary boundaries and learn from business administration and political science. This, indeed, is the suggestion. Without such interdisciplinary alliances, I doubt whether public affairs/administration will be able to decipher the new CPA.

REFERENCES

Brooks, A. 1990. "South Carolina's Special Schools." *AACJC Journal* (Feb./Mar.).

Cleary, R. 1990. "What Do Public Administration Masters Programs Look Like? Do They Do What Is Needed?" *Public Administration Review* 50 (6):663–673.

Dahl, R. 1947. "The Science of Public Administration: Three Problems." *Public Administration Review* 7:1–11.

Garrison, D. 1993. Unstructured telephone interview, President, Tri-County Technical College, South Carolina, January 6, 1993.

Gulf of Maine Council on the Marine Environment. 1991. "Council Approves Gulf of Maine Action Plan at July Meeting." *Turning the Tide* 3 (4):7.

Hillenius, D. 1990. "The Amsterdam Model." *Western City* 66 (6):8–11.

Nothdurft, W. E. 1992. "The Export Game." *Governing* 5 (11):57–61.

Riggs, F. 1991. "Public Administration: A Comparativist Framework." *Public Administration Review* 51 (6):473–477.

Rimer, E. 1992. "Early Lessons on Teaching Comparative Public Policy in an Interdependent World." *SPAE Forum* 3 (1):4–5.

Rivlin, A. M. 1992. "A New Vision of American Federalism." *Pubic Administration Review* 52 (4):315–320.

Roeder, P., and G. Whitaker. 1993. "Education for the Public Service: Policy Analysis and Administration in the MPA Core Curriculum." *Administration & Society* 24 (4):512–540.

Ryan, R. 1990. "The Internationalization of Domestic Policy Issues: Will Public Affairs/ Administration Respond?" *International Journal of Public Administration* 13 (1 & 2):127–153.

_____. 1992. "Transboundary Intergovernmental Management: The Application of Intergovernmental Management to Transborder Issues." Paper presented at the American Society for Public Administration National Conference, Chicago, Ill., April 15.

Tucker, R. W. 1990. "A World Transformed: 1989 and All That." *Foreign Affairs* 69 (4):93–114.

Waldo, D. 1968. "Comparative Public Administration: Prologue, Problems, and Promise." *Papers in Comparative Public Administration*. Special Series: Number 2.

Waterman, M. 1990. "The Gulf of Maine Action Plan." Prepared for the Council on the Marine Environment, Augusta, Maine.

Werlin, H. 1992. "Cultural Engineering: Singapore's Approach to America's Problems." Paper presented at the American Society for Public Administration National Conference, Chicago, Ill., April 15.

Wynne, G. G. 1992. "Idea Imports." *State Government News* 35 (12):11–12.

4

Why Has Bureaucracy Not Smothered Democracy in the United States?

Fred W. Riggs

Is this not a ridiculous question? Despite the harsh rhetoric of presidential campaigns, and the severe attacks on our bureaucracy that one sometimes hears from the candidates, I doubt if anyone seriously thinks that the American bureaucracy can smother our democracy. Rather, it is viewed as a big nuisance, a source of red tape and an obstacle to action, a self-serving apparatus, or just plain inefficient. But our democracy is surely too vibrant to be smothered by a bunch of appointed public officials!

To the contrary, when Americans discover that important new programs are needed, we typically expect government—by which we usually mean public officials, bureaucrats—to come to the rescue. The great tasks of public administration are those which require the services of appointed officials—both military officers and civil servants. These include national defense, emergency management, maintaining law and order, building and maintaining highways, fighting crime and drugs, managing our natural resources, handling foreign policy, and many other activities. The last thing we expect or fear of our public officials is that they would seize power, suspend Congress, and destroy our constitution.

THE RECORD

Nevertheless, just such a fear came to my mind several years ago when I counted coups in Third World countries. I found that about 110 countries had republican forms of government, and I discovered that almost 50 (44 percent) of them had experienced one or more coup d'etat. My definition of a coup is a narrow one: it includes only events in which public officials, headed by a few military

Some portions of this paper are adapted from Riggs (forthcoming).

officers, grab power, suspend the constitution, and smash congress. Admittedly, the word can mean other things too—even a vote to change the leadership of a city council or state legislature—but the only sense of the word that I have in mind here is the one defined above.

Well, you may say, "Even if 44 percent of the republics in the Third World have had coups, that doesn't really frighten me. After all, we expect their new constitutions to be fragile, and most of them inherited well-established imperial bureaucracies before they got their independence. But our constitution has already survived for over 200 years—it will surely last for centuries to come."

"But wait," I have to answer: "You havn't heard the whole story yet." If you analyze the fate of Third World republics according to the type of regime they had, you will find something that is both puzzling and frightening. First, and most astonishing, I found that single-party dictatorships were almost immune: of about 35, less than a fifth (six) had experienced coups. When I counted only the 17 countries in which independence had been won after an extended revolutionary struggle, I found that just one of them (Guinea—1958–1984) had experienced a coup (i.e., 6 percent)—you will find all this data in Riggs (1993, 218).

Single-Party Regimes

Surely this has nothing to do with the United States, you may think. But I believe we can learn a lesson from it. I suspect, though I cannot prove, that the bureaucracy in all these countries was extremely weak politically—you could call it powerless. It's not hard to find the reason. A single-party system, by definition, forbids genuine opposition parties, although it may permit some token parties that pose no real threat to those in power. That means that the party leadership is able to dominate an elected assembly (created to legitimize the party's decisions), and it can therefore always have its way—it does not have to confront congressional opposition, as we do in our presidentialist system. Moreover, unlike our bureaucrats, its appointed officials do not have to deal with often contradictory mandates from each of the three branches of our government: the executive, the legislative, and the judicial. Do not the cross-pressures generated by having a multiplicity of "bosses" anger officials who, if they could do so, might gladly push them aside in order to make decisions the way they think proper?

Notice also that a dominant ruling party can assign trusted party officials (commissars, the "reds") to work at the side of bureaucrats (the "experts"). Consequently, anyone who shows signs of resistance or willingness to support a coup can be eliminated right away without waiting for tedious judicial proceedings. In short, bureaucrats in any single-party system are, indeed, powerless. How could they support a coup?

But also, how could they administer effectively? Would they not always be taking a big chance if their expertise were to tempt them to go against the ideological preferences of their party monitor? I believe that the result is, almost universally, that public administration in a single-party regime has to be faulty, even disastrous. Yes, disastrous! Eventually the whole population becomes disappointed by administrative failures and angry at the ruling party—even though they dare not display their anger publicly. But, eventually, I suspect, when matters really go from bad to worse, even the party leaders will realize that something terribly wrong has happened and they will begin to disagree among themselves about how to correct the situation. At some point in this process, internal arguments among these leaders will precipitate a huge crisis and the regime will come tumbling down. There will be no coup, but there will be a crash. I believe that is what happened recently in the various countries of Eastern Europe and then in the Soviet Union. It is likely to happen also in the single-party regimes of the Third World.

Multi-Party Republics

When we deduct single-party regimes from the 111 republics that I counted in 1985, we find that 43 of 76 multi-party republics had experienced coups—that is, 56 percent. Why, we may well ask, were public officials able to seize power in so many countries? Part of the answer, surely, is that all of the public bureaucracies are far more powerful than are the powerless apparatuses of the single-party regimes. We don't think about this possibility, I believe, because the American myth of a dichotomy between politics and administration leads us to assume that bureaucrats are nothing more than the agents of a political system which establishes and uses them as its pliant tools for purely administrative purposes. This assumption also reflects the fact that bureaucrats in America are, indeed, exceptionally powerless. We need to discover why this is true, and why bureaucracies in other countries are normally much more powerful than ours.

Of course, any government that is limited by constitutional restraints is less able to dominate and repress its bureaucracy than is a single-party system. All of their officials are able—within limits, no doubt—to exercise the civil rights which protect their interests as well as those of other citizens. The right to organize, which everyone has in a democracy, normally extends to public officials too. In the absence of a single official ideology, bureaucrats typically have as much freedom of thought and opinion as other citizens, and their views, as experienced experts, may actually count for more. Indeed, insofar as civil rights are protected and public servants identify their own interests with those of the state as a whole, they begin to think that what is good for officials is also good for the state. If these premises are correct, then officials in any representative government are likely to claim and to achieve much more power than their counterparts in single-party regimes.

One welcome consequence of bureaucratic empowerment is better public administration. The more experts in government service are able to use their special knowledge to support the implementation of public policies, the more satisfaction they will derive from their work and the more effective they will be. Two observations follow: a major advantage and a serious limitation.

The advantage involves the reduced risk of coups. The more effective a polity's public administration is, the lower the prospects of a coup. There are two reasons for this conclusion. First, to the degree that the general public is satisfied with the quality of public administration and accepts the policies that its government implements, there will be less popular demand for a radical regime change. No doubt, policy debates can be loud and even angry, but we will not see revolutionary movements or major demonstrations for radical change. And second, so long as the officials themselves are relatively content—they feel satisfaction in public office and they are well paid, secure, and safe in their jobs—they will not support any coup group striving to overthrow the government. Without strong backing from a large number of civil servants, no military group can expect to stage a successful coup.

The limitation follows from the essential dynamics of any modern organization, including governments viewed as a whole. Bureaucracies are not whole organizations, although we carelessly use the word, sometimes, to mean just that. Rather, bureaucrats are staff members working for any organization, private or public. Here, however, I shall limit the meaning of this word to government employees. As employees, they accept an obligation to support and facilitate the implementation of the goals or policies expressed by the state. No doubt, they often contribute significantly to the elaboration of these objectives, which is why they do need power, but they cannot formally legitimize their preferences.

THE PROBLEM OF LEGITIMACY

In order to legitimize public policy in any state, an extra-bureaucratic source of authority is needed. In traditional monarchies, the king, as sovereign, provided this source, and bureaucrats worked under royal authority. The source of this authority was, ultimately, supernatural—coronation ceremonies were used to enthrone a monarch and establish his or her sacred legitimacy (Hocart 1927). In our rationalistic and secularized age, however, sacred monarchic authority has been discredited—it survives only in a dozen oil-rich or miniature states.

Instead, the myth of popular sovereignty has taken its place. This myth can only be implemented through concrete institutions, typically centering in an elected assembly. Although we identify this myth with democracy, single-party regimes actually accept it too. They do "elect" members to an assembly, but without competing parties, the members have no choice but to serve as a legitimizing "rubber stamp" body, voting to accept all the laws proposed by the ruling party. This leaves real power in the hands of the party's leaders, one of whom is named to hold the largely ceremonial post of head of government. By contrast, in the most common and successful forms of democracy, the government is, essentially, a committee of the elected assembly and may be discharged by it at any time, simply by a vote of no-confidence—this is what we mean by a parliamentary system.

In presidentialist regimes, by contrast, the head of government is elected independently of the assembly and serves for a fixed term, not subject to discharge by a no-confidence vote—impeachment proceedings are for crimes, not policy, and they do not change the party in power. This rule produces the separation of powers which we customarily identify with "presidentialism." Incidentally, I use this rather awkward word instead of presidential simply because parliamentary systems often have elected presidents (as head of state) and even single-party regimes have "presidents." The American type of presidential system is presidentialist, but the Austrian or Iraqi presidential polities are not.

Constitutive Systems

Regardless of which formula for selecting the head of government is adopted, the basic political configuration in all modern republics is the same. It always centers on an elected assembly and a head of government, institutions that can only be established by elections and, typically, a party system. Because we need a term for this configuration (i.e., an elected assembly and head of government neither plus elections and a party system), I proposed one more than 20 years ago. I chose *constitutive system* to name the total machinery of government that links citizens, as constituents, to the polity as a whole, normally following a set of basic laws set forth in a constitution. Constitutive systems are, in fact, constitutive for all modern states. Anyone who finds this term awkward or confusing may well recommend and use a better one.

However designated, the concept is needed for the comparative analysis of all modern governments. Because we don't use such a term, we tend to study only the parts of a constitutive system and consequently have difficulty understanding how its parts are linked together. Anyone who attends a conference of the American Political Science Association will find confirmation: it offers innumerable panels on such parts as the "president," the "congress," "parties," "elections"—and even the "bureaucracy"—but virtually no panels on how all these parts fit together and affect each other—that is, no sessions on our constitutive system!

A Bureaucratic Polity

The holistic concept of a constitutive system is particularly important when we analyze the effects of a coup d'etat. No doubt coup leaders sometimes permit a purely formalistic constitutive system to remain, or even install a new one, but such actions only conceal the new reality, namely that appointed officials dominate a government without having any means to legitimize their authority—neither a traditional monarchy nor a modern constitutive system. To clarify the discussion that follows, I use *regime* in a Lasswellian sense to refer only to polities which have a workable constitutional basis, whether it be monarchic or rooted in a constitutive system. By contrast, when a state is controlled, without any such authority, by military officers and other bureaucrats who have simply seized power, we need a different term. Unfortunately, again, we lack one. Lasswell uses bureaucracy in its original sense to mean a polity dominated by appointed officials, but because the later meanings of this word are needed now, I substitute *bureaucratic polity* (Riggs 1966, 311–366).

In order to sustain its constitutive system, therefore, a modern state must keep its bureaucracy under effective control. However, bureaucrats need power in order to administer effectively—they cannot do so when they are powerless, as we have seen in the single-party regimes. But it is not easy to maintain control over a powerful bureaucracy, especially during times of real crisis. With this in mind, it becomes relevant to compare the experience of presidentialist with parliamentary regimes in the Third World. According to my analysis, in 1985, 30 of the 33 countries that had adopted presidentialist forms of government (i.e., 91 percent) had experienced coups, whereas less than a third (31 percent) of the 40 countries that had adopted parliamentary systems of government had experienced a breakdown by means of a coup d'etat—and none of them broke down by any other means. The countries are listed and further details can be found in Riggs (1993, 223–225). The difference is so striking that it needs to be analyzed.

Although all democratic governments in the Third World are fragile and vulnerable to the seizure of power by public officials, presidentialist governments following the American model are far more likely to experience such disasters than are parliamentary regimes. One obvious conclusion is that, perhaps, the capacity of parliamentary regimes to control their bureaucracies is significantly greater than that of presidentialist regimes. The basic reason for this difference is not difficult to see. The fusion of executive/legislative powers in a parliamentary cabinet enables it to speak with a single voice whenever problems involving the government's ability to control its bureaucracy are involved.

Separation of Powers as a Liability

By contrast, in presidentialist regimes the separation of powers that results from the fixed term of its head of government ("president") means that the regime's real power over the bureaucracy is fragmented. Moreover, because of its huge agenda, any congress cannot hope to debate and decide all issues in plenary session—by contrast, a parliament that limits itself primarily to yes/no votes over government-sponsored bills, relying heavily on party discipline, can have a relatively restricted agenda.

To overcome this handicap, Congress needs to partition its decision-making responsibilities among a host of relatively autonomous committees, each of which becomes, therefore, the source of authority for laws and budgets which control the actions of individual government agencies. Moreover, the separation of judicial powers also saddles public administrators with restrictive court decisions. We tend to view the resulting fragmentation of governmental powers over the bureaucracy from an administrative point of view, noting how it imposes cross-pressures on officials that handicap and frustrate their ability to act (Rohr 1986). However, this fragmentation also has a profoundly important political consequence: it severely handicaps every presidentialist regime in its efforts to control its bureaucracy.

Better control over their bureaucracies by parliamentary regimes means, of course, that they are normally able to implement public policies more successfully than presidentialist regimes. It follows that the motives for both popular and bureaucratic rebellion against parliamentary regimes will be significantly less than those found in presidentialist regimes.

EXPLAINING THE EXCEPTION

Taken together, these considerations explain why almost all of the world's presidentialist regimes have experienced coups. But it leaves unanswered a giant question: why has the United States not experienced the same fate? In short, why has bureaucracy not smothered American democracy as it has virtually all other presidentialist regimes? The question, in my opinion, has two parts:

First, why has the American constitutive system, despite the handicaps inherent in its regime design, been able to control its bureaucracy more effectively than have the constitutive systems in other presidentialist regimes? How can we explain this exception?

Second, why has the American bureaucracy been less powerful than the bureaucracy in other presidentialist regimes and therefore less able to mount a coup d'etat? Why has it been semi-powered rather than powerful?

Overcoming the Handicaps

The answer to the first question is quite complicated and I cannot deal with it here. Some critics argue that the U.S. democracy has not succeeded. However, although the regime has experienced severe internal crises—such as those generated by the Civil War, the Great Depression, and international conflicts—it has maintained itself through all of them. No doubt, some American presidents have, during emergencies, exercised powers of questionable constitutional legitimacy. Nevertheless, for over 200 years presidents have been elected every four years and the Congress has never been suspended. By the simple and most obvious criteria, the regime has survived.

Some scholars take the survival of presidentialism in the United States for granted. They assume that if other polities have not succeeded in making our formula work, there must be some cultural, economic, social, geographical, or other noninstitutional causes which, in each case, have led to disasters. More radical critics assume that American imperialism is the main villain, or that the world capitalist system and the dependency syndrome can explain all the breakdowns.

However, when we compare the American case with other presidentialist regimes, we find, I believe, that catastrophic breakdowns are normal for any polity committed to our constitutional system—but there are some para-constitutional practices (Riggs 1988; 1994) in the United States that account for the survival of this exceptional case. They include, for example, single-member electoral districts that support a centripetal two-party system that produces a Congress whose members are at least willing to negotiate and compromise with the president, even though, as a result, many minority groups cannot be represented in the political process and are deeply alienated. Other presidentialist republics typically use some kind of proportional representation scheme which leads to the proliferation of political parties or party factions that intensify ideological commitments and aggravate the unavoidable tensions between any president and Congress.

Another practice that is universally deplored involves widespread abstention from voting. No doubt this results from the feeling of many minority groups that they cannot win any real power. However, their abstention permits the two major parties to focus their campaigns on efforts to win support from independents—the moderate center—producing a centripetal party system whose relatively moderate representatives people a congress that is willing, sometimes, to bargain with and support the president.

The seniority principle in congressional committees and the frequent reelection of incumbents also strengthens the American Congress in a perennial contest where the president, as commander-in-chief and head of government, typically holds much stronger cards. Although such practices are widely condemned as "un-democratic" and they have been rejected in other presidentialist regimes, they have contributed significantly to the American regime's legitimacy and its ability to control its bureaucracy. For a full discussion see Riggs (1994).

A SEMI-POWERED BUREAUCRACY

Let us turn now to the second question: Why is the American bureaucracy less powerful than its counterparts in virtually all other presidentialist regimes? The reasons for the evolution of a semi-powered bureaucracy in America can be discovered only when we recall several decisive historical transformations which were not replicated in other presidentialist regimes. These transformations involve the introduction of rotation in 1829 during the administration of President Andrew Jackson and the subsequent enactment of the Pendleton Act in 1883. These landmark events divide American bureaucratic history into three stages, each of which needs to be understood in relation to the others.

The Retainer Stage

During the first 40 years of our existence as a state, public officials, appointed on a patronage basis, were able to keep their jobs indefinitely. As Leonard White has clearly explained, "The spirit of the Federalist system favored continuity of service from the highest to the lowest levels. . . . No property right in office was ever established or seriously advocated, but permanent and continued employment during good behavior was taken for granted" (White 1951, 369).

Strangely, despite the ubiquity of job retention under patronage systems, we lack a generally accepted term for the practice. However, in European monarchies, the personal retainers or servants of a king or lord often assumed governmental administrative functions and were still called *retainers*. Why not use this word also to refer to patronage appointees in a republic whenever they remain in office indefinitely? Until a better term is proposed, therefore, I shall use retainer to refer, specifically, to patronage appointees in a bureaucracy who retain their positions indefinitely. Ironically, we keep the word servant in the phrase "public servants"— but it lacks the explicit sense of continuity in office retained by retainer.

When a bureaucracy is constituted primarily of retainers, it can become very powerful. No doubt, because of their long-term experience in office, some retainers become proficient administrators. Nevertheless, their lack of preappointment qualifications often handicaps public administration. Moreover, because of the absence of tenure rooted in legal safeguards, retainers are often insecure and they worry about their job security. Predictably, therefore, retainers have strong reasons to establish networks and support structures that will enable them to keep their positions. As a result, retainer bureaucracies, over the years, become quite cohesive and politically powerful.

The Rotation Stage

When President Andrew Jackson came into office in 1829, he was able to stifle the further development of retainer power by introducing the rotation system. Leonard White gives Jackson credit for this landmark transformation, acknowledging that he "did not introduce the spoils system," but, he says, "he did introduce rotation into the federal system" (1954, 4–5). The word "spoils" is not only pejorative—it carries two meanings that make its use confusing. Here White clearly equates "spoils" with "patronage." No doubt all the early retainers were, themselves, beneficiaries of "spoils" when they were first appointed to an office. What subsequently became salient was the link between rotation and patronage, acceptance of the practice of discharging appointees to create vacancies for newcomers. Let us refer to the new spoilsmen as *transients*. Although many American retainers no doubt remained in office throughout the nineteenth century, the overriding fact was that many of them were also replaced by transients.

Discussing the new practice of rotation, White claims that it "was a rational remedy in 1829 for an admitted problem of superannuation, but the cure introduced evils of greater proportion" (1954, 4–5). What White could not see becomes apparent only when you compare the American experience with that of other presidentialist regimes. The "problem of superannuation" was really trivial compared with the growing menace of bureaucratic power rooted in the efforts of insecure retainers to safeguard their jobs, a danger that other presidentialist regimes were unable to avoid. As for the "evils of greater proportion," they were actually mixed evils. No doubt, the partisan transients who came into office between 1829 and 1883 frequently betrayed the public trust and proved to be incompetent administrators. However, unintentionally, they performed a great public service.

First, their very incompetence and corruption fueled a growing demand for reform, which led to the Pendleton act. Where retainers prevailed, as in all the other presidentialist regimes of the last century, some degree of competence emerged simply as a result of experience, and I suspect that there was less corruption, or at least it was less conspicuous. Because transients are in a hurry, they are often clumsily corrupt and become notorious. By contrast, retainers have time enough to learn how to mask their venality, and they don't need to make a quick "killing." I suspect this contrast, rather than cultural differences, helps us to understand why anti-officeholder protest became so much stronger in the United States than it was in the regimes where retainerism prevailed.

Second, and perhaps even more importantly, partisan transients radically reduced the prospects for bureaucratic power in America, thereby facilitating the preservation of its presidentialist regime. Transients in public service are inherently incapable of generating bureau power—although they might want to preserve their positions, they know they cannot remain in office long enough to create the networks needed to exercise real power. Moreover, to the degree that they accept rotation as a fact of life, they look for new job opportunities outside of government, an activity that virtually strangles the development of bureaucratic power.

The Functionary Stage

The rotation system established in 1829 by President Jackson paved the way for the Pendleton Act in 1883 (Hoogenboom 1961), which created a new and truly American mode for recruiting and promoting civil servants who can properly be called *functionaries*. To understand the very exceptional character and consequences of this innovation we need to contrast it with the British mandarin model. The role of "functionary" differs from that of a "mandarin" because it is based on specialized or professional knowledge plus career ladders which permit functionaries to rise to the top within their own field of specialization, avoiding rotation into other subject-field domains. (We cannot use "functional" for this type of system because this word has other familiar connotations. As a replacement adjective, I use the awkward construction, "functionist.")

Had the British model been followed, graduates of prestigious liberal arts ("Ivy League") colleges would have monopolized appointments in a growing class of American "mandarins." Two consequences would surely have followed. First, and most importantly, this new "administrative class" of generalist administrators would soon have become so powerful that, in concert with military officers, it could have dominated the presidency and, I believe, the Congress. The results would have been damaging if not catastrophic for the survival of representative government in America. A managerial elite of generalists would have easily gained control over the bureaus and departments and even the still unformed executive office of the president.

Had an American mandarinate been created, moreover, there would have been little or no reason to develop public administration as a field of professional education. The Ivy League colleges would have been immensely strengthened at the expense of emergent professional schools, and their classic scholarly traditions would have been viewed as quite adequate preparations for bureaucratic careers. Moreover, powerful bureaucrats, preserving their secrets and privileges, would have blocked the embarrassing research in public administration that continues to probe their sanctuaries and question their special privileges.

With an American mandarinate, moreover, there would have been no need for schools specializing in the preparation of future public administrators. Our leading bureaucrats would have been liberally or legally trained generalists who assumed that good administrators are born (typically in upper-class families) and not produced by any kind of specialized (vocational!) education. No doubt some technicians (operators) under their jurisdiction would have been professionals— including staff specialists—but they could never have become top-line "administrators."

The Pendleton Act

As Paul Van Riper has clearly explained, although the British idea of a merit system was accepted, it was remarkably changed by the Pendleton Act of 1883 so as to provide for practical open exams on a nationwide basis (Van Riper 1958, 96–112). This change was "accidental" in the sense that the members of Congress who supported the innovation could not have foreseen the inherent risks a mandarin system would pose for a presidentialist regime. Rather, they were preoccupied with patronage issues: decisively, they were able to stipulate that recruits be apportioned among the states (Van Riper 1958, 101). The idea of open exams enabled new candidates at virtually any age to enter a classified service. Thus young Ivy League graduates could not create a mandarin class, as their Oxbridge counterparts did in the British system.

Perhaps most importantly, the idea of practical exams was designed to replace the academic experience offered by the old-line liberal arts colleges (such as Harvard, Yale, Princeton, and Columbia) with a new kind of professional certification based on expertise in the type of work recruits would be expected to do. This stipulation reflected a grassroots anti-elitist sentiment that prevailed in Congress.

Actually, Congress had already laid the groundwork for the academic preparation of professionals in agriculture, engineering, public health, transportation, forestry, education, etc., by means of the Morrill Land-Grant College Act of 1862. This act awarded substantial "land grants" to "the several states" to enable them to establish and fund colleges whose goal would be "to teach such branches of learning as are related to agriculture and the mechanic arts . . . in order to promote the liberal and practical education of the industrial classes in the several pursuits and professions in life" (Edmond 1978, 15–16). The embryonic professional schools spawned by this act soon flourished, with government service as a magnet and professionals in office as allies.

As the merit system grew during the 1880s and the following decades, a steady flow of candidates applied, well prepared to take the new "practical" exams that would qualify them for tenured positions in government. "As specialisms in education and in governmental functions proliferated during the present century, top administrative posts were increasingly preempted by professionals in appropriate fields" (Mosher 1975, 9). Not all career bureaucrats are professionals, but virtually all are functionaries in the sense that they are specialists who pursue their careers within a few program agencies. They differ from the mandarins who, from an early age, can rotate between assignments as they move into elite cadre positions as generalists. The functionist orientation of the American bureaucracy drives its centrifugalized semi-powered status. Writers like James Q. Wilson (1989), Francis Rourke (1984), and Eugene Lewis (1977), among others, have written about the power of professionalism in the American bureaucracy.

A Centrifugal and Semi-Powered Bureaucracy

Although the professionalization of the nonpartisan career services in the United States has a host of administrative implications, a major consequence is political. It contributes mightily to the durability of our fragile presidentialist constitution. It does so by imparting an extra-bureaucratic orientation to many American officials. As James Q. Wilson points out, "Because the behavior of a professional is not entirely shaped by organizational incentives, the way such a person defines his or her task may reflect more the standards of the external reference group than the preferences of the internal management." So strong is this external influence on professionals that Wilson proposes we not call them bureaucrats, a term to be reserved for "someone whose occupational incentives come entirely from within the agency" (Wilson 1989, 60).

To me, all appointed officials (public personnel) are bureaucrats and no doubt many of them are not professionals, but professionalism has nevertheless centrifugalized the American career bureaucracy—perhaps more so than any other bureaucracy on earth. Just as Leonard White failed to note how rotation and spoils had drastically reduced the power potential of a retainer bureaucracy, so Wilson does not report on the political effects of professionalism in the U.S. bureaucracy—they have simply prevented it from becoming an integrated and therefore a powerful force in American government. Certainly it is far from powerless but, as noted above, it is semi-powered.

One might assume that students of bureaucratic politics would call attention to this fact, but they have not. Their usual preoccupation is with how officials gain and exercise influence in policy-making, especially in their relations with interest groups, lobbyists, and members of Congress, or how elected politicians seek to control and monitor the conduct of bureaucrats. Francis Rourke asserts that "bureaucrats do not have a monopoly over policy making," but they do "have a strategic role in the process by which decisions are made" (1984, 190). He therefore rejects, as extremist, the view that "bureaucrats will come to occupy so commanding a position in the policy process as to become in effect a power elite, dominating all government decisions in which they participate" (Rourke 1984, 189).

Assuredly the limitations on American bureaucratic power created by its status as a mixed bag of transients and professionals will block any efforts by its leaders to seize power. They are reinforced by two other factors which I am not discussing here, though they clearly are very important. First, the partitioning of the American bureaucracy because of federalism and innumerable local governments means that, organizationally, we are not dealing with a single bureaucracy but with a great many. Moreover, heavy reliance on nongovernmental organizations—both private corporations and nonprofit associations—to perform many of the functions that in other countries are typically performed by public officials means that, comparatively speaking, the U.S. bureaucracy is relatively small for a big country.

CONCLUSION: A SEMI-POWERED BUREAUCRACY

A simple answer to the question posed in the title to this essay is that the American bureaucracy has, exceptionally, been semi-powered from the very beginning. Although it began leaning toward a retainer bureaucracy, just as all the other early presidentialist regimes have, the growth of bureau power was abruptly halted when President Jackson succeeded in introducing the rotation principle. Subsequent reliance on partisan transients radically curtailed any further empowerment of the American bureaucracy—no doubt, it actually reduced it.

Rotationism, moreover, fueled the movement to create a career system, but the Pendleton Act rejected the mandarin model as manifest in the British career system, replacing it with a functionist model that proved hospitable to professionalism and the subsequent development of externally oriented interest networks. Taken in conjunction with continued reliance on transients to staff the top position in the bureaucracy—plus the weakening effects of federalism and privatization—this uniquely mixed bureaucracy has never achieved a strong enough power position to carry out a coup d'etat.

Comparisons with other presidentialist regimes indicate that, for our type of constitutional system, breakdown by a coup d'etat is an ever-present possibility. Yet the exceptional features of the American semi-powered bureaucracy make it extremely unlikely here. Nevertheless, students of American public administration need to be aware of the sacrifices we have had to make to achieve this degree of stability. The American government is less able to adopt and implement many extremely important public policies than are most parliamentary regimes. The capacity of the government to coordinate its activities and achieve even a modest level of integration is severely limited. Many democratic values associated with the goals of social justice and equality have been sacrificed. Certainly, the U.S. system of public administration cannot be put forward as a model for emulation abroad. Its achievements, which are indeed impressive, have been won at a very high price.

One of these achievements involves the extensive development of public administration as a field of research and teaching. I believe that specialists in this field have a useful role to play overseas—their methods and special insights can help governments and scholars in other countries analyze and solve their own problems. But they can do so only after they have achieved a far deeper understanding of the exceptional circumstances that have generated the truly unique American system of public administration than they now have. To do that, I believe, they must abandon the parochialism of the traditional approach which equates the American experience with a truly universal understanding of public administration. Instead, they need to join with colleagues in all countries of the world, using a universally applicable comparative approach, in order to gain deeper insights into the special problems and phenomena of the semi-powered bureaucracy found in the United States, as well as those of more powerful bureaucracies in other countries.

REFERENCES

Chapman, Richard A. 1970. *The Higher Civil Service in Britain*. London: Constable.

Dogan, Mattei. 1975. "The Political Power of the Western Mandarins." In *The Mandarins of Western Europe*, ed. M. Dogan. New York: John Wiley, 3–24.

Edmond, J. B. 1978. *The Magnificent Charter: The Origin and Role of the Morrill Land-Grant Colleges and Universities*. Hicksville, N.Y.: Exposition Press.

Heclo, Hugh. 1977. *A Government of Strangers: Executive Politics in Washington*. Washington, D.C.: Brookings Institution.

Hocart, A. M. 1927. *Kingship*. Cambridge: Oxford University Press.

Hoogenboom, Ari. 1961. *Outlawing the Spoils: A History of the Civil Service Reform Movement, 1865–1883*. Urbana, Ill.: University of Illinois Press.

Kaufman, Herbert. 1981. *The Administrative Behavior of Federal Bureau Chiefs*. Washington, D.C.: Brookings Institution.

Lewis, Eugene. 1977. *American Politics in a Bureaucratic Age*. Cambridge, Mass.: Winthrop Publishers.

Mackenzie, C. Calvin, ed. *The In-and-Outers: Presidential Appointees and Transient Government in Washington*. Baltimore: Johns Hopkins University Press.

Mosher, Frederick C. 1975. *American Public Administration: Past, Present, Future.* University, Ala.: University of Alabama Press.

Riggs, Fred W. 1964. *Administration in Developing Countries: The Theory of Prismatic Society.* Boston: Houghton Mifflin.

_____. 1966. *Thailand: The Modernization of a Bureaucratic Polity.* Honolulu: East-West Center Press.

_____. 1969. "The Structures of Government and Administrative Reform." In *Political and Administrative Development*, ed. Ralph Braibanti and Associates. Durham, N.C.: Duke University Press, 220–324.

_____. 1970. "The Comparison of Whole Political Systems." In *The Methodology of Comparative Research*, ed. Robert Holt and John Turner. New York: Free Press.

_____. 1979. "Shifting Meanings of the Term 'Bureaucracy.'" *International Social Science Journal* 31(4):563–584.

_____. 1988. "Survival of Presidentialism in America: Para-constitutional Practices." *International Political Science Review* 9(4):247–278.

_____. 1992. "Coups and Crashes: Lessons for Public Administration." Paper presented at the American Political Science Association convention, September 1992.

_____. 1993. "The Fragility of the Third World's Regimes." *International Social Science Journal.* 136:199–243.

_____. 1994. "Presidentialism: An Empirical Theory." In *Comparing Nations: The Pendulum between Theory and Practice*, ed. Mattei Dogan and Ali Kazancigil. London: Basil Blackwell.

_____. Forthcoming. "Bureaucracy and the Constitution." *Public Administration Review.*

Rohr, John A. 1986. *To Run a Constitution.* Lawrence, Kan.: University of Kansas Press.

Rourke, Francis E. 1984. *Bureaucracy, Politics, and Public Policy,* 3d. ed. Boston: Little, Brown.

Teng, Ssu-Yu. 1943. "Chinese Influence on the Western Examination System." *Harvard Journal of Asiatic Studies* 7:267–312.

Van Riper, Paul A. 1958. *History of the United States Civil Service.* Evanston, Ill.: Row, Peterson.

Waldo, Dwight. 1968. "Scope of the Theory of Public Administration." In *Theory and Practice of Public Administration*, ed. James C. Charlesworth. Annals, Monograph #8. Philadelphia: AAPSS.

White, Leonard. 1951. *The Jeffersonians.* New York: Macmillan.

_____. 1954. *The Jacksonians.* New York: Macmillan.

Wilson, James Q. 1989. *Bureaucracy: What Government Agencies Do and Why They Do It.* New York: Basic Books.

5

Democracy Versus Bureaucracy: Transforming the Nature of the Civil Service in Bulgaria

Randall Baker

INTRODUCTION

It is often the case, in Western democracies, that the focus of public and academic interest is on policy and ideology, rather than on bureaucracy. However, the bureaucracy is the arm of government that ultimately has to deliver the promises and face the public in day-to-day matters. Furthermore, the old notion that somehow the public service is a professional machine, insulated from the vicissitudes and character flaws of politics, blissfully neutral and objective—if it ever were true—certainly has not been true since the War in Eastern Europe. There concern relating to the nature and role of the bureaucracy has been overshadowed by the alarming speed with which unemployment, inflation, shortages, reactionary backlashes, organized crime, and nationalistic violence have stolen the public scene since the heady days of 1989. It is hardly surprising that there is little time or thought for the "administrative machine." Rice addressed some of these issues in his 1992 article in *Public Administration Review* on capacity constraints in key public institutions (Rice 1992). My article reviews the roots of the distorted bureaucracy inherited at this time of transition to democracy: a bureaucracy ironically now given a central role in the process of transition away from the very distortions it was specifically created to protect! In some parts, especially in Russia, there is a deep-seated belief that the flaws of the machine are ineluctable, inevitable, and endemic to the nature of *all* bureaucracy. The gray indifference of the *apparatchiks* of the socialist bureaucracy merely coopted the gigantic and often grotesque bureaucracy that had been the butt of writers such as Gogol and Chekoff (and in Czechoslovakia, Kafka). So the more immediate specter of economic and political chaos and the folklore of grudgingly accepting the inevitability of bureaucratic indifference and its byzantine obstacles form a considerable barrier to reform of the public service. On the other hand, this situation provides a powerful laboratory for reexamining the fundamentals of operational democracy, and a mirror for considering our own values and system.

Civil service reform is an intrinsic part of the whole national and political reform ethic. Csaba writing about technocratic reform under the old Soviet-bloc regimes observed "One of the fundamental reasons for the failure of technocratic reforms [in communist Eastern Europe] was the opposition of the apparatus of the mighty party state to any change that could, even partially, have substituted them as arbiters in coordinating socioeconomic processes" (Csaba 1990, 203). Lacking clear, reformist values, strategies, policies, and legislation, the "easiest" approach to civil-service reform is to opt for technical gimmicks using some supposedly generic basic package of computing or management skills. At present Bulgaria is awash with management seminars, often run by outsiders who have absolutely no time, nor often inclination, to understand the historical provenance, nor do they have effective local counterparts who understand this broader need. All too often the counterparts yearn only for "state-of-the-art" skills. This approach of buying-in totally alien packages reflects a naive belief in the universal application of certain all-purpose "models" of the public service.

The provision of technical expertise in the interest of "rebuilding democracy" may be well-meaning, but is frequently culturally unrealistic and highly dangerous without an extraordinary amount of contextual work and a powerful decision-making core of *local* people who are not seduced by foreign values in this time of change. In short, Bulgaria does not become democratic by becoming American. However, comparative consideration of the principles and ideas underlying the working and evaluation of the public service in an established democratic, market economy situation elsewhere provides a useful *starting point* for the origination of a home-brewed set of guidelines and, eventually, reform programs.

In what follows consideration is given explicitly to the nature of the historical and political ecology of Bulgaria's administrative history—which is reasonably typical of what happened in most of Eastern Europe after the onset of Communism. At the same time, the chapter tries to deal in practical realities.

The reality is that Bulgaria has a public service: it is not going to go away, and for the moment this is all the country has, for better or for worse, except for changes at the very top and considerable shrinkage due to the impoverishment of the public purse. So the first principle in the consideration of options is to accept that it is necessary in the medium term to work with the people who are there; we must accept this and do our best to bring them around from the negative attitudes inherited from the past that some have traditionally demonstrated almost as a badge of office. Realism is essential, and this involves many compromises that individuals, understandably, may find hard to bear. But the alternatives are (1) a continual compromising of reform by a cynical rump bureaucracy, (2) an endless process of recrimination, and (3) a witch hunt that will absorb the energies and resources that should be directed toward creative change.

Our starting point is to comprehend how the existing public service was selected, trained, and ideologically oriented; how it related to the former political process; how it viewed itself as relating to the public at large; and the basis on which its members were promoted to the senior positions that most continue to hold at present—if they have not been seduced away to the private sector leaving a dangerous vacuum. This is the human resource with which reform programs must deal, if we are not to be like the Albanians and "abolish religion," or Pol Pot and "abolish cities." Jan Winiecki, nevertheless, writing in 1988, recommended buying out the old nomenklatura in order to free an East European economy from its traditional bureaucratic interferences, and the Poles turned many secret police into taxi drivers (Winiecki 1988).

Also at the root of our thinking is the fact that the public service, whatever else it may or may not be, is a fundamental element in the operation and maintenance of sound democracy. It is not all up to the politicians and the courts. It is also up to the bureaucracy to adopt that attitude of *service* that should symbolize a system of public empowerment and bureaucratic accountability and not a system of perpetually demonstrating *control*. In this way it is essential that those in the public service understand the reasons why they are there in the broadest political sense, which is not just to issue permits, or collect garbage, or deliver the mail. This is far more important than honing "management skills."

THE NATURE OF PUBLIC ADMINISTRATION UNDER THE SOCIALIST SYSTEM: THE BULGARIAN INHERITANCE

The Constitutional Dimension

Since 1947 Bulgaria, like many of its counterparts in Eastern Europe, was part of the socialist group of countries, and this was the defining influence on the public sector, which was in reality the *only* sector. In some respects the socialist monopoly accentuated some dangers latent in any public sector monopoly situation, taking them to extremes of alienation that contributed, eventually, to the forces that brought down the system. The "state," after all, was superior to all other considerations, and the Party was, in effect, the state for all practical purposes. Consequently the relationship between government and public administration was incestuously intimate, and there was no suggestion of "neutrality," "objectivity," or any of the other words used to suggest a separate existence of these two elements. Furthermore there was almost no distinct separation of powers because all branches served the same exclusive ideology and system. Clearly, public administration reform must deal with the fundamental reconstructions of the relationship between government and public administration as well as the legal basis of the state, citizens' rights, and the accountability of those in office.

The previous situation (1947–1989) was a control system *par excellence* allowing for no real dissent, and by the end, almost no creative thought of any sort was tolerated as the dogma ossified into callous indifference and, ultimately, the pursuit of massive personal gain. Bulgaria's bureaucracy took its orders from an unaccountable political leadership that was corrupted by its power, an intellectual charade, and a total lack of accountability. Such a service concept, as it existed in the public administration at all, was service to the state and party as *master*. Responsibility is taken by the system, so there is little idea of personal responsibility. This alienation was expressed in Bulgaria by the slogan "we work for the system, the system does not work for us." Since, by the end, the entire system was ultimately perceived as corrupt, then there was no need for individuals within it to feel personally corrupt or guilty, and this is an alarmingly dangerous situation of excuse by collective guilt. Ironically, exploiting this attitude may provide the most productive pathway for reform. Cynicism had long been established as a coping mechanism by those on the receiving end of socialist absolutism usually manifesting itself in black humor, which the Bulgarian elevated to a national culture that even had its own institute at Gabrovo! But the cynicism was also endemic to those *operating* the system. This has left a legacy of terrible fatalistic pessimism among Bulgarians who believe, like the Russians, that their public service is a reflection of the human condition and is therefore one of life's inevitabilities and burdens.

The ideological purity and adherence to the Party line were the only form of "accountability" in the system. The state spent two generations drilling into peoples' minds that there was only one right way to do things, and this had already been worked out for them by an ideological elite. Such an *ex cathedra* view of decision making consolidated and heightened the conventional bureaucratic emphasis on rules and procedures in the public service elevating it to almost religious ritual. Indeed questioning of almost anything in such an environment is a dangerously heretical business. So when it comes to talking about "management" and other dynamic concepts in the public sector, people must overcome almost five decades of profoundly prudent reticence. This discreet invisibility phenomenon is particularly noticeable in meetings such as seminars, workshops, classes, and so on. Once the formal instruction is over and the opportunity for creative interchange occurs, there is a deep and lasting silence, and evidently this is the expected form of behavior, unless the question is "harmlessly" technical or procedural. The only previous opportunity for any public statement would be to endorse the proposition of your superior in ringing, ideologically correct terms. Kohák described the phenomenon thus:

Our biggest problem is not our leaders but ourselves. After forty years of Communist rule we have developed habits, skills, and attitudes that were adaptive when surviving under imposed rule but that have become hopelessly maladaptive now that we are our own masters. One of our most detrimental habits is our inclination toward anonymity—our inability to express any distinctive, forceful personal identity, our avoidance of any initiative, of any decision, any responsibility. Under Communist rule any spontaneous act . . . was treated as suspect. The adaptive strategy was to think nothing until told what to think, and then to agree, though not too vehemently. . . . Another maladaptive holdover from "real socialist" society is the inability to distinguish between illusion and reality, between fantasy and truth, between "real" and "just pretending." For twenty years the ability to erase that distinction was an essential survival skill. (Kohák 1992, 15)

This ritual has emptied much of the language of any meaning and has set up parallel meanings for other terms, all of which provide a veritable minefield for someone coming in from outside this culture of shadows. Indeed in some ways people in professional groups, or almost any semiformal gathering, appear intimidated, or at least embarrassed, by their new-found freedoms and more comfortable accepting instructions rather than responsibility. Bureaucrats were previously *instructed* to go or not to go to meetings, and one of the new-found freedoms is the freedom to stay away since the traditional meeting was just a ritualistic empty gesture. The only exception might be where the meeting is now teaching some advanced electronic technique or practice that might offer a ticket out the door and into the private sector.

The Operational Dimension

Bulgaria's public sector operated, therefore, within a system—indeed it can be called a culture—that was obsessed with petty secrecy and that carefully controlled, distorted, and managed information to disguise inadequacies, root out dissension, exaggerate performance, and deceive. At another level "real" information was exchanged, at some personal risk, by other channels such as late-night parties, subsidiary plots in plays, double entendres, surrogates (such as the environmental movement), and so forth. This builds on an old Bulgarian tradition learned during the 500 years of Ottoman Turkish occupation. Then the Bulgarians set up all sorts of double-function operations such as the *chitalitsas*, or reading rooms, where revolutionary verve was concealed in play readings, poems, and choral groups. It is very interesting how quickly the avant-garde theater and the environmental parties fell upon hard times throughout Eastern Europe and Russia once the institutions of democracy were realized and it was no longer necessary to function through "coded" language and surrogate institutions.

It will be difficult, therefore, to inculcate into such a system an almost revolutionary approach to information management. Even the term "management" is distrusted here, since it was one of those co-opted words that acquired a negative parallel meaning. The informational revolution, so fundamental to change in the West, is not just a question here of better techniques, more computers, sharper skills, and so on. It is clear that the whole ecology of information has to change. It has, so to speak, to come out of the closet and be accepted as part of the democratic process. The "real" information must not be the information that was historically concealed by official statistics: it must be official statistics. Where the whole system was a lie, truth is an almost indefinable commodity. "Official truth" will be an extraordinarily hard psychological shift for the population at large to accept, not unlike telling them that all the left-turn signs now mean "turn right." Clearly an essential part of any information theory, management, and practice reform in this situation is the need to consider very carefully, as part of the curriculum, the question of human rights and the need to protect these rights from abuse by people misusing improved information systems. Bulgaria was, after all, an "informer" society where information was power and part of a huge process of betrayal. Better information may so easily be equated with more efficient control as, perhaps, in China where the population of the whole country, plus photographs, is being entered into a central computer in Beijing.

The ownership and control of the factors of production and distribution by the state during socialism was an extreme form of the interventionism also seen in many parts of Western Europe after the war. This exclusive power in turn, like unregulated monopoly in any situation, emphasized the latent indifference of the employees and management of monopolies toward the provision of service, negative attitudes toward the public, and so on. Although the system was not specifically designed to bring out the worst in human nature, it sometimes seemed that it was perfectly suited to do so. Again, everything functions in parallels: services are performed for other *sub rosa* services outside the orbit of recorded activity. In this context, the public service offers, through universal monopoly, a unique opportunity for brokering petty power. "You want something from me, then what will you do for it?" Licenses, permits, tickets—the whole gamut of the bureaucratic monopolistic paper chase— provide endless fodder for this hungry monster. In such a world the bureaucracy has a vested interest in *increasing* the opportunities for erecting hurdles since this increases the potential for spoils. Elaborate detection-foiling and inefficiency- protecting mechanisms become embedded in the system. Efficiency as a handmaiden of democracy and modern management, in this traditional spoils context, works against the perceived interests of those benefiting from exploiting their positions in the public service by cutting down the number of lucrative hurdles (Gregory 1989). Losing this spoils and patronage system represents a personal setback for the people who benefited powerfully from the way it functioned before 1989. And so it would be normal to expect more than just indifference and lassitude from them: We may well expect to see obstruction arising from genuine resentment of the changes that caused the loss of privilege from top to bottom of the system. Resentment will be a natural consequence of reform under these circumstances, and it has to be seriously considered. The value of a resentful and alienated public service is really questionable.

One area of public service where such a loss could be particularly dangerous would be in the public security services, and this may be seen in Bulgaria in the preference shown by the traffic police for stopping cars with official government plates! In previous times they would not have dared to stop such cars, but now these cars are believed by the police to contain the people who have stripped them of their role of menacing the population. One reformist mayor of a major town in north central Bulgaria, for instance, received death threats over the telephone following his investigations of socialist misappropriation of property, and so he took to carrying a weapon and had his official car fitted with a secure emergency phone linked only to police headquarters. The next death threat came over *this* phone. The bulk of the personnel in the security services other than those at the very top, of course, remain the same whatever has happened to the nature of politics in the last few years.

One important consideration to bear in mind in terms of the original construction of the public service concerns the prior basis for advancement. This was first and last through demonstrated loyalty to the Party and the center. Thus, the higher one moves in the existing public service, the more implacably loyal to the old ways the incumbents, in theory, must surely be. This raises some profound problems concerning leadership and management in the public service in the short to medium term.

Local government was, under the former regime, largely a myth. Instead it took the form of the local representation of both central government and a central budget within the total central planning system. In fact the local government system was the grassroots end of the national Party control and patronage system, ensuring ideological purity and internal "security." Here officialdom operated on a very personal level; terms like "state," "Party," and the like could not easily be detached from the office holders who held sway in the village. At this local level the corruption of the system would be inseparable from the corruption of the individuals who represented it, and this was better known and understood than it was with the more remote individuals higher up, who could hide behind the party verbiage machine and disinformation services such as radio and television. At the local level, through village tyrants, the most venal of all distortions of the concept of service occurred, and the patching up will therefore be most difficult and even dangerous sometimes, but it is here that the roots of democracy must establish themselves.

THE ROLE OF PUBLIC ADMINISTRATION IN THE TRANSITION TO DEMOCRACY AND THE FREE-MARKET ECONOMY

It is not possible to define the precise and detailed contemporary role of the public sector in Bulgaria because the nature of the free-market economy still has to be defined in the context of that country. Now there is a massive economic upheaval with the almost total wholesale legal restitution of private property of all sorts to those who can claim legal title predating the socialist "revolution." This vast restitution has left much of agriculture and the distributive sector in turmoil. Most of the state-run retail outlets collapsed when confronted with their first "realistic" rental bill from the new owners of the buildings in which the stores were situated. By mid-1992 well over two-thirds of the store fronts on the major streets in Sofia were empty, but within them new retail and service businesses have been emerging at astonishing speeds. Garages, basements, indeed any available street-front space, are all being converted to petty capitalism. The streets are lined with stalls selling every sort of foodstuff and consumer goods. The repression of the last four decades has not killed the entrepreneurial spirit. On the other hand the municipal authorities have tried to suppress street trading, even though most of the retail outlets have closed, because they are considered unhygienic and untidy. The mayor of Sofia claimed this streetside capitalism made the city look like Istanbul, which is an unfortunate remark in a country whose largest minority is Turkish, and where the Turkish party holds the deciding votes in the democratic majority in the National Assembly. It was also claimed that these traders were charging unfairly high prices. It shows little understanding of the market economy to sweep these traders away by fiat and expect fairer prices to prevail. No economist has yet showed how the price mechanism is made fairer by reducing competition. This incident simply reveals the unhappy compromise of new democratic, free-market ideals in an inherited psychosis of the need to control.

But to what extent privatization, restitution, and the other liberating forces will effectively carry Bulgaria toward the free-market system is hard to say. It seems fairly certain that Bulgaria will end up much more of a Western European welfare state than something resembling the United States. Furthermore, the democratic stance is preserved through a loose-knit assembly called the Union of Democratic Forces (SDS), while former communists still hold a third of the vote. So the pressure will be there for strong compromise on continuing state intervention in many sectors. Furthermore, it is not at all clear where the capital would come from to "privatize" many of the moribund industries dotting the land that now make totally uncompetitive products. There is a naive expectation in Bulgaria that foreign investment is just waiting on the borders. Unfortunately for Bulgaria it has Serbia, a Macedonia that nobody wishes to recognize, an angry Greece, and Romania on its borders, and Hungary and former Czechoslovakia between it and Western Europe. Whatever the eventual shape of the democratically inspired Bulgarian economy, it is evident that the state sector has one essential role: it must ensure the maintenance of the conditions of fair competition. Once more, how this is to be defined is a matter for the Bulgarian political process to decide. But, whatever it decides, the public sector must help facilitate this change, prevent abuse, and maintain the prerequisites of a solid economy (sound money, the legal framework, and so forth). Enabling things to happen is a different state of affairs from insisting, as a public service, on doing them yourself, and it requires different attitudes and skills such as flexibility, a dynamic approach, aiming at results rather than procedures, etc. These are hardly qualities to be found in a former monopolistic, highly centralized intimidation machine seeking out opportunities for corruption, privilege, nepotism, and gain. But that is what is being suggested: that one system evolves into the other. It is not difficult to see why Bulgarians become easily depressed at the prospect of effecting real change through the public sector.

In this context it is important that the public sector not just be given a new set of rules to replace the old ones, but be given a set of *principles* to govern their role, attitude, perceptions, and behavior. Perhaps the basic guiding principle is that which states that the control should rest with the public to the greatest extent possible. This is almost unimaginable to senior bureaucrats at present in Bulgaria. The control psychology dies hard.

There are many ways in which the period of transition is going to highlight the inadequacies of the existing skills base. For instance there is likely to be a proliferation of contact between government and foreign bodies, public and private, at almost all levels. In the past, for obvious reasons, this was strictly controlled and limited. Now, in contrast, local governments increasingly have to seek out their own investment and revenue sources, and many of these lie outside Bulgaria. The process will involve entering a competitive and rather aggressive area in which other democracies have long honed their skills. There was still a belief even among many local government officials attending seminars during July 1992 that the ˙ foreign investors were waiting to come to Bulgaria, and little appreciation of what would have to be done to get them. The whole area of bargaining, investment promotion, contract negotiation, and international trade law will have to become much more diffused.

PROBLEMS AFFECTING THE PUBLIC SERVICE
IN THE TRANSITIONAL PERIOD

The first challenge in making the change from the conditions described above is to recognize publicly that they existed. History cannot be swept under the carpet along with all the busts of Georgi Dimitrov, Lenin, and friends. The previous regime left a living, breathing legacy locked into the body politic in the form of the civil service, a creature that they fashioned to their needs. So the first step is to be clear and open about this fact, to appreciate and understand it, and decide just what is to be done about it. Otherwise, instead of the public service facilitating change and democracy, it will—through inertia—*obstruct* reform. Some of this obstruction may be wilful, but a lot of it will derive from the fact that for the last 50 years for most people this is how public administration "was done." Change in the previous system, except by fiat from the center, represented a threat, and so it will not be greeted enthusiastically by many of the incumbents still warming the seats of the bureaucracy. Some broad and bold statement will have to be made about just what is the role of the public service vis à vis the public and the political ethos of the new Bulgaria. And the public is going to want to know how these bureaucrats are to be held responsible for their actions, since they could hide behind a shield of total indifference under the previous systems. How is it to be different now?

Unfortunately, as was pointed out at the beginning of this article, the focus of the national debate is overwhelmingly on policy and the compromise among ideological paradigms and parties, not with the nature of the body that must, ultimately, deliver most of these services. Indeed, as stated earlier, the preoccupation with hardware, software, styles, and gimmicks is likely to produce a public service that is more *efficiently bad* than it previously was, and that may not be a blessing—in an unreconstituted internal security and surveillance force for instance.

During the period of reforms in Eastern Europe since 1989, there has been a growing dilemma. As prices, unemployment, inflation, and crime rise, the public may either continue to hold to the belief that this is part of the pain of *transition*, or it may be excused for thinking that what it sees is more akin to emerging *anarchy*. Even in Poland where much of the leadership rose through the trade-union movement and where they were used to carrying the people with them through hard times confronting well-defined opposition, the reformers have been democratically shunted aside to bring back the former hard liners. Meanwhile, in much of the rest of Eastern Europe, the musicologists, dramatists, and lawyers have no such experience of populism and are being set aside (Landsbergis in Lithuania, Havel in the Czech and Slovak Federal Republic, and Philip Dimitrov in Bulgaria) in favor of "strong government" to check the rise of perceived anarchy and organized, very real threats to the public order (the "mafia"). Kohák described the dilemma this way:

One explanation . . . is the quality of our leadership. In central Europe today the morally pure are hopelessly inexperienced, while the expert and experienced are morally tainted by collaboration with the old regime. Central European dissidents would have greatly benefited from a decade of gradual democratization, which would have allowed them to slowly reenter public life and gain the expertise and experience needed to govern. Instead, the transfer took place in a few days, leaving the new governments in disarray. (Kohák 1992, 15)

People become extremely nervous and frightened under these conditions; the horizon of the government gets dramatically shorter: the key survival issues become much sharper and more alarming. Discussion on the nature of the public service, in these circumstances, does not figure very prominently. Thus it is much too early to say that Western-style democratic institutions have taken root in Eastern Europe yet, and there may well be a period of heavy compromise with previous incumbents simply because they demonstrated the ability to *control*. They offer the "strong government" alternative, and they have a proven record of "control."

In this condition of terrible uncertainty, and the fact that there is no secure majority in the National Assembly for the coalition of democrats, time becomes the enemy of real reform. During this time of headlong change in Bulgaria, expectations are pitted against the daily reality of enormous uncertainty and change and the vastness of the task of retooling 50 years of psychological engineering. Writing about the United Nations Development Program's recent comparative experience on public administration in transitionary situations, Paul Collins (1992, 1) has stated:

The risks of failing to keep up the momentum in retraining and reorienting critical cadres are great. . . . [W]hatever the time horizon or the pace of reform at the institutional level, unless we maintain the investment in enhanced public management capacities, the time lag between the initial adjustment programme and the actual enjoyment of benefits will be great. This can only endanger the whole process of reform—both political and economic.

It is essential then, for the reasons discussed above, that policy debate on public administration reform takes place at the highest levels so that there can be agreement on the rules and principles. Indeed, there is usually fairly swift movement toward updating the rules because of the need to pass new laws governing the public service; but the questions remain as to the basis on which the laws and rules will be constructed, and whether or not the public service needs more than laws to give it direction and momentum.

THE PARTICULAR IMPORTANCE OF THE ROLE
OF LOCAL GOVERNMENT

The local government system is the key to democracy. It is at this level that people most directly feel empowered or controlled, and so it is important to think how the system is to function at this level and not to imagine that it will be some miniaturized replica of the national government. The temptation has been to structure the system almost totally in a vertical way, limiting integration at the lower level. In general there is a replication of central government services at different levels without any modification for scale, and there is no device to enable communication horizontally among the offices functioning in a community. Indeed the socialist system never encouraged horizontal linkage, since it was the vertical link that strengthened the command structure. The local government line of command and reporting was, and to a large extent still is, upward. There is also no questioning of whether this degree of division of responsibility makes any sense at any and every scale. At the smaller community level the separation of people into bureaucrats and citizens is almost impossible because everyone is personally identified with the actions they are authorized to carry out. In the local government domain there is a need for a fundamentally new approach embodying (1) thinking about innovative ways of combining public sector skills at the lower levels into teams, groups, and so on; and (2) the broad range of skills that are going to be needed to service local governments with totally new revenue-raising and disbursing functions, local accountability, and management needs. No longer can officials sit there and administer central commands and their allocation from a central budget. That may have been more comfortable, but it belonged to the defunct control model.

WHAT TO DO?

Apart from the fact that the government leadership must issue a bold statement on the role of the public service, and the reform necessary to achieve this reform, there remains the question of "selling the package." As noted above, the civil service already exists and has been there for a long time. On the one hand there is little to be gained by accusing everyone of being time-serving party lackeys. One may feel good for a day or so afterwards, but the country either grinds to a stop or there is now an implacable and powerful group opposed to reform. The key may be that the entire system was corrupt formerly, and since that was the only system in town, even good people had to accept its distortions if they were to serve the greater good of their country. Toma Tomov has summarized this situation as follows:

There is a group of influential people belonging to the reformist factions within what were formerly called the Communist Party. These people display: open-mindedness, a feeling of personal responsibility, a strong position within the Communist Party, and high professional and social standing, attained by virtue of competence, dedicated work, and impeccable morale. Their names are not in the headlines and, I believe, never will be. They were quietly working to precipitate an open crisis but prevent bloodshed, long before awareness of dissident thinking. Now that the balance is tilted, however, these people are faced with the pressing demand to step down from the political scene and into oblivion, the stated reason being their undeniable link with the previous regime. (Tomov 1991, 14)

The alternative was to take to the hills with a rifle. Also, in such a system there were many *convinced* socialists who truly wanted society and their country to advance. If one now proclaims the corruption of the old system, and declares that the bureaucracy is now "liberated" from its tyranny, then everyone has an opportunity to be "born again," nascent democrats and old-school opportunists alike. This may seem cynical, but in the short term, the reform movement must touch the bureaucracy and carry it with it. Confrontation will not help, but here we have an "out" for all those willing to take it.

The longer-term perspective comes, in company with the spreading roots of democracy and the market, through training and retraining. The scope exists for many innovative courses, not just in database management, including an explicit examination of the national psychosis of the last 50 or so years. This has already been proposed as part of the country's first professional degree in public administration at the New Bulgarian University. This catharsis approach to reform is far more basic to the needs of the country than the mechanics of better budgeting or personnel methods, though these are important too.

CONCLUSION

Examining a situation such as Bulgaria, or indeed any of the newly democratic nations of the former communist world, throws into sharp relief the functioning of the market system and the democratic process. These are normally internalized or taken for granted in much of what we teach in the United States. Perhaps the best way of understanding and appreciating the strength of the public service in a functioning democracy is to see what happens when the basic principles do not apply and work backwards from there. Perhaps courses on American government should start with a short course on Albanian government!

REFERENCES

Collins, P. 1992. "Management Development and Change in Centrally-Planned Economies: A Review of Selected International Experience." Paper presented at the International Institute for Administrative Science annual conference, Vienna, Austria, July 1992.

Csaba, L. 1990. "The Bumpy Road to the Free Market in Eastern Europe." *Acta Oeconomica* 42:197–216.

Gregory, P. R. 1989. "Soviet Bureaucratic Behavior: Khozyaistvenniki and Apparatchiki." *Soviet Studies* 41(4):511–525.

Kohák, E. 1992. "Central Europe's Post-Captive Minds." *Harper's Magazine* (June):15–20.

Rice, E. M. 1992. "Public Administration in Post-Socialist Eastern Europe." *Public Administration Review* (March/April):116–124.

Tomov, T. 1991. "The Impact of Political Change in Eastern Europe on Behavioral Sciences and Psychiatry." *British Journal of Psychiatry* 159:13–18.

Winiecki, J. 1988. *Gorbachev's Way Out?* (working paper). London: Center for Research into Communist Economies.

6

Theory and Methodology in the Study of Comparative Public Administration

B. Guy Peters

This paper addresses methodological and theoretical problems in the study of comparative administration. This is difficult, given the varied meanings of key words such as "comparative" and "administration." To some degree, this must be a paper about some general questions and problems in comparative social research, given that only the particular subject matter differentiates the concerns of this paper from other research in comparative government. The difference of subject matter is, however, sufficiently important that some of the intellectual roots of comparative administration must be explored. Further, as I and others (Lundquist 1985; Heady 1991) have argued elsewhere, theoretical and methodological issues are central to the failure of comparative administration to fulfill the expectations many scholars had for it during the 1960s and 1970s. That is to some extent true for comparative politics as a whole, but is particularly true for comparative administration. Fred Riggs's optimistic forecast (1976) of comparative public administration becoming "the master science" in the field of public administration is not yet close to being realized.

INTRODUCTION: THE INTELLECTUAL ROOTS AND THEIR IMPACT ON THE STUDY OF COMPARATIVE ADMINISTRATION

The study of comparative public administration involves elements of at least two broader strands of social inquiry. First, the principal substantive focus of comparative administration is the structure and activities of public administration and public administrators. This concern raises a number of related questions about the efficiency and effectiveness of administrative systems. In this first body of literature, the variables and subjects of investigation are either at a micro level (human behavior within organizations or between clients and administrators), or are premised on shared and largely unquestioned values of a single political system.

Although administration occurs within a particular socioeconomic and cultural setting, those external values are largely irrelevant for most studies of public administration. On the other hand, most comparative public administration examines organizational structures and administrative behavior within more than one cultural and political setting. At a minimum comparative public administration involves comparison of the administrative system in one country different from that of the researcher and involves at least an implicit comparison with the researcher's own national system. This second intellectual root of comparative administration requires attention to questions of comparative research of all types, albeit with an emphasis on the comparison of institutions and the behavior of actors within institutions. Coming as it does from these two backgrounds, comparative public administration contains some elements of each and some of the intellectual problems of each. Further, blending the two traditions presents some additional intellectual problems.

Public Administration

First, from the perspective of public administration, there are important questions about the definition of administration and of bureaucracy and about where the researcher can delimit his or her concerns. For example, should we include political appointees in the United States as a part of "administration" because they occupy roles at the head of administrative organizations, or should we consider them as a part of the political executive (Heclo 1977; Aberbach and Rockman 1983)? Should we, in fact, include ministers with the political responsibility for managing public organizations as a part of administration, or are they better dealt with as part of the "political" government? At the other end of the spectrum, do we include clients within the system and assess the impact of their characteristics on the functioning of public organizations? To what extent should private organizations performing public functions be included as a part of administrative apparatus of government (Hood and Schuppert 1988; Milward 1991)? This question becomes even more acute as numerous scholars advocate "networks" and "polycentrism" as the best approaches to public administration (Laumann and Knoke 1987; Klijn and Teisman 1991). These are all definitional questions with substantial impacts on what we can uncover when inquiring into comparative administration.

In addition to empirical, definitional questions, there is a question of where the boundary between normative and empirical questions exists in public administration. Indeed, the fundamental question is whether there is, or should be, such a boundary. To what extent should public administration be primarily concerned with the analysis and description of existing structures? Conversely, what role should the study of public administration play in the design of new government institutions (Leemans 1976; Pollitt 1984; Lane 1990; Olsen 1990), and in changing managerial behavior within existing bureaucracies? These questions exist whether administration is being studied in the United States or any other country, but become especially acute in a comparative analysis. Public administration does have a practical and reformist side that comparative political science rarely has, at least overtly, and the important role for comparative research in policy prescription must be addressed. This is true even after the untimely demise of much of our interest in development administration (Esman 1980). Adopting a reformist and involved stance, however, quickly puts us crosswise with our more "pure," scientific colleagues doing comparative politics and comparative sociology.

Comparative Politics

The research questions arising in comparative politics are even more vexing for the scholar. First, much of the tradition of comparative politics has been that, in practice, "comparative" means politics somewhere else, rather than an emphasis on genuine comparison; I have characterized this tendency elsewhere (1988) as the "stamps, flags and coins" approach to comparative politics. Therefore, the field has been predominantly descriptive rather than analytic. There are, of course, numerous important exceptions to that unkind generalization about the state of the field (Collier and Collier 1991). In addition, many single-country studies in comparative politics have potential theoretical importance and address theoretical issues from interesting perspectives (Power 1990). The pronounced need remains, however, to emphasize the direct comparison of political systems. This continuing need is especially damning given that comparison is the only laboratory open to most social scientists, and the generation of comparative statements appears to be the principal route to theory construction (Lijphart 1971; Dogan and Pelassy 1990). At present the comparison of administrative systems is even more primitive than the comparison of whole political systems or of other components of political systems such as elections and legislative behavior (Dalton 1988; Laundy 1989). We simply have not had either the theoretical approaches for deductive analysis (other than the ideal types mentioned below), or comparable data for inductive analysis, that might make directly comparative work in public administration readily "doable." While the existence of usable deductive models, for example, public choice, may be questioned (Bendor 1990), it appears clear that the we have not had the databases nor the agreed conceptualizations necessary for more empirical work. Further, the relative state of ignorance of even many country and area specialists about administrative systems (sometimes including their own) implies that descriptive analyses of public administration in individual countries can be of greater value than similar descriptions of parliaments or party systems.

Associated with the descriptive character of much of comparative politics is a static quality in much of the work. The existing literature is much better at describing the status quo than it is in explaining the dynamics of the political system(s) in question. While the literature on Third World countries often has a prescriptive element concerning change and "development," little of the literature on the First World is useful for understanding changes and particularly not for advising governments engaged in reform efforts. This is true despite the importance of continuing efforts at change and reform in most political, and especially administrative, systems (Olsen 1990; Caiden 1991; Peters 1991). We as scholars of comparative politics are faced with massive political changes, but often appear to lack the tools or the inclination to do very much to shape those changes. To be of greater utility, therefore, comparative politics, and comparative public administration, needs to be able to speak more effectively, both descriptively and prescriptively, to the problems of change.

A final question about the study of comparative politics relevant here concerns the relationship between the systemic and individual levels of analysis (Jackman 1985). Scholars often skate between ecological and individualistic fallacies and may fall into one or both. Researchers characterize whole systems and assume that individuals occupying roles within those systems behave correspondingly. On the other hand, we can characterize the behavior of individuals in political roles empirically and then assume that the encompassing systems will behave similarly. Therefore, a major challenge to comparative politics continues to be developing an ability to link the micro and the macro levels of analysis and to be able to make meaningful statements about both.

Mixing Comparative Politics and Public Administration

It should not be surprising, given the descriptions of the two fields offered above, that melding them is also difficult. One is a field (public administration) that tends to be ethnocentric, micro-level for much of its work, somewhat descriptive, but at the same time is normative and ameliorative. The other (comparative politics) is also often descriptive but presses vigorously and self-consciously toward nomothetic statements. It strives (often with limited success) not to be based solely on the experiences of industrialized democracies and to be "scientific" rather than practical or reformist in its orientation. Further, comparative politics tends to focus its attention on the macro level, and countries constitute a major unit of analysis, as well as the major (presumed) source of variance in its studies even if the data themselves are micro-level. The flowering of comparative public administration during the heyday of development administration meant that it acquired more of a practical and reformist bent, but the roots of the field in comparative politics might make it less practical.

The variety of intellectual problems facing comparative public administration has generated numerous scholarly doubts concerning the viability of the field (Aberbach and Rockman 1983; Sigelman 1976). This current skepticism follows several decades of great optimism and enthusiasm about the contributions of, and prospects for, comparative administration. I have argued elsewhere (Peters 1988) that much of the current malaise is a function of the apparent absence of accepted and easily operational dependent variables. Published work in comparative public administration rarely looks as "scientific" as that published in other areas of comparative inquiry. The observation of the "unscientific" nature of comparative administration often was made in contrast to the apparent successes of comparative public policy studies. Interestingly, there is now substantially more skepticism about the progress of comparative policy studies, especially that work based on easily identified and utilized quantitative data such as public expenditures. The world of public policy may actually be more complex, and require substantially greater contextual and institutional knowledge (Ostrom 1991), than has been assumed by some analysts. Rather than being peculiar to comparative public administration, the malaise of comparative studies may be a very widespread phenomenon.

Although it has more company than often thought, comparative public administration appears to remain in the doldrums (Aberbach and Rockman 1983). This apparent malaise is not a function of an absence of interest, as the recent successes of some journals and other scholarship in the field clearly indicates. Further, the connections of comparative administration to several broader strands of inquiry are not entirely disadvantageous. Although some problems are shared across these fields, some strengths are also shared. There is no lack of interest and research opportunities, but a number of important theoretical, methodological, and substantive questions remain unanswered about comparative administration. These questions must be addressed if this area of inquiry is to progress. After this perhaps excessively long preamble, I will now discuss some of those questions. As well as detailing the problems, I will try to provide at least some inklings of answers that may be beneficial for the continuing work in this field.

THEORETICAL PROBLEMS
FOR COMPARATIVE PUBLIC ADMINISTRATION

The first set of questions we will raise about comparative public administration are primarily theoretical. These to some extent return to the questions already discussed (Peters 1988) about the appropriate focus of inquiry for this field of study. What are we trying to explain? What is the appropriate boundary of our study, and how does it relate to other concerns within public administration and comparative politics? We will discuss these questions from a theoretical perspective here, but any choices made about the focus of inquiry will have ramifications for the methodological stances that are required. There are some basic questions about methodology implied in the selection of theoretical foci, because certain methodologies usually associated with the "scientific" thrust of the social sciences may be inappropriate for approaches concerned with more holistic and humanistic questions. In the complex world of administration, identifying independent and dependent variables may require as much faith as science, so that somewhat less precise methods and language may be useful.

What Do We Want to Know?

The most basic question is what do we want to know about comparative public administration? As Richard Rose once wrote, "First, Catch Your Dependent Variable." As noted, most of the history of this field, as indeed of comparative politics more generally, has been descriptive. There are a number of excellent descriptions of the structure of administrative systems (Timsit 1987) and of the behavior of individuals within those systems (Suleiman 1974). If that were the focus of our work, we might terminate the paper here, for there would be little need for an extensive discussion of theory and methodology. Even if the focus were descriptive, however, we might have some implicit theoretical questions and associated methodological questions. Single country studies, even if descriptive, can have substantial theoretical importance if selected properly and motivated by appropriate questions (Lijphart 1975; George 1979). If, however, what we want to know is more theoretical and analytic, then theoretical and methodological problems become paramount.

If we assume for the time being that what we are after is more nomothetic statements about administrative life, then we must confront the substance of that desired knowledge. On the one hand, we may not want real comparative knowledge, but instead may be seeking universals about the behavior of individuals within public organizations. At the end of research that level of theoretical knowledge might still be the outcome if we are able to remove the nominal country titles from variables (or actually packages of variables) and assign to them other, more conceptual, names. In the short run, however, the questions remain about what can we learn within particular national or subnational contexts that can be used to build broader theoretical statements about administration and its relationship to the rest of policy-making and politics. A universal theory of public management will have to wait.

I once (Peters 1988) offered a set of four possible dependent variables—people, structures, behavior, and power—that captured some of what we would want to know. First, we need to know who is in public administration—their skills, values, and socioeconomic backgrounds. This is important not only for sociological voyeurism but also because who is there will influence what can and does happen. Also we need to know something about the structures of public organizations. Despite heroic efforts we still lack usable and comparable means of classifying the structures of government departments or of the entire populations of public organizations in a country. We also need to know what the members of the public service do, in the quotidian administration of programs and in their roles as organizational, if not partisan, politicians. Finally, we need to know something about the powers of the public service relative to other policy-making institutions and how that power is exercised in the policy process.

These are all important topics, but it is not clear that taken together they capture the essence of the administrative system of a country. Further, if we move away from these rather simple categories, we need to ask more basic questions about administrative systems and the knowledge we need about them. Many of those questions are relational. We need to understand how administration fits with the remainder of the political system, and how it "interfaces" with the social system. The fit with the remainder of the political system goes beyond simple questions of power and goes to the match of bureaucratic elements in administration with the remainder of the system; in essence a large contingency theory question. This match is especially important in less-developed political systems but is also crucial for understanding the politics in industrialized democracies. Likewise, the issues of meshing with the social system will extend beyond administrative recruitment to consider how societal demands are processed and how decrees issued from government are processed in the social and economic system.

Level of Analysis

One of the most fundamental questions we need to ask about research in comparative public administration is at what level of analysis do we want to proceed; where will we find our dependent variable? The existing literature on public administration, or "bureaucracy," or civil service systems, is replete with examples of macro-level research. At the most basic there is an assumption that the nominal categories of countries are meaningful and useful in explaining observed variations in administrative behavior. At a somewhat lower level, the concept of *bureaucracy* is also macro-level and is an attempt to describe a set of structural properties of administrative systems found in (Weber presumed) developed societies or perhaps in all societies (Berger 1957; Crozier 1964; Etzioni-Halevy 1983; Page 1985; Wilson 1989). This macro-level research is important and useful, provided that our purpose is to make comparative statements about countries or statements about the impacts of the structural properties of regimes.

Likewise, the public administration literature is filled with micro-level concepts and analyses that focus attention on the individual working within the public service and on his or her behavior in office. The (by now vast) work on "images" and role perceptions in public administration (Aberbach, Putnam, and Rockman 1981; Aberbach and Rockman 1983; Muramatsu and Krauss 1984; Campbell and Peters 1988; Mayntz and Derlien 1989) are all concerned with the attitudes and behaviors of individuals as they function within government. The managerial literature is also largely micro-oriented and is concerned with how best to motivate workers and gain their participation and compliance (Perry and Wise 1990). Finally, the literature on representative bureaucracy is largely oriented toward the collection of micro-level information. There is no right or wrong answer about what level of analysis at which to work, but the selection of one or another does imply something about the types of findings the research on comparative administration can produce.

Concentrating on macro-level of analysis, for example, directs attention to the connectedness of administrative institutions to other important social and political institutions in society. Thus, when we focus on the macro level, we are concerned with accountability or responsibility (Day and Klein 1987) and the way in which administrative organizations are involved in the governance of their societies (Peters 1981; Lieberthal and Oksenberg 1988). Further, we are concerned with the extent to which administrative organizations are embedded in the social system and reflect the characteristics of that system. Thus, for example, although the data used to study representative bureaucracy are individual level, their utility is to characterize whole systems and to say something about whether the civil service reflects the social structure from which it is drawn. These research questions are all important for understanding the civil service, or the bureaucracy, and for understanding the place of those institutions in the governing system, but they are not the only important questions about the civil service.

PROBLEMS OF LINKAGE AND CROSS-LEVEL INFERENCE

There are two elements of special importance in this discussion of the levels of analysis problem in comparative political analysis. The first is that civil service systems and the individuals who work within them are linked to a number of different elements of the social system. The civil service system, as a system, shares some of the properties of the government as a whole, and that in turn shares some attributes of the surrounding society, economy, and culture. Individuals within the civil service have some portion of their behavior determined, or at least influenced, by being members of the civil service, but their behavior is also affected by the society and their personal and professional linkages with other social institutions. This portrayal of the connections of the civil service and its members should help forestall attempts toward quick overgeneralization and determinism based primarily upon its structural or even personnel characteristics.

The embeddedness of public administration in the broader social and political systems presents difficult methodological problems. Those surrounding systems are composed of a number of properties, some of which would be measured in our analyses and many of which would not. Therefore, when we find that there is a relationship between some x and some y in our analysis, we assume that is the "real" relationship that exists. It may be, however, that the relationship is spurious and the product of some as yet unmeasured z. So many z's are tied up in any social system that, particularly when we use countries as an implicit analytic variable, there is a very high probability of making false inferences about relationships. This is, of course, a problem in any comparative research (Ragin 1987), but is perhaps greater for comparative administration because of the multiple connections with society— politics and management—and the difficulties in measuring our dependent variables. Further, the civil service like all other social institutions will have a symbolic significance within the culture that may be difficult to understand outside the culture.

The embeddedness raises the additional troublesome ramification that some philosophers of social science (Kaplan 1964) have referred to as *act meaning* versus *action meaning*. That is, actions taken within a particular social setting may have meanings that are not the same as would be imputed by observers not fully familiar with that social system. Thus, similar behaviors taken by an American and a Dutch civil servant might signal different things to other members of their organizations. The research methods needed for effective research on the civil service might therefore be more those of the "squat anthropologist" than the more conventional social science researcher. That is, we may need to do as Kaufman (1981) did and virtually live the lives of our subjects to gain greater insight into their administrative behavior.

In addition to the general problem of action meaning, in a political setting such as that inhabited by civil servants, there may be multiple meanings for any set of actions as the individual is engaged in multiple "games" (Tseblis 1990) that are a function of his or her multiple roles in a public bureaucracy. Even without the rationalistic logic embodied in much of this literature, these multiple and often conflicting linkages across levels and across segments of roles (Peters 1991) can be crucial for interpreting behavior within institutions. Thus, the need to contextualize administrative behavior not only within the society but even within the multiple roles and games of the average senior civil servant makes understanding outcomes of the process that much more difficult for outsiders. This will again require close observation of behavior within context, rather than the more conventional survey and descriptive analyses.

Although we need to keep our analysis at the appropriate level, it is also important to remember the interactions among levels. This is especially true when we remain cognizant of the fact that citizens and private organizations (firms or whatever), are also important components of the administrative system. Most systems models of social and political life include a feedback loop that links actions back to inputs, and for public administration the loop is usually closed through citizens. The outputs and consequences of administrative action may be individual (benefits denied, regulations not enforced, or whatever) but the cumulation of those actions may be systemic. Thus, when we attempt to measure the individual behaviors of civil servants vis à vis clients, which is certainly an important aspect of administrative behavior and administrative outputs, we may also be measuring some items that are of great consequence for the entire political system.

The second error that is important is to guard against the tendency to make improper inferences across levels of analysis. There is a common tendency in social research, and not just research about public administration, to make such unjustified inferential leaps (Robinson 1950; Retzlaff 1965). It is all too easy to assume that if the majority of individuals, or perhaps even all individuals, occupying roles in an administrative system think and behave in certain ways, the system will then behave in a similar manner. Bureaucrats may think in certain ways, but it is not always certain that *the bureaucracy* will function in that manner. Given the traditions of comparative politics characterizing entire systems, the ecological fallacy is even more common, and researchers assume that because they can characterize the system as a system, the individuals within it will behave as they should. This is often the case, but by no means is it always the case, and deviance from the prescribed roles may be extremely important in explaining some aspects of the behavior of the system, most especially the ability to produce change.

The growth of public choice approaches to political phenomena has made the question of cross-level inferences even more important. The question of "methodological individualism" is especially evident in the work of scholars such as William Niskanen (1971) who posit that "budget maximizing bureaucrats" dominate bureaucracies and determine the outcomes of administrative decision making. There are numerous critiques and elaborations of this basic model (Jackson 1982; Blais and Dion 1991), and it holds sway over a good deal of thinking in the field. The reason that it is mentioned here is that it illustrates problems of cross-level inferences. The model assumes that micro-level motivations (budget maximization), if existant among top-level bureaucrats, define systemic properties. It appears, however, that the structural characteristics of regimes and civil service systems within which these purported maximizers operate have as much or more impact on the actual performance of the system (Peters 1991).

Equivalence—The Traveling Problem

One of the most familiar problems in comparative analysis, but still one of the most important, is the equivalence problem. It is part of the more general validity problem in social research; how can we have confidence that we are measuring what we think we are measuring? Even if we are able to validate concepts and their indicators within a single society, can we be sure that the concepts have the same meaning, or indeed any meaning at all, in different societies? To some degree this problem may be more manageable for comparative administration than for other social phenomena. The tasks assigned to public administration are somewhat more comparable than expectations about, say, legislatures in different settings. Even then, however, the nature of administrative organizations and the social meaning attached to those institutions may be widely divergent among societies, even those that appear very similar on socioeconomic and political characteristics.

One of the most obvious examples of the equivalence problem in public administration arises around the issue of "corruption" in the public service. One observer's corruption often is another person's conception of acceptable behavior or even of proper and obligatory behavior. There are numerous examples of scholars studying administration in the Third World and assuming that corrupt behavior was rampant and detrimental to "development." For the participants, however, it was expected that they take care of their relations with administrative problems, and various forms of extracurricular payments were factored into the decision about the official rate of pay from government (Abueva 1966). We may argue that, after a period of transition, these systems would function better with a more Weberian system of administration, but the claims of corruption and immorality are probably not justified in the terms of the society. It is not just in the cases of Third World countries that differing moral conceptions arise. Public servants and scholars socialized in the Anglo-American tradition of civil service "neutrality" often look askance at the manifest political involvement of civil servants in countries such as France and Germany (Mayntz and Derlien 1989).

While bureaucratic corruption is an interesting and important example of the difficulties of generating equivalent measures across cultures, it is by no means the only example, and a good deal of our investigation into comparative administration is influenced by this fundamental problem. Even terms with which we are very familiar and use without much cogitation, such as democracy, have rather different interpretations in different countries and therefore require specification if used comparatively. If we are interested in the senior civil service as a component of the total civil service, for example, it may make a substantial difference if there is a unified concept of the service, or if senior officials enter as "high flyers" with little connection to the remainder of the personnel system.

The notion of mid-range theory is applicable here. It may be that concepts are stretchable within a particular geographical setting, or within a range of functional concerns, but lose their meaning when forced to travel farther. We may want, however, theories and measures that can span a greater intellectual distance. That goal may require first doing the work necessary to generate the broader theories about public administration that are applicable and meaningful in a variety of cultural settings. We must inquire, however, whether such a goal, worthy though it may be, is really attainable within the bounds of existing resource availability and human capacity. Indeed, focusing on middle-range concerns—whether defined by geography or particular aspects of civil service systems—may be a more fruitful avenue even without consideration of resource and intellectual constraints. We may need to begin with better understanding of smaller parts of the intellectual puzzle before we are capable of understanding the larger entity. As Wildavsky argued about planning, if the theory can encompass everything then maybe it is nothing.

IMPACTS ON APPLICATION
OF PUBLIC ADMINISTRATION RESEARCH

In addition to its impacts upon the scientific aspects of our work, the equivalence problem also has very important impacts on applied comparative administration and the penchant of some scholars of administration for "reform-mongering" (Hirschman 1969). A great deal of the reform activity around civil service systems follows intellectual fashions (Astley 1985), or political fads, with little attention to the difficult problems of matching the reform to the particular problem and sociopolitical system within which it must be administered. This absence of concern with cross-national learning about reform points to two glaring weaknesses in the study of comparative administration. One is the tendency to give insufficient attention to the ideational aspects of policy and administration. Governments differ in large part because the mental pictures that people (elites and ordinary citizens alike) carry around in their heads are different. Social constructionists have gained a foothold in the study of substantive policy issues (Nelson 1984; Best 1989), but have been less successful in persuading people that administrative reality is as much socially constructed as, for example, is the drug problem or child abuse. Thus, a reform that is perfectly reasonable and effective in one setting is likely to be ineffective or counterproductive if tried in another setting simply because the change is not conceptualized in the same manner.

In addition to the impacts of cross-cultural differences on learning, there are strong impacts of ideational differences across time. The administrative structures of most countries represent numerous overlays of ideas that were considered the latest concepts at one time or another, but which have since been deemed to be outmoded or even wrong. These overlays, however, do make adaptation slow and more difficult than it might otherwise be, but they must be understood if organizational change is be successful. The principal administrative theorists adopting such a perspective are the institutionalists, guided in large part by their concept of "appropriateness" for administrative action. If administrative reform is to be the search for appropriate institutions (March and Olsen 1989), then that appropriateness must be understood within the context of the national and organizational histories of the setting in which the search takes place.

The other glaring weakness in the literature highlighted by the desire to transplant reforms is the failure to investigate adequately the conditions of policy learning, here using administrative reform as a type of policy. Some efforts have been undertaken (Rose 1990; Wolman 1992) to rectify this problem, specifically for social and economic policies, but there is as yet little attention to its implications for administrative reforms. This is true despite the frequent occurrence and significant impact of administrative change on governance. Even for more developed aspects of "policy learning," there is as yet little development of methods for analyzing the crucial attributes of social and economic reforms that may make them amenable to transplantation (Dommel 1990). This is in part because there is as yet little development of ideas about social and economic factors that lead to successful policies, nor of the attributes of policies themselves. We believe, for example, that administrative reform may be different than other policy reforms, yet we have little idea of what are the relevant variables that define that difference. Further, we are not sure if the variables defining the differences are readily manipulable. If they are not, then attempts at transplanting reforms may not be worth the effort. We are probably correct that there are significant differences between administrative reforms and other policy changes, but if this insight is to be useful we need to understand why that is true. We are faced with another problem when we try to understand what social and economic conditions are related to particular administrative systems.

This question is discussed in the anthropological literature as "Galton's problem" and derives from the observation of similar social patterns in different cultures (Naroll 1970; Eyestone 1977; Klingman 1980). Did the observed patterns arise autonomously, or was there a diffusion of a social innovation across cultures? This problem is increasingly evident in the contemporary political and administrative world in which communications and organizations such as the OECD and the World Bank diffuse administrative innovations rapidly. While establishing the intellectual pedigree of an organizational pattern or a reform proposal is interesting, it is not so important intellectually as understanding the conditions that generate and support those patterns. Even if the identified administrative innovation is transplanted, it has been at least minimally successful if it persists.

What can that success tell us about planned transplantation of organizational patterns? We should consider the work of administrative reformers and organizational designers around the world as a natural laboratory for further planned reform efforts. Attempting to codify and integrate these findings will require better methodologies for deriving lessons from the experiments and understanding what can be transplanted successfully and what can not. That will require identifying cultural and social elements central to the success of the reform, as well as better classifications of the elements of reforms themselves. Further, we also need somewhat clearer criteria of success if this indeed to be an effective laboratory for change. At the most basic level success is the persistence of the reform, but we would also need to employ measures based more on attainment of prespecified reform goals.

GENERIC ADMINISTRATION

We commonly think of comparative administration as being cross-national comparison, but some of the same theoretical and methodological issues arise if we seek to compare across policy areas. One issue that frequently arises in the study of public administration is whether all administration is the same, or so similar that differences in policy areas need not be considered. This question often arises for administration in the public and private sectors (Allison 1986; Bozeman 1987) but is also relevant for administering different types of policy within government. The generic view that all policies are the same can be contrasted with the view that the policy problems, and associated administrative problems, of each policy area are unique and therefore must be conceptualized differently. This differentiated view has substantial appeal, given the diversity of public functions that even the most casual observer can identify. For example, Page and Goldsmith and their collaborators (1987) found that particular policies administered in different countries were more similar than different policies administered in the same country; policy rather than country was the better predictor (see also Rose 1990). The difficulty is that we do not yet possess an adequate conceptual scheme for identifying the relevant differences among policy areas for either policy-making or administrative purposes (Kellow 1988; Peters 1991).

The most common means of classifying policy areas or policy problems is functional, or the names that we see on government buildings—defense, education, environment, etc. For analytic purposes, however, the variation within each of these categories may be as great as the variation among them. In most countries (even the United States) health policy includes a mixture of direct service provision, regulation, subsidies, loans, etc. Health policies also deal with a range of target populations including the medically indigent, the aged, hospital administrators, and medical students. It is by no means clear that a policy profile and an administrative pattern effective for one policy intervention or one target population will be equally effective for others within the one policy area. What we need is a more conceptual means of dealing with policies and with their targets.

Lowi's classificatory scheme for policies is a major attempt at developing such a conceptual device for public policies. That work has spawned a huge corpus of literature in political science (Kjellberg 1977; Peters, Doughtie, and McCulloch 1977), but also appears severely flawed. First, as with the nominal classification of policies, there may be as much variance within as among the cells of the typology (Spitzer 1987; Kellow 1988). Further, it is not clear if the variables used to classify policies, especially the proximity to coercion, are really the most effective variables of this purpose. Coercion has been used as a means of classifying the instruments of government (Phidd and Doern 1978; Woodside 1986), but even there the concept appears to miss the subtle differences existing among policies and the many alternative means of achieving policy goals. Thus, we believe that policy studies, and the associated administrative science, should look further for schemes to classify policy.

Based upon the above description, and my own earlier work (Linder and Peters 1984, 1991), I would argue that using nominal titles of policy problems, or Lowi's (or Wilson's) classifications as a labelling device, is unlikely to be productive in comparative administration. Rather, a better strategy may be to look at the instruments that government uses to reach policy goals as the basis for a more useful classificatory scheme of administration. We argue that for policy studies per se, alternative and more problem-focused schemes would be necessary to link with instrument choices, but for *administrative* purposes instruments constitute an acceptable basis for classification. If we consider that governments attempt to influence their economies and societies through one or another instrument, then these become the central content of administration.

As well as capturing the content of policy, there is substantial variance in the manner in which instruments are administered. At one end of the spectrum some government programs, albeit a declining number, are provided directly to clients, and government is responsible for their staffing and implementation. At the other end of the dimension, a number of public programs (e.g., tax expenditures) are provided indirectly and rely upon private organizations or citizens themselves to take up the benefit offered. Whereas the first category of programs is administratively intensive and requires complex hierarchies of service providers, the latter type of program requires relatively little direct administration but a great deal of monitoring and review. Between the two extremes are public programs provided in whole or in part by the private sector. These require some direct administration, as well as a means of monitoring private compliance with public policy intentions. Thus, the selection of one or another instrument will tell us a great deal about the policy preferences of governments, as well as something about the administrative needs of those governments. This may be a place to start when looking at classificatory schemes for policies that can assist in understanding administrative differences.

RELATIONAL ISSUES

The role of instruments is perhaps especially important since many of the truly significant questions about comparative public administration are boundary and relational questions. That is, what are the boundaries of the administrative system, especially the public administrative system, and what are its relationships with other significant actors? As the state increasingly becomes "hollow" and dependent upon the private sector, or other governments, to implement its policies and programs, then the absence of clear definitions of the state are all the more evident. Further, within governments themselves issues of accountability and the role of the "political" institutions in controlling the more privatized and decentralized state abound. This is perhaps especially evident in the United Kingdom where "Next Steps" appears to have altered long-standing traditions of ministerial responsibility for policy and administration. Similar reforms in New Zealand (Scott, Bushnell, and Salle 1990) have even more greatly changed relationships between the political masters and the instrumentalities of policy implementation. A focus on the instruments of governing would provide a common focus for analysis, regardless of what type of organization is actually wielding the tools.

One danger of any conference concentrating on the comparison of civil service systems alone is that these components of governance do become isolated from other important components of the process, and the relational aspects are not sufficiently attended to. We risk doing a disservice to our own understanding of the civil service and of other components of comparative politics if we disaggregate the institutions of government too much. This concern with linkages may need to extend even beyond the formal institutions of government as the experience of corporatist states and corporatist political theory has demonstrated. Clearly, there is something to be gained by a particular focus on the civil service, but we also need something of the big picture of the total system of politics and government.

As with so many of the questions in comparative research, for example, grand theory versus mid-range theory, there is a problem of balance. How wide does our theoretical and empirical net need to be to capture enough of the total systems within which administration is embedded, and how particular do we need to be to focus sufficient expertise on the topic? These are difficult questions to answer definitively.

Again, we need an iterative approach, using some research designs that are more anthropological as well as some more positivistic ones. The former may help us frame better questions and better measures, while the latter may enable us to provide at least preliminary answers to those questions.

APPROACHES TO METHODOLOGY

We have discussed a number of methodological points, but at this point there is a need to raise some final points about the way in which to build knowledge in this area of inquiry. As we have been discussing the field, we have been implicitly contrasting it with the more "scientific" parts of the social sciences with their emphasis on indicator construction, measurement, and statistical relationships. We raised a number of doubts about the ability to reach that level of scientific development in this area. Therefore, this section will discuss briefly some of the alternative methods that may provide much useful information but which need not conform to all the requirements that our colleagues in voting behavior or even judicial behavior might impose on themselves. Further, we will make some arguments that such levels of "development" might really be counterproductive.

Ideal Types

If we move from the idea of building classificatory schemes inductively, we can go back to the roots of administrative science and use the method of ideal types as the means of understanding differences among real-world administrative systems. By moving back to our roots I obviously refer to the importance of Weber's ideal type model for the development of bureaucratic theory. The method of ideal types has the virtue of providing a standard against which real world systems can be compared. Even if the "model" is rather ethnocentric (as Weber's certainly is), the comparison is meaningful. We can clearly tell that country X has an administrative system that does not conform to Weber's idea of rationality. The question then becomes why, and what difference does it make? The danger, of course, is that the ideal type analysis is converted into a different type of ideal, with the assumption that the Western conceptions of "good" administration become normative standards rather than empirical referents.

A good deal has been achieved in public administration through the careful analysis of Weber's work and the comparison of real-world experiences with the ideal-type model he created. Page (1992), for example, used Weber's ideal types to explicate a number of important comparative differences among European political systems. Likewise, Torstendahl (1991) utilized Weber's ideas somewhat less precisely as an instrument to examine administrative change in Scandinavia. Earlier, Berger (1957) used the Weberian ideal to understand the emergent bureaucracy of Egypt. No author went into their exercise expecting to find a perfect

Weberian system, and indeed no one should have, but seeing the deviations in different countries and in different time periods does help explain administrative development. This is especially true given the developmental logic that undergirded much of Weber's model (Mommsen and Osterhammer 1987).

Weber's model has been the intellectual gold standard against which real-world bureaucracies have been compared most often, but there are other options that may be more meaningful for political scientists seeking to understand the role of public administration in the governing process. Ferrell Heady, for example, demonstrates the use of a number of models of civil service systems for comparative purposes. Further, the model of the *administrative state* offers one view of the tasks that bureaucracy must perform in government and can be used to identify the manner in which those tasks are performed (Waldo 1948). As with Weber, there is something of a developmental perspective embedded within this framework, with the assumption that not only will "modern" administrations perform these tasks, but they will perform them in certain ways. Even if this is regarded as excessively ethnocentric, the "model" does provide a basis for comparison. Much the same is true of our own (Peters 1981, 1991) ideas about "bureaucratic government" as a means of examining the role of the civil service in governance. The model is derived from the experience of Western democracies, but has fewer factors peculiar to those systems. In fact, given that many Third World countries have bureaucracies that are strong relative to the political institutions of their governments, a notion of bureaucratic government may be particularly useful in those settings. Also applicable would be the growing body of work on steering, whether taken from a more centralist position (Linder and Peters 1984) or a more decentralized position (Kickert 1991).

The Theoretical Case Study

We warned above of the dangers of concentrating attention on the single case and assuming that the one country is either so particular that no others need be compared, or is so general that all others are like it. Americans researchers, for example, tend to do the former for other countries and the latter for the United States. The advocates of case study methodology appear to say that this strategy of "comparative" research is not desirable in many settings, and opponents do tend to outnumber the advocates. The difficulties encountered with case studies can, however, be ameliorated by the use of theoretically driven case studies (Walton 1973; George 1979; Agranoff and Radin 1991). Such studies attempt to use the same methodology and the same research questions in a number of settings and then later induce generalities from the findings (George 1979). Again, this research design cannot be applied unless there is already some theoretical and conceptual guidance; the researcher must know in advance what questions to ask (Yin 1984). On the other hand, this approach can be useful for either theory "testing" or theory elaboration after an initial stage of deduction or simply cogitation has been completed.

A variant of the theoretical case study is the "comparable" case study (Lijphart 1975). The idea is very similar to the theoretical case but rather than necessarily being so specifically informed by theory, and concerned with the elaboration of a particular theory as the product of the exercise, the comparable case study strategy is more concerned with comparison per se. Of course, comparison can be argued to be the principal tool for theory development for the social sciences (Smelser 1976), but this is really a matter of emphasis. The idea is to build theory by looking at a number of comparable cases and extracting generalizations from that research.

The theoretical case study is a useful and relatively cheap way of generating more directly comparable research in comparative politics, but also has pitfalls. One is that the "instrument" in a series of case studies will be different and is a source of error (Campbell and Stanley 1966). Each researcher will be an expert in his/her area and therefore will bring to the research situation vested interests and pre-conceptions about what the findings should be. If that is the case, then there is a strong probability of bias in the findings. We can guess about the directions of the biases, but attempting to counteract them or adjust for them may simply add another type of bias. The alternate strategy of using nonexperts has some appeal, but has obvious countervailing disadvantages. Again, the problem for comparative research is how best to balance breadth and depth. How can we marshall sufficient expertise for each case without making the research outcomes just another set of incomparable studies of different political or administrative systems? The iterative approach between more descriptive studies by country experts and more theoretical studies by functional experts would appear to be one way around this methodological conundrum.

The "comparable case study" strategy has some special pitfalls. The most obvious is that we are placed in the difficulty of having to define "comparable" (see Sartori 1970; DeFelice 1980). On how many dimensions must cases be similar before they are close enough? Must the researcher assume that he or she knows in advance that the cases are comparable? If not, there is a need for (expensive) sampling of cases to have a sufficient number that are truly comparable. This statement of the problem also would return us to the familiar Przeworski-Teune (1970) territory and the need to ask ourselves whether "most different" or "most similar" cases are the best for comparison. Comparable in the usual sense of the term means similar, but comparable may also mean that the cases should maximize variance on some (presumed) independent variable so that we find differences on the (presumed) dependent variable. Given the relatively low level of scientific development (especially of usable indicators) in much of comparative administration, we may well want to adopt strategies that do maximize observed variance.

False Scientism?

A final point here is whether the expectations raised in the preceding portions of the paper are not inappropriate, and whether we should aspire to less sweeping developments of theory and methodology. There have been a number of arguments advanced that public administration is not amenable to the quantitative techniques associated with the social sciences and is better understood phenomenologically (Denhardt 1981; Hummel 1987). At a less extreme position, it can be argued that the emphasis placed on quantitative methodologies and indicators is misplaced, and we should place greater emphasis on qualitative methodologies (Miles 1979) and on methods ("meta-analysis") that permit cumulation of case study materials. On the other hand, it might be argued that this is much too easy an admission of defeat and that we should merely push ahead searching for full scientific development of this field rather than retreat so quickly.

The barriers facing any attempt to build "science" in comparative public administration are formidable. We are (usually) denied the experimental method as a means of establishing causation between change in the external environment and administrative behavior, although internal changes within organizations can be treated as experiments. Even with statistical analysis, we have more variables than cases, especially given that using country as an implicit control variable packages together a huge number of variables—some of which are not identified or even imagined (Frendreis 1983; Jackman 1985). Such models are at best indeterminate statistically so that the usual canons of social scientific research do not apply well. Therefore, we often are in the position of *illustrating* theoretical arguments with comparative examples (Smelser 1976) rather than really being able to test theoretical arguments systematically using comparative data. The illustration may well illuminate the theory being considered, but it cannot be said to "test" the theory in the usual sense of that term.

At an even more basic level, our understanding of public administration and its milieu may not be sufficiently well developed to distinguish independent and dependent variables so that a statistical "test" could even be conceived properly. Above, I advised that we should catch our dependent variable first, but that may beg the question of how one knows where the factors fall in a presumed causal sequence. For example, do recruitment patterns for the civil service replicate the social structure, or do they help to create or perpetuate social patterns? Are certain "less-developed" patterns of administrative behavior a function of lower levels of economic development or are they causes of that low level of development? We could make arguments both ways in the above examples and in many others where we would want to establish causation. It may be that rather than seeking the precision and parsimony sought by science, we should instead search for thicker and more useful descriptive statements about systems with the hope first of some descriptive generalization and then perhaps *science*.

DO WE WANT AVERAGE PERFORMANCE?

It could be argued that the purpose of comparative administration research is not to generate generalizations about public administration that will push back the frontiers of social science. Rather the purposes are more ameliorative and reform oriented; we need to know what works. If that is indeed the case, then scientific generalizations are not the appropriate target for analysis. Instead, finding exceptional performance is the goal. Miller (1984) made this point about the study of public policy, and much the same can be said about administration. That is, we may want to identify civil service reforms, or continuing administrative arrangements, that have been unusually successful rather than identifying modal patterns or even stable patterns among factors in administration. If we can do this, then the possibilities of offering useful advice are enhanced. This research pattern would not be well tolerated by the more "scientifically" oriented scholars' departments, but it is still a viable and meaningful approach to research in comparative civil service systems.

Just as we want to identify patterns of exceptional performance if the goal of the inquiry is to improve practice, we must also be concerned about which variables are manipulable. Research in comparative policy studies often has identified economic development as the best predictor of public spending for education, health, etc. The lesson then is to get rich, but that is not particularly useful advice for developing countries that were trying to do that anyway. The point is that if research is to be useful for policymakers, they must be given strings to pull that will produce results rather than be told that some remote factor X is the root cause of the problem. Again, good social science may not always be particularly good policy or administrative science.

CONCLUSION

This paper has plowed a good deal of ground, much of which will be very familiar territory to most readers. Indeed, most of the issues that confound students of comparative public administration in 1994 are the same issues that have plagued us for decades and that have plagued students of comparative politics in general for that same length of time. That continuity does not make the questions and problems any less important. Also, it does not mean that the problems raised are necessarily insuperable. What it does mean is that there is no quick technological fix for most of our research questions, nor any methodological medicine that will cure all our ills. That form of easy salvation does not exist in this social scientific vale of tears.

It appears the real hope for deliverance will come not from quick fixes but from an interaction between theory and data. Social scientists have a history of denigrating "barefoot empiricism," and often that has been justified. On the one hand, there is much to be said for actually having data that speak to a real issue even if the data are not as neatly packaged for theoretical purposes as we might like. On the other hand, more empirically minded colleagues tend to devalue the work of theorists as being excessively disconnected from the reality of the world or as being so broad as to be useless in practice. Some of those complaints have been valid, but have assigned perhaps too little value to the generation of meaningful generalizations that can guide future empirical work. Clearly the need is to connect the two strands of thought and work. Further, that connection may need to come initially at a rather low level of generalization—at the level of mid-range theory. We noted above the possibilities of developing such theories, organized around geography, instruments, or substantive administrative issues. There is no shortage of things to be done, and this volume and the associated collaborative research represents an excellent way in which to start the enterprise.

REFERENCES

Aberbach, J. D., R. D. Putnam, and B. A. Rockman. 1981. *Bureaucrats and Politicians in Western Democracies.* Cambridge, Mass.: Harvard University Press.

Aberbach, J. D., and B. A. Rockman. 1983. "Comparative Administration: Methods, Muddles and Models." *Administration and Society* 18:473–506.

Abueva, J. V. 1966. "The Contribution of Nepotism, Spoils and Graft to Political Development." *East-West Center Review* 3:45–54.

Agranoff, R., and B. A. Radin. 1991. "The Comparative Case Study Approach in Public Administration." In *Research in Public Administration*, vol. 1, ed. J. L. Perry. Greenwich, Conn.: JAI Press.

Allison, G. T. 1986. "Public and Private Management: Are They Fundamentally Alike in All Unimportant Respects." In *Current Issues in Public Administration*, ed. F. S. Lane. New York: St. Martin's.

Astley, W. G. 1985. "Administrative Science as Socially Constructed Truth." *Administrative Science Quarterly* 30:497–513.

Bendor, J. 1990. "Formal Models of Bureaucracy: A Review." In *Public Administration: The State of the Discipline*, ed. N. B. Lynn and A. Wildavsky. Chatham, N.J.: Chatham House.

Berger, M. 1957. *Bureaucracy and Society in Modern Egypt.* Princeton: Princeton University Press.

Best, J. 1989. *Images of Issues.* New York: De Gruyter.

Blais, A., and S. Dion. 1991. *The Budget Maximizing Bureaucrat.* Pittsburgh: University of Pittsburgh Press.

Bozeman, B. 1987. *All Organizations are Public: Bridging Public and Private Organization Theories.* San Francisco: Jossey-Bass.

Caiden, G. 1991. *Administrative Reform*, 2d ed. New York: De Gruyter.

Campbell, C., and B. G. Peters. 1988. "Images of the Administrative Process: Politics, Administration and Image IV." *Governance* 1:80–101.

Campbell, D. T., and J. C. Stanley. 1966. *Experimental and Quasi-Experimental Designs for Research.* Chicago: Rand-McNally.

Collier, R. B., and D. Collier. 1991. *Shaping the Political Arena.* Princeton: Princeton University Press.

Crozier, M. 1964. *The Bureaucratic Phenomenon.* Chicago: University of Chicago Press.

Dalton, R. J. 1988. *Citizen Politics in Western Democracies.* Chatham, N.J.: Chatham House.

Day, P., and R. Klein. 1987. *Accountabilities.* London: Tavistock.

DeFelice, E. G. 1980. "Comparison Misconceived: Common Nonsense in Comparative Politics." *Comparative Politics* 13:119–126.

Denhardt, R. B. 1981. *In the Shadow of Organization*. Lawrence, Kan.: University of Kansas Press.

Dogan, M., and D. Pelassy. 1990. *How to Compare Nations*, 2d ed. Chatham, N.J.: Chatham House.

Dommel, P. 1990. "Neighborhood Rehabilitation and Policy Transfer." *Government and Policy* 8:241–250.

Esman, M. J. 1980. "Development Assistance in Public Administration: Requiem or Renewal." *Public Administration Review* 27:271–278.

Etzioni-Halevy, E. 1983. *Bureaucracy and Democracy*. Boston: Routledge and Kegan Paul.

Eyestone, R. 1977. "Confusion, Diffusion and Innovation." *American Political Science Review* 71:441–447.

Frendreis, J. P. 1983. "Explanation of Variation and Detection of Covariation: The Purpose and Logic of Comparative Analysis." *Comparative Political Studies* 16:255–272.

Fried, R. 1990. "Comparative Public Administration: The Search for Theories." In *Public Administration: The State of the Discipline*, ed. N. B. Lynn and A. Wildavsky. Chatham, N.J.: Chatham House.

George, A. 1979. "Case Studies and Theory Development: The Method of Structured, Focused Comparison." In *Diplomacy: New Approaches in History, Theory and Policy*, ed. G. P. Lauren. New York: Free Press.

Heady, F. 1991. *Public Administration: A Comparative Perspective*, 4th ed. New York: Marcel Dekker.

Heclo, H. 1977. *A Government of Strangers*. Washington, D.C.: The Brookings Institution.

Hirschman, A. O. 1969. "Models of Reform-Mongering." *Quarterly Journal of Economics* 63:236–257.

Hood, C., and G. F. Schuppert. 1988. *Delivering Public Services in Western Europe*. London: Sage.

Hummel, R. P. 1987. *The Bureaucratic Experience*, 3d ed. New York: St. Martins.

Jackman, R. W. 1985. "Cross-National Statistical Research and the Study of Comparative Politics." *American Journal of Political Science* 29:161–182.

Jackson, P. M. 1982. *The Political Economy of Bureaucracy*. Oxford: Philip Allan.

Kaplan, A. 1964. *The Conduct of Inquiry*. San Francisco: Chandler.

Kasfir, N. 1969. "Prismatic Theory and African Administration." *World Politics* 21:295–314.

Kaufman, H. 1981. *The Administrative Behavior of Federal Bureau Chiefs*. Washington, D.C.: The Brookings Institute.

Kellow, A. 1988. "Promoting Elegance in Policy Theory: Simplifying Lowi's Arenas of Power." *Policy Studies Journal* 16:713–724.

Kickert, W. J. M. 1991. *Complexiteit, Zelfsturing en Dynamiek*. Alphen aan den Rijn: Willink.

Kjellberg, F. 1977. "Do Policies (Really) Determine Politics? And Eventually How?" *Policy Studies Journal* (special issue) 554–570.

Klijn, E. H., and G. R. Teisman. 1991. "Effective Policymaking in Multi-Actor Settings: Networks and Steering." In *Autopoiesis and Configuration Theory: New Approaches to Societal Steering*, ed. L. Schaep, M. v Twist, C. Temer, and R. J. in't Veld. Dodrecht: Kluwer.

Klingman, C. D. 1980. "Temporal and Spatial Diffusion in the Analysis of Social Change." *American Political Science Review* 74:123–137.

Lane, J.-E. 1990. *Institutional Reform*. Aldershot: Dartmouth.

Laumann, E. O., and D. Knoke. 1987. *The Organizational State.* Madison, Wis.: University of Wisconsin Press.

Laundy, P. 1989. *Parliaments in the Modern World.* Aldershot: Dartmouth.

Leemans, A. F. 1976. *The Management of Change in Government.* The Hague: Martinus Nijhoff.

Lieberthal, K., and M. Oksenberg. 1988. *Policymaking in China: Leaders, Structures and Process.* Princeton: Princeton University Press.

Lijphart, A. 1971. Comparative Politics and the Comparative Method. *American Political Science Review* 65: 682–693.

_____. 1975. "The Comparable Cases Strategy in Comparative Research." *Comparative Political Studies* 8:158–211.

Linder, S. H., and B. G. Peters. 1984. "From Social Theory to Policy Design." *Journal of Public Policy* 4:237–259.

_____. 1989. "Instruments of Government: Perceptions and Contexts." *Journal of Public Policy* 9:35–58.

Lundquist, L. 1985. "From Order to Chaos: Recent Trends in the Study of Public Administration." In *State and Market: The Politics of Public and Private,* ed. J.-E. Lane. London: Sage.

_____. 1988. "Privatization: Towards a Concept for Comparative Policy Analysis." *Journal of Public Policy* 8:1–20.

_____. 1989. "The Literature on Privatization." *Scandinavian Political Studies* 12:271–277.

March, J. G., and J. P. Olsen. 1989. *Rediscovering Institutions.* New York: Free Press.

Mayntz, R., and H.-U. Derlien. 1989. "Party Patronage and Politicization of the West German Administrative Elite 1970–1987: Toward Hybridization?" *Governance* 2:384–404.

Meyers, F. 1985. *La politisation de l'administration.* Brussels: Institut International de Science Administrative.

Miles, M. 1979. "Qualitative Data as an Attractive Nuisance." *Administrative Science Quarterly* 24:590–601.

Miller, T. C. 1984. "Conclusion: A Design Science Perspective." In *Public Sector Performance: A Conceptual Turning Point,* ed. T. C. Miller. Baltimore, Md.: Johns Hopkins University Press.

Milward, B. 1991. "Managing the Hollow State." Paper presented at annual meeting of the American Political Science Association, Washington, D.C.

Mommsen, W. J., and J. Osterhammer. 1987. *Max Weber and his Contemporaries.* Boston: Allen and Unwin.

Muramatsu, M., and E. S. Krauss. 1984. "Bureaucrats and Politicians in Policymaking: The Case of Japan." *American Political Science Review* 78:126–146.

Naroll, R. 1970. "Galton's Problem." In *Handbook of Method in Cultural Anthropology,* ed. R. Naroll and R. Cohen. Garden City, N.J.: Natural History Press.

Nelson, B. 1984. *Making an Issue of Child Abuse.* Chicago: University of Chicago Press.

Niskanen, W. 1971. *Bureaucracy and Representative Government.* Chicago: Aldine/Atherton.

Olsen, J. P. 1990. "Modernization Programs in Perspective: Institutional Analysis of Organizational Change." *Governance* 4: 125–149.

Ostrom, E. 1991. "Rational Choice Theory and Institutional Analysis: Toward Complementarity." *American Political Science Review* 85:237–243.

O'Toole, L. J. 1986. "Policy Recommendations for Multi-Actor Implementation: An Assessment of the Field." *Journal of Public Policy* 6:181–210.

Page, E. C. 1985. *Political Authority and Bureaucratic Power.* Brighton: Wheatsheaf.

_____, and M. J. Goldsmith. 1987. *Central and Local Government: A Comparative Analysis of West European States.* London: Sage.

Perry, J. L., and L. R. Wise. 1990. "The Motivational Bases of Public Service." *Public Administration Review* 50:367–373.

Peters, B.G. 1981. "The Problem of Bureaucratic Government." *The Journal of Politics* 43:56–82.

_____. 1988. *Comparing Public Bureaucracies: Problems of Theory and Method.* Tuscaloosa, Ala.: University of Alabama Press.

_____. 1991. "Public Bureaucracy and Public Policy." In *Context and Meaning in Public Policy,* ed. D. E. Ashford. Pittsburgh, Pa.: University of Pittsburgh Press.

Peters, B. G., J. C. Doughtie, and M. K. McCulloch. 1977. "Types of Democratic Systems and Types of Public Policies." *Comparative Politics* 9:327–355.

Phidd, R., and G. B. Doern. 1978. *The Politics and Management of Canadian Economic Policy.* Toronto: Macmillan of Canada.

Pollitt, C. 1984. *Manipulating the Machine.* London: George Allen and Unwin.

Power, J. 1990. *Public Administration in Australia.* Sydney: Hale & Iremonger.

Przeworski, A., 1987. "Methods of Cross-National Research, 1970–1983: An Overview." In *Comparative Policy Research,* ed. M. Dierkes, H. N. Weiler, and A. B. Antal. New York: St. Martins.

_____, and H. Teune. 1970. *The Logic of Comparative Social Inquiry.* New York: Wiley-Interscience.

Ragin, C. C. 1987. *The Comparative Method: Moving Beyond Qualitative and Quantitative Strategies.* Berkeley: University of California Press.

Retzlaff, R. H. 1965. "The Use of Aggregate Data in Comparative Political Analysis." *Journal of Politics* 27:797–817.

Riggs, F. W. 1964. *Administration in Developing Countries: The Theory of the Prismatic Society.* Boston: Houghton-Mifflin.

_____. 1976. "The Group and the Movement: Notes on Comparative Development Administration." *Public Administration Review* 36:641–645.

Robinson, W. S. 1950. "Ecological Correlations and the Behavior of Individuals." *American Sociological Review* 15:351–357.

Rose, R. 1990. "Prospective Evaluation Through Comparative Policy Studies." *Studies in Public Policy* 182. Glasgow: University of Strathclyde, Centre for the Study of Public Policy.

Sartori, G. 1970. "Concept Misinformation in Comparative Politics." *American Political Science Review* 64:1033–1053.

Scott, G., P. Bushnell, and N. Salle. 1990. "Reforms of the Core Sector: The New Zealand Experience." *Governance* 3:138–165.

Sigelman, L. 1976. "In Search of Comparative Administration." *Public Administration Review* 36:621–625.

Smelser, N. 1976. *Comparative Methods in the Social Sciences.* Englewood Cliffs, N.J.: Prentice-Hall.

Spitzer, R. J. 1987. "Promoting Policy Theory: Revising the Arenas of Power." *Policy Studies Journal* 15:675–689.

Suleiman, E. N. 1974. *Politics, Power and Bureaucracy in France.* Princeton: Princeton University Press.

Timsit, G. 1987. *Administrations et états: étude comparée.* Paris: PUF.

Torstendahl, R. 1991. *Bureaucratisation in Northwestern Europe, 1880–1985.* London: Routledge.

Tseblis, G. 1990. *Nested Games.* Berkeley: University of California Press.

Waldo, D. 1948. *The Administrative State.* New York: Ronald Press.

Walton, J. 1973. "Standardized Case Comparison: Observations on Method in Comparative Sociology." In *Comparative Social Research,* ed. M. Armer and A. Grimshaw. New York: John Wiley.

Wilson, J. Q. 1989. *Bureaucracy.* New York: Basic Books.

Wolman, H. 1992. "Understanding Cross-National Policy Transfers." *Governance* 5:27–45.

Woodside, K. 1986. "Policy Instruments and the Study of Public Policy." *Canadian Journal of Political Science* 19:775–793.

Yin, R. K. 1984. *Case Study Research.* Beverly Hills, Cal.: Sage.

7

Comparative Civil Service Research: The Strategic Agenda

Eugene B. McGregor, Jr., and Paul Solano

Civil service systems are once again under scrutiny around the world. At issue are both the practical designs of government and the research programs of public administration scholars. This short paper seeks to discover why the subject of comparative civil service research commands attention and what the current significant research questions might be.

The renewed call for a comparative analysis of the "multiple and dynamic roles that civil service systems play" is both timely and correct (Morgan and Perry 1988, 95). The civil service system is one of the core concepts around which the public administration profession is organized. It is an institution not claimed by the other social science fields with which public administration art and science must interact and compete. Moreover, since all civil service systems act as the bridge between the "polity or state and specific administrative organs" (Morgan and Perry 1988, 86), the ability to deal confidently and authoritatively with civil service matters stands as a core public administration requirement. The converse is also implied: inability or unwillingness to confront current issues of civil service design and management threatens our common enterprise.

Not since the 1960s and early 1970s has the scholarly community made a significant attempt to comprehend on anything approaching a comparative basis the "rules, structures, roles and norms" (Morgan and Perry 1988, 89) that characterize this strategic public administration institution. Since the late 1970s and 1980s, research can be characterized as either a continuation of earlier work (Heady 1984) and long-standing debate (Riggs 1980) or country-based analyses of the higher civil service echelons (Koh 1985). With few exceptions (Aberbach, Putman, and Rockman 1981; Rose 1985; Peters 1989), truly comparative empirical analyses of civil service systems have been few and, for the most part, they have been one-time studies with limited objectives. The Morgan-Perry argument is certainly correct that little scholarly investment has been made in the development of comparative studies built up from common agreements about nomenclature and how a cumulative research agenda can be fashioned. Moreover, the absence of a strong comparative civil service literature weakens the practical guidance scholars might provide about how civil service systems might be designed and managed at a time when the structure and function of whole public service systems are now being reexamined by policymakers and practicing managers.

The insinuation of practical notions into a research agenda is intended to suggest a possible beginning point for comparative civil service analysis. This strategy simply requires that one acknowledge a premise underlying much current public affairs discussion: the 1990s will continue to see turbulence in the public affairs environment (Kaufman 1985, 35–64) and an acceleration in the power and impact of public affairs perturbations on public administration operations (Kooiman and Eliassen 1987, 1, 5; Peters 1989, 289–296). In some cases, the premise is acknowledged in the negative as in the case where doubt is expressed as to whether a successful and smooth transition from a static administrative culture to a dynamic management culture can be negotiated (Metcalfe and Richards 1987). Regardless of testimonial, the point is that the practical task environment now requires that public decision makers come to terms quickly with strategic decisions about how to design, develop, and manage complex social systems charged with doing public work in an era of great change and challenge (Peters 1989, 289–296). Thus, what makes the recent call for comparative civil service systems knowledge timely is the unscheduled appearance of a large-scale, public problem-solving agenda. The agenda includes global problems that do not respect either current or future national boundaries, the search for winning positions in the economic competitiveness race, and sporadic popular demands for government excellence and performance. Moreover, the agenda is constrained by the reality of fiscal scarcity. For better or worse, a global scrutiny of civil service and public service systems is under way by examiners whose ambitions involve the solving of problems rather than the accumulation of knowledge.

Nowhere is the practical character of the agenda more clear than in two recent reports, the 1989 report (*Leadership for America 1989*) of the National Commission on the Public Service (the Volcker Commission) and the report (Vonhoff Committee 1980; Breunese 1988) of the 1980 Committee on the General Structure of the Government Services (the third report of the Vonhoff Committee). The report assesses the public services and public administration systems of the United States and the Netherlands, respectively. There are doubtless other reports from other countries articulating parallel themes—the cases of Britain (Fry 1990) and Germany (Seidentopf 1986; Eilsberger 1989) are most relevant—but these two are illustrative even though the two country cases are obviously different in size, scope, and substance.

The opening statements of both reports make very clear why a strategic examination of their public service systems is required: the external world is pressing challenges and problems on their respective public sectors that cannot be adequately met by continuing static administrative and civil service operations designed for the problems and policies of earlier more stable eras. While the two reports focus on different issues and action items, the two reports agree on two conclusions: first, effective public policy and government depend on public activity that is swifter, smarter, and better coordinated than ever before in responding to problems which are bigger, more complex, and constantly changing. Second, the design and operation of complex systems of public employment stand at the junction where public problem-solving, government decision making, politics, and public administration converge. Failure to cope adequately with the need for an effective public service endangers the whole society.

A further point emerges from current public management discussions (Hollingsworth 1982; Raksasataya 1985; Rice 1992; Baker 1993; DiIulio, Garvey, and Kettl 1993; Gore 1993; Morley 1993; National Commission on the State and Local Public Service 1993). Public service and not simply *civil* service is on trial. Whereas "civil" service most generally refers to the system of employment that binds people to the authoritative machinery of the state, "public" service is the more comprehensive term. Public service certainly includes civil service, but it also includes the competitors of civil service who may be thrown into the business of government in order to produce the action and results that *public* service demands and requires. Indeed, in the pursuit of government effectiveness and public productivity, the design and operation of modern civil service "systems" may even contemplate competition among a multiplicity of civil *services*, each with distinct and different founding principles. Thus, civil service is but one player in the public affairs play, and while it is perhaps correct to say that there will always be a civil service as surely as plays need players, set designers, and stage hands, there are clearly many possible roles and tasks to be performed. The allocation of major and minor parts involves a playwright and producer's judgments about how the public play is to be put on.

Where does all of this leave the comparative analysis of civil service systems? At least three research agendas are indicated. First, civil service is perhaps most obviously a system of employment. Second, it is also a political system in which public *officials* perform a governance function. Finally, insofar as civil service is expected to do useful work, it is an instrument of public policy. For each of these three perspectives, comparative research involves different questions, concepts, theories, and units of analysis. The first two perspectives are traditional in the sense that previous research efforts have focused on the politics and the administration of public employment operations—respectively, the politics and administration duality that anchors all civil service system analyses.

The third perspective is relatively unexplored, but is suggested by the two commission reports noted above. The idea of a civil service *system*, however, must consider the interactions and connections among all three agendas.

CIVIL SERVICE AS A SYSTEM OF EMPLOYMENT

Whatever else civil service systems are, they are mechanisms for placing workers on a public payroll. Viewed from an employment perspective, civil service systems have been extensively, if not recently, compared in terms of the size of public employment (Rose 1985), the rules of employment that bind employees to the state and government service (Sayre 1964; Suleiman 1974), and the nature of higher civil service. The unit of analysis in these studies is typically the individual employee, or employee cohort, and the appointing authority that represents the system through which personnel are employed and careers are defined.

One clear finding is that there are a large number of personnel designs by which people may be directly engaged to perform government work (McGregor 1991, 75–102). What is also clear is that although much descriptive research and some comparative research has already been done, there are many unanswered questions regarding the contingencies under which one employment system design or another is more or less desirable. The questions below merely serve to illustrate many of the employment system possibilities:

- *Recruitment*: Is it open or closed?
- *Selection basis*: Selection for a career or program?
- *Job evaluation*: Are rank and pay vested in positions or persons?
- *Training and development*: Shall the basis for training and upward mobility be done on an elitist or nonelitist basis?
- *Performance appraisal*: Shall there be merit pay or a fixed pay formula?

The key research question does not revolve around a simple description of which employment system attributes can be found among the world's administrative systems, although that is a significant enough undertaking. The critical need is for contingency knowledge that comes from assessing *combinations* of design attributes. Thus, the major issue revolves around evaluating the effectiveness and performance characteristics of personnel system design packages in an environment where many combinations are now possible.

In addition, there is also a whole series of research issues related to the scope of employment system design. For example, the question of whether a given design shall cover the whole or only part of a civil service system has never been resolved or fully researched. Current U.S. practice seems headed for increasing levels of experimentation even within a single "system." The U.S. Civil Service Reform Act (CSRA) of 1978, for instance, authorizes experiments with alternative personnel system designs. While the record shows that during the first ten years of the CSRA little use was made of the research and demonstration project authority embedded in the statute, there are somewhere between five and ten demonstration projects currently under way or on the drawing boards of federal agencies. These decentralized experiments involve trial runs with variously redesigned systems of classification, recruitment and employment, compensation administration, and performance management. Under a system of decentralized personnel operations, more experimentation can be expected than under centralized administrative designs.

Many other employment systems questions abound. For example, there is the question of realigning the degree of eliteness captured by the civil service vis-à-vis other labor markets; this question is raised most recently by the Volcker Commission whose defense of career public service implies a deliberate enhancement of the eliteness of the entire U.S. public service establishment. A variation on the question of civil service eliteness concerns its very definition; for example, the debate about whether higher civil service ranks are best staffed based on a general liberal arts education or on the strength of "relevant" professional training is an example of one of the great debates in civil service design (Fry 1990)—the issue turns on an underlying substantive disagreement about what civil service eliteness really means. Finally, there is perennial interest in the degree to which civil and public services—whatever their putative eliteness—are equitable in terms of being representative of the populations served; this is particularly in cases where the civil and public services constitute important avenues of upward social mobility (Wise 1990).

As a general appraisal, the impression one has from the work in the "civil service as a system of employment" area is that the list of research questions is well-developed, and that a substantial amount of research has already been done, if not recently, on many issues. Certainly, however, a firm research base of descriptive country studies has been developed over several decades. Thus the basis for ambitious comparative research on employment operations has already been established. What has not been done, however, is to develop contingency models linking the environmental demands made of public and civil servants to the combination of employment system variables that are prospectively powerful predictors of public sector performance. This issue is taken up again at the end of the paper.

CIVIL SERVICE AS AN INSTRUMENT OF GOVERNANCE

All comparative analyses of civil service systems acknowledge the blatantly political functions attached to any institution that serves as a "bridge between the polity or state and specific administrative organs" (Morgan and Perry 1988, 86). After all, the whole function of the civil and public service depends largely on an authoritative competence to know and do things and on the powers exercised as a consequence of managing public explicit grants of authority. In this respect civil service exercises a governance function.

Some of the critical and recurring questions that emerge from this agenda include the following:

- The extent to which public and civil systems are neutral with respect to political processes (Morgan and Perry 1988, 87–88).
- The relationships between bureaucracies, policy-making, and the political environment of public administration (Aberbach and Rockman 1987, 474).
- The extent to which systems of public and civil service promote bargaining and mediation across subgovernments and policy networks (Aberbach and Rockman 1987, 499–502).
- The extent to which planning and coordinating authority is centralized or decentralized (Aberbach and Rockman 1987, 496–499; Toonen 1990) as aresult of public and civil service system design.

At issue is the design and operation of the "core central state" for which numerous institutional configurations are possible (Dunleavy and Rhodes 1990). Each of the many possible designs envisions different roles, decision processes, power positions, and pathologies that depend on whether chief executives, executive cliques, cabinet ministers and department heads, or career civil servants are the central actors in executive decision making (Dunleavy and Rhodes 1990, 6–7).

It risks simplification to say that one of the most critical governance questions revolves around whether civil servants are cast in the role of neutral servant or agent of a corporate state. The servant model appears particularly prevalent in Anglo-American models of accountability, although service to crown and service to fellow citizens appear as variations on a common theme. Furthermore, as often pointed out in popular accounts of bureaucratic machinations (Lynn and Jay 1984), the designation of "nonpartisan humble servants" can be misleading inasmuch as civil service command of government operations can, in the end, determine both executive decisions (Dunleavy and Rhodes 1990, 15–16) and the exercise of political power. Public servants acting as possibly partisan agents of some kind of state, by contrast to the Anglo-American tradition, appear to have been more in keeping with continental practice.

Both types of governance models may be changing over time. Thus, research that deals with theories of agency (Ross 1973) should prove useful to discussions of bureaucratic power and politics as the pressure for policy change and civil service effectiveness penetrates the operating systems of the United States and Europe, as well as the rest of the world. Indeed, the exercise of democratic power depends on the outcomes of discussions that begin with the attempt to define the meaning of political "principals" and their respective "agents." The answers to these questions also form the basis for developing systems of public service ethics that set standards of acceptable and unacceptable behavior.

In sum, research following a governance approach to civil service comparison invokes a standard list of well-developed questions on which some substantial research about the "profession of government" in different countries has already been done. It also invokes units of analysis that are different from the micro detail found in the employment-system approach. For example, the governance approach also includes as relevant such units of analysis as the dominant institutions of government, the decision arenas, and the many political roles through which power in public bureaucracy is exercised. While some research has been done on the governance agenda, the truly comparative research and theory formulation that systematically show the relationships among public bureaucracy, policy-making, and the political environment have yet to be done. Moreover, the governance agenda appears to be changing. This is precisely the area targeted by current political and governmental redesign efforts under way around the world. Examples of an experimental attitude toward the governance agenda abound. For example, the Vonhoff Committee report (1980) hints broadly at the need for substantial administrative change, although its implementation is problematic (Breunese 1988). The Volcker Commission speaks directly about the development of a new governmental and political elite in a strengthened career executive (National Commission on Public Service 1989, 16–19), even though the official status of recommendations proffered by a self-appointed commission remain unclear. Finally, to take a third example, the Thatcher impact on core executive decision making (Dunleavy and Rhodes 1990) merely adds to the finding that both ferment and the potential for substantial change lurk beneath the surface of most, if not all, of the traditionally stable Western democracies. Political changes and restructurings under way around the world merely underscore the significance of the governance issue. Precisely what changes will be made and might be predicted remains one of the interesting questions.

CIVIL SERVICE AS AN INSTRUMENT OF PUBLIC POLICY

A third agenda results from the fact that neither of the first two agendas directly addresses the question of what, after all, public and civil servants do and produce. Governance and employment are incomplete statements of civil service productivity, although the earlier determination that civil servants preside over processes of governance, for example, dictates a design based at least in part on the idea of a "profession of government." Yet the productivity role of public officials appears at the heart of the current global debate about civil servants and public bureaucracy. Does the civil service, for example, "merely" serve as a steel—or graphite, magnesium, or bamboo—frame for authoritative decision making? Or, does it also produce final products? Obviously, commitment of civil servants to the delivery and production of final products and services dictates designs that include operations management and other business-oriented attributes. Thus, definitions of civil service performance and productivity also determine how large civil and public service systems are required, as well as the boundaries and interactions among multiple civil and public service delivery systems (Dunleavy 1989a; 1989b).

Clearly, public service education and training also depend on the selection of productivity instruments. For example, if the job of the higher civil servant is "essentially political" (Fry 1990, 188)—meaning that civil servants merely preside over policy and administrative processes and arrange for productivity to occur—then the case for extensive professional education in technical and managerial areas is undermined. Professional education and training are required only when one is being recruited to engage in the production of a complex final product, service, or result. Thus, the traditional civil service debate about the relevance of formal, professional education and training as civil service employment criteria presumably hinges on an implicit notion about the productivity role of its personnel. The long-standing British debate about "preference for relevance" appears, for instance, to turn on this pivotal issue (Fry 1990).

Unlike the first two agendas, where some comparative literature has built up over many years, comparative public policy and productivity research has only begun to get under way on the productivity agenda. For one thing, research progress rests on advancements in comparing very complex issues associated with defining the goals and objectives of government and administrative agencies. Some progress has been made here. To date, a comparative public policy literature has been developed about definition and range of public programs (Rose 1984) and the extent to which a variety of government "tools" (Hood 1983; Savas 1987) are usefully engaged in the production of public goods. Furthermore, current empirical investigation reveals an enormous variety of productive roles played by government bureaus and agencies even in unitary and seemingly uniform administrative systems (Dunleavy 1989a); thus, the characterization of "bureau types" as service delivery, regulatory, transfer, contracts, and control agencies for any given policy area suggests some of the complexity of defining and operationalizing the productivity contribution of public service systems (Dunleavy 1989b).

Not surprisingly, the least progress has been made in this third research agenda. The questions are hard to answer because they involve comparisons of the core administrative functions of government (Dunleavy 1989a; 1989b). Moreover, the units of analysis are different from research on either employment or governance issues. For example, in the "civil service as public policy instrument" perspective, the units of analysis include a long list of policy authorizers, implementers, fixers, payers, producers, arrangers, and clients and consumers who define both the domain of *public* service and basis for purposive *civil* service activity. This agenda does not undermine or deny the importance of the official *civil* service, so important in the first two agendas, but it does establish the framework within which civil service is used, if at all.

In summary, it is axiomatic that all comparative research productivity depends upon the questions asked. The intermediate conclusion here is that civil service comparison involves at least three types of questions. Each type, in turn, focuses on different dimensions of civil services, invokes different units of analysis, and reaps different payoffs in the derived answers and generalizations. A corollary conclusion is that the indiscriminate intermingling of agendas, research questions, and units of analysis probably dooms the prospects for successful comparative research.

TOWARD A THEORY OF SYSTEMS

The foregoing discussion does indeed suggest that civil service and public service systems play "multiple and dynamic roles" (Morgan and Perry 1988). The problem, however, is that if the roles are truly "multiple and dynamic," then developing a firm understanding of a "system" is not a trivial undertaking. By definition, systems involve the interactions and transactions connecting interdependent pieces of an operating whole. Yet if all three research agendas, mentioned above, are in some way critical both to the design and understanding of a public service "system," then explicit connections among the three research agendas must be defined and operationalized.

Linking the three agendas is difficult enough for static public service systems. Dynamic systems pose an even greater challenge. However daunting the challenge, at least three general strategies for systems development might be considered. First, analysis can concentrate on the social roles played by civil and public services in society (Morgan and Perry 1988). The three agendas suggest three role sets within which there are many possible variations. For example, public service systems are most obviously sources of employment, and thus, without "producing" anything, the salient "role" of civil and public service might be defined as providing economic opportunity and upward mobility opportunity for parts of society whose prospects would otherwise be limited.

A second role possibility is that public service systems are useful in terms of governance. This is a distinctly political formulation in which civil servants perform a steerage and decision-making function as guardians of democratic processes. In this case, civil service might be viewed as serving a maintenance, or process, good (Morgan and Perry 1988, 92–94), where officials are employed to protect institutions of sovereignty and legitimacy that, in turn, maintain community and public order. Comparison of precisely how this role has been played in the past and might be played in the future is another direction that could be taken by role research.

In a third possible casting of "role," civil and public services are to be viewed as instruments of public goods production. Production is a slippery concept for which a final definition is not required here, but civil service "productivity" might be loosely defined in terms of the final object and result of organized work effort. Thus, productivity research would focus on the contributions of administrative work systems to intermediate administrative outputs (e.g., cases processed) as well as final policy outcomes and public goods. Clearly, civil service systems can play many roles with respect to public production. For example, civil servants might serve as arrangers, payers, and producers of final products that increase public goods and decrease public ills. Furthermore, productivity roles clearly vary as public policy employs the instruments of direct service delivery, contracts, grants, transfer payments, tax expenditures, and so forth, in order to achieve its aims.

A second general strategy for understanding a whole public service "system," or configuration, is to examine the tension between the pieces and the whole of a public. This strategy emphasizes the salience of the governance agenda, since the act of resolving the inherent tension between the "public interest" and constituent factions comprising the public is inherently political. The tension between top-down and bottom-up budgeting and management models is illustrative, for the implicit conflict between aggregate spending constraints promulgated by a whole fiscal policy and general management strategy, on the one hand, and the grass-roots resource claims of constituent agencies and programs, on the other, are an enduring fact of public management life.

Another illustration is found in the classic pressure group struggle where the governance of a whole public often competes with the goals and pressures of organized interests. The United States is traditionally regarded, for example, as a system in which the constituency interests and subunit pressures have dominated decisions about the interests of the whole (Aberbach and Rockman 1987, 501–502). However, circumstances change. One way to read the Volcker Commission report, for example, is to view its recommendations to strengthen the top career executive system as a move to increase the leverage a chief executive of a whole government enjoys with respect to divergent factions. Whether other countries, such as the United Kingdom, France, Germany, or the Netherlands (Breunese 1988), display similar or contrasting configurations and changes remains an important issue.

A third research strategy by which public service configurations can be understood is in terms of the contingency links that connect a public policy "environment" to a public service "system." Here, the unit of analysis becomes a whole polity and the task environment in which a nation, state, or city must operate. The basis for this strategy depends on a fundamental axiom: all public service systems must respond to the opportunities, threats, and challenges posed by their task environments or they cannot survive in the long run. We avoid here the difficult question of whether public services can "die" in the same manner that resource-starved organizations can cease to function (Kaufman 1985). Creating precise models of a public "environment" is prospectively difficult. A basic construct would need to take into account the complexities of measuring the turbulence, stability, competition, scarcity, power, and strategic threats and opportunities that comprise the task environment of any public agency or polity.

Notwithstanding difficulties, there is precedent for a strategic environmental approach. The contingency management research literature on private sector industrial management is well developed. One promising public sector application of this "outside-in" logic can be found in an emerging literature on European public management (Kooiman and Eliassen 1987). Here, one finds attempts to create models of policy environments that involve determining whether or not substantive policy issues are critical to survival and whether the social environment is competitive. From such determinations are derived judgments about the public service configurations that best fit environmental demands (Bekke 1987). For example, decisions about centralizing and decentralizing public service systems derive from such environmental judgments.

Environmental typologies need not be static. It is theoretically possible to create models where changes in environmental characteristics clearly signal the need to redefine and redesign systems of management and public service. This third strategy is also appealing because of the face validity of its premise: internal organization and management do indeed depend on the characteristics of the task environment. It is clear, for example, merely from the nonrandom sampling of two public service commissions and committees (Vonhoff Committee 1980; Volcker Commission 1989), that it is precisely because of changing public task environment that reexamination of the basis for public and civil service was deemed necessary in at least two countries. One suspects that policymakers in other countries have reached similar conclusions and that the active reappraisal of public service systems is under way around the world.

What summation can be reached about comparative civil service *systems*? It has been suggested here that each of the three comparative research agendas is, by itself, a kind of system—an employment system, a political system, and a policy implementing system, respectively. In reality, these are only partial systems. The current list of problems being pressed on policymakers—politicians and public managers alike—cut across the three agendas. Thus, real world problem-solving requires experimentation with more than one agenda *at the same time*. Solving problems of government productivity, for example, also has implications for governance *and* employment system design. Whether each agenda should be treated separately or as part of a single systemic configuration depends upon whether a strategic overlay can be developed that can link the three agendas. A multilevel research approach appears to be indicated.

A final conclusion is that there appears to be some mutual gain in attempting to link practitioners and scholars. The practioner's need for answers to important questions in advance of the development of a secure knowledge base will prove problematic to many scholars. Nevertheless, willingness to accept the challenge of joining two agendas may enrich scholarly insight rather than leaving scholars and the academy alone to pursue a seemingly dispassionate and presumably scientific quest for pure knowledge unconnected to any practical agenda. If research links can be established, then both practicing and scholarly communities will be strengthened for different reasons but to the benefit of all.

REFERENCES

Aberbach, J. D., R. D. Putnam, and B. A. Rockman. 1981. *Bureaucrats and Politicians in Western Democracies*. Cambridge, Mass.: Harvard University Press.

Aberbach, Joel D., and Bert A. Rockman. 1987. "Comparative Administration Methods Muddles and Models." *Administration and Society* 18 (4):473–506.

Baker, Randall. 1993. "Democracy Versus Bureaucracy: Transforming the Nature of the Civil Service in Bulgaria." Bloomington, Ind.: School of Public and Environmental Affairs, Occasional Paper #31.

Bekke, Hans. 1987. "Public Management in Transition." In *Managing Public Organizations: Lessons from Contemporary European Experience*, ed. J. Kooiman and K. A. Eliassen. London: Sage Publications, 17–32.

Breunese, Jaap N. 1988. "Administrative Reforms in the Netherlands." In *Public Infrastructure Redefined*, ed. L. J. Roborgh, R. R. Stough, and Th. A. J. Toonen. Leiden: Groen, 251–261.

DiIulio, John J., Jr., Gerald Garvey, and Donald F. Kettl. 1993. *Improving Government Peformance: An Owner's Manual*. Washington, D.C.: The Brookings Institution.

Dunleavy, Patrick. 1989a. "The Architecture of the British Central State, Part I: Framework for Analysis." *Public Administration* 67:249–276.

_____. 1989b. "The Architecture of the British Central State, Part II: Empirical Findings" *Public Administration* 67:391–418.

_____, and R. A. W. Rhodes. 1990. "Core Executive Studies in Britain." *Public Administration* 68:3–28.

Eilsberger, Rupert. 1989. "Education for Public Administration in the Federal Republic of Germany." Bloomington, Ind.: School of Public and Environmental Affairs, Occasional Paper #23.

Fry, Geoffrey. 1990. "The Fulton Committee and the 'Preference for Relevance' Issue." *Public Administration* 68:175–190.

Gore, Al. 1993. *Creating a Government That Works Better and Costs Less*. Washington, D.C.: Report of the National Performance Review.

Heady, Ferrell. 1984. *Public Administration: A Comparative Perspective*, 3d ed. New York: Marcel Dekker.

Hollingsworth, J. Rogers, ed. 1982. *Government and Economic Performance*. Special issue of *The Annals* of the American Academy of Political and Social Science 459 (January).

Hood, Christopher, C. 1983. *The Tools of Government*. Chatham, N.J.: Chatham House Publishers.

Kaufman, Herbert. 1985. *Time, Chance, and Organizations: Natural Selection in a Perilous Environment*. Chatham, N.J.: Chatham House Publishers, Inc.

Koh, B. C. 1985. "The Recruitment of Higher Civil Servants in Japan: A Comparative Perspective." *Asian Survey* 25:292–309.

Kooiman, Jan, and Kjell A. Eliassen. 1987. Preface to *Managing Public Organizations: Lessons from Contemporary European Experience*, ed. J. Kooiman and K. A. Eliassen. London: Sage Publications, 17–32.

Lynn, Jonathan, and Antony Jay, eds. 1984. *The Complete Yes Minister: The Diaries of a Cabinet Minister*. London: BBC Books.

McGregor, Eugene B., Jr. 1991. *Strategic Management of Human Knowledge, Skills, and Abilities: Workforce Decision Making in the Post-Industrial Era*. San Francisco: Jossey-Bass.

Metcalfe, Les, and Sue Richards. 1987. "Evolving Public Management Cultures." In *Managing Public Organizations: Lessons from Contemporary European Experience*, ed. J. Kooiman and K. A. Eliassen. London: Sage Publications.

Morgan, E. Philip, and James L. Perry. 1988. "Re-orienting the Comparative Study of Civil Service Systems." *Review of Public Personnel Administration* 8 (3):84–95.

Morley, Don. 1993. "Strategic Direction in the British Public Service." *Long Range Planning* 26:77–86.

National Commission on the Public Service (Volcker Commission). 1989. *Leadership for America: Rebuilding the Public Service*. Washington, D.C.

National Commission on the State and Local Public Service. 1993. *Hard Truths/Tough Choices: An Agenda for State and Local Reform.* Albany, N.Y.: The Nelson A. Rockefeller Institute of Government.

Peters, B. Guy. 1989. *The Politics of Bureaucracy,* 3d ed. London: Longman.

Raksasataya, Amara, ed. 1985. *Special Number on Government Organization and Personnel Management Reform in Asia.* Special issue of the *Thai Journal of Development Administration* 25 (December).

Rice, Eric M. 1992. "Public Administration in Post-Socialist Eastern Europe." *Public Administration Review* 52:116–124.

Riggs, Fred. 1980. "Three Dubious Hypotheses: A Comment on Heper, Kim, and Pai." *Administration and Society* 12:301–326.

Rose, Richard. 1984. *Understanding Big Government: The Programme Approach.* Beverly Hills, Cal.: Sage Publications.

_____. 1985. *Public Employment in Western Nations.* Cambridge: Cambridge University Press.

Ross, Stephen A. 1973. "The Economic Theory of Agency: The Principal's Problem." *American Economic Review* 63:134–139.

Savas, E. S. 1987. *Privatization: The Key to Better Government.* Chatham, N.J.: Chatham House Publishers.

Sayre, Wallace S. 1964. "Bureaucracies: Some Contrasts in Systems." *The Indian Journal of Public Administration* 10:219–229.

Siedentopf, Heinrich. 1986. *Public Administration in the Federal Republic of Germany.* Speyer: Speyerer Arbeitshefte 69.

Suleiman, Ezra N. 1974. *Politics, Power, and Bureaucracy in France: The Administrative Elite.* Princeton: Princeton University Press.

Toonen, Theo A. J. 1990. "The Unitary State as a System of Co-Governance: The Case of the Netherlands." *Public Administration* 68:281–297.

Vonhoff Committee. 1980. Third Report by the Committee on the General Structure of the Netherlands Government Services. The Hague.

Wise, Lois R. 1990. "Social Equity in Civil Service Systems." *Public Administration Review* 50:567–575.

8

Administrative Reform

Gerald E. Caiden

Public managers everywhere profess to search continuously for improved government performance in general, and improved managerial performance in particular. If one looks into their actual conduct, one will immediately recognize two distinct and opposing attitudes to administrative reform. The crusading entrepreneurs are always on the lookout for new ideas, better methods, innovations and promising designs. They are open to novelty. They study what others do to identify what they might be able to copy or adapt. They are prepared to take risks to do even better. Indeed, so eager for change are they that they are often suckers for the untried, and they fall victim to the fads and gimmicks that often sweep through public management without rhyme or reason.

In contrast, the reactionary bureaucrats show excessive caution. They rarely indicate willingness to try anything new. Indeed, they oppose anything that threatens to upset routine. They are closed to novelty, and they will find excuses why foreign practices cannot work in their circumstances. They are not prepared to risk present achievements for possible future gains that may well turn out to be losses. Whereas the crusading entrepreneurs back administrative reform, the reactionary bureaucrats obstruct it. They don't believe in administrative reform at all, and their stubborn resistance to reform usually succeeds. They are not easily fooled, and they will go for the well tried and proven every time in preference to the untried and experimental no matter how promising. Both sides fight to capture the middle ground with the conservatives favored by vested interests in the status quo and popular fear of the unknown and aversion to disruption.

Although the chances for successful administrative reform are poor, there are always crusading entrepreneurs in every generation who are willing to try their hand and some of them beat all the odds. If ever circumstances looked unpromising, they were for Florence Nightingale who without backing, experience, professional management skills, and position, can be considered one of the most successful administrative reformers of all time in what she instigated once her initial proposals were implemented. She transformed the delivery of public health and medical services, and her example remains an inspiration for all reformers since. A reading of her autobiography (Woodham-Smith 1955) is a good starting point in the comparative study of administrative reform, for here was a rank amateur who stuck to her guns, overcame tremendous odds and benefited untold millions of succeeding generations.

Florence Nightingale's story is a classic case study of what administrative reform entails, the qualities required in reformers, the forces garnered against reform, the strategies used to overcome stubborn resistance, and the different instruments employed to shape the final product, if ever finality can be identified in this or any other case for the story of public health administration reforms continues. Unfortunately, administrative reformers don't make good copy and biographies even of crusading entrepreneurs in public management are rare anywhere. In their absence, we begin at quite a different point, namely, dissatisfaction with government performance.

PUBLIC DISSATISFACTION
WITH GOVERNMENT PERFORMANCE

A common and justifiable complaint around the world is that governments, irrespective of regime, are not and have not been performing well for some time. People generally are disappointed in government performance even though government manages somehow to avoid fouling up altogether. Governments promise much but deliver much less. They rarely come through as expected. They borrow large sums of money and impose more and more taxes, but they cannot prove value for money. They employ large numbers of people and command much talent, but few seem to contribute much to the general welfare or appear productive. On the contrary, they diminish the quality of life with their insistence on so much red-tape even for the simplest transactions. In many countries, people dread the thought of dealing with government agencies and employ intermediaries to do their business for them. Open a conversation anywhere and people will soon voice their dissatisfaction with government performance.

How justifiable are such universal attitudes? Nobody really knows. No satisfactory way of measuring government performance has yet been devised or agreed upon and even if it were, facts are unlikely to convince all the doubters who go on instinct, perhaps an instinctive dislike of government and what government represents. Most governments do not care enough to provide any channels for public grievances to be aired let alone investigated. Many governments which do provide complaint handling systems don't really take much notice of them and starve them of the resources needed to do a good job. Those that really take public complaints seriously and provide proper grievance machinery, such as the ombudsman fraternity (Caiden 1983), show that while in their case there is a good deal of ignorance about what government can and cannot do, and what citizens are or are not entitled to, significant wrongdoing evades public management systems devised to capture and correct it. Much avoidable injury is caused, and the victims are right to complain. Ombudsman offices uncover injustices mostly of a minor nature, but every so often they also came across major instances of public maladministration. They worry whether or not the few people who complain represent merely the tip of the iceberg of all those who really should complain but don't.

An interesting exercise is to observe public complaint mechanisms at work, what they do, who takes advantage of them, how complaints are handled and if justified how they are settled or resolved, what gives rise to complaints, what people most complain about, and, most important, managerial attitudes toward complaints, complainers, and investigations. If no mechanisms are easily accessible, then inviting a sample of the public to talk about government or what they feel is wrong with it will usually cover much the same ground. Everyone, it seems, has his or her favorite story about public maladministration and needs little bidding to share it. The same thing is also largely true of people who work within government administration or who do business with government agencies, providing they do not fear victimization or punishment for revealing what they know about government operations. If there is so much smoke around, surely there must be fire somewhere.

UNCOVERING SERIOUS PUBLIC MALADMINISTRATION

Of course, there is fire. It would be miraculous if government organizations ran as smoothly as people expect. For a start, people's expectations are probably too high. Further, public mismanagement is probably much more prevalent than anyone suspects. As long as government is run by human beings and human beings are imperfect, then mistakes are bound to occur. In all human arrangements, there is always room for improvement; none is perfect. All organizations operate with imperfections; all are infected with bureaupathologies. This does not stop them performing well, but if left untreated the bureaupathologies will spread and intensify and eventually impede performance noticeably. It is relatively easy to identify bureaupathologies (Caiden 1991b, 492) infecting public organizations, but it is not so easy to determine which are serious enough to impede performance and to require corrective treatment.

If bureaupathologies were identified, traced down, and treated before they got out of hand (and this is a basic obligation of public sector managers), there would be little need for administrative reform. Things would not get so out of hand that simple corrective actions would no longer suffice. But untreated bureaupathologies accelerate into serious public maladministration that sooner or later becomes all too obvious. Bad accidents happen; public works collapse; epidemics break out; battles are lost. Public places become unsafe and private places insecure. The public suffer and are outraged. Political capital is lost if nothing is done to assuage public discontent. Further temporizing just will not do. Action is called for, at least an inquiry into what brought about such a situation and what might be done to avoid any recurrence or to turn things around. In short, serious public maladministration does not need uncovering: eventually it reveals itself. Unfortunately, the public has to endure the pain which smarter public management might have averted.

THE GRAND DIAGNOSIS

When obvious breakdowns in government administration occur, the public seeks retribution and governments offer scapegoats. But none of this gets to the heart of what went wrong and which bureaupathologies have to be treated. Governments call on respected and trusted experts to tell them. They appoint official inquiries to uncover the facts, reveal the shortcomings, and suggest remedies in the grand diagnosis—grand because the inquiry is sweeping in scope and fully empowered to investigate thoroughly. Most countries have had at least one such grand diagnosis in recent decades and several have them frequently. During the mid-1980s, for example, the Commonwealth Government of Australia had a rash of them and before that, most governments in Australia had grand inquiries specifically into their public management systems (Smith and Weller 1978). They are landmarks in administrative history wherever they report. They are quoted for generations afterward.

Some grand diagnoses are more important than others. Those conducted by the superpowers of the time and the traditional fashion leaders in administrative matters receive most attention. What they decide to do reverberates around the globe and lesser powers copy them. Others less fortunate cannot afford to hold such elaborate inquiries and even if they had the means to publicize their own grand diagnoses, perhaps only their immediate neighbors would take notice because no far away country would. In recent years, many of the superpowers and fashion leaders have held such inquiries (Caiden 1991a, 168), which have received inordinate publicity and attention. Comparing their results and findings alone makes fascinating reading. Their reports (sometimes in multiple volumes) constitute administrative textbooks superior often to academic literature in quality of writing and depth of research. To outsiders, they reveal more than can be found elsewhere; they are a mine of information. They also hide things. So it is better to read them together with mass media comment at the time of their release, as well as the later reports, to get the real flavor and context of the reports. It is also important to compare them with any predecessors just to see whether the same bureaupathologies occur again and again and whether the same remedies are repeated.

For a proper understanding of such grand diagnoses, it is useful to keep a checklist in mind. It is impossible to find out the whole truth behind grand inquiries and alas all too often one is not able to go much behind the final report. Nonetheless, the following items should appear in any checklist:

- What were the circumstances bringing about the appointment of an inquiry?
- Why were the terms of reference framed as they were? What was included and what was deliberately excluded? By whom? Why? With what impact on the subsequent inquiry?
- Who was appointed to head the inquiry? How were other members selected? What qualifications did they possess pertinent to the inquiry? How did they view the inquiry? What part did they play in conducting the inquiry?
- What supports did the inquiry have? Who owned the inquiry? Who identified with it? What powers were given to the inquiry? What restrictions were placed? What access to resources and research did the inquiry have? How dependent was the inquiry on information received? Could the inquiry independently validate evidence? Did witnesses cooperate and comply or were they reluctant and evasive?
- How much is known about the internal politics of the inquiry? Who took the lead? Who compromised? Who was ignored? Who largely drafted the report?
- What is the nature of the report? How was it released? How many copies were printed? To whom were copies sent? How was the report distributed?
- What was the follow-up? Who was required to act on the report? How were the findings implemented?
- Who has assessed the long-term impact of the inquiry? What measures of success have been applied? By whom? What do the critics charge?

Answers to these questions should reveal the worth of the grand diagnosis and point to the obstacles that were placed before administrative reform.

OBSTACLES TO REFORM

The circumstances giving rise to bureaupathologies are likely to inhibit the progress of administrative reform. Here is the paradox—countries most in need of administrative reform are the least able to implement it. If they had what it took to maintain competent public management able to reduce public maladministration and lessen the need for reforms, they would not find themselves in such a mess and would be better able to adopt the necessary remedies and antidotes. In them, everything seems to conspire against reformers. Circumstances are never propitious. The timing is never appropriate. Resources cannot be found. Competence is at a premium. The so-called Third World fares the worst. What does one do in a country like India, the world's largest democracy, where the then prime minister said this about his public bureaucracy in December 1985:

We have government servants who do not serve but oppress the poor and the helpless . . . who do not uphold the law . . . but connive with those who cheat the state and whole legions whose only concern is their private welfare at the cost of society. They have no work ethic, no feelings for the public cause, no involvement in the future of the nation, no comprehension of national goals, no commitments to the values of modern India. They have only a grasping mercenary outlook, devoid of competence, integrity and commitment. (Gandhi 1985)

He had, earlier that year, introduced a sweeping administrative reform program monitored by a new Department of Administrative Reforms within a new Ministry of Personnel, Public Grievances and Pensions that spearheaded a Twenty Point Programme. It should have been no surprise to him that like all previous administrative reform campaigns, this one also soon floundered due to bureaucratic resistance and inertia.

On the other side of the globe in the English-speaking Caribbean, another set of democracies, this time small states, were not faring much better. They were suffering many problems familiar to Third World countries, such as uncontrolled growth of the public sector, declining status of public employment, scarce management skills, overcentralization, lack of coordination, chronic misuse and underutilization of skills, poor facilities, slovenly service, low productivity, and corruption. They badly needed to improve public sector management particularly in running public enterprises, reducing the dominant clerical mentality, educating politicians about the need to invest in public management, and providing for greater public participation. Again countless reform campaigns had floundered due to bureaucratic resistance and inertia. Again case studies of failed reform attempts would produce long lists of obstacles ranging from cultural factors (such as poor work ethic) to population movements (in this case, brain drain) that would make reform virtually impossible if it were not for the fact that all countries have in fact implemented reforms that have stuck, and some Third World countries have done well in combatting corruption, institutionalizing the ombudsman, and empowering the poor (Caiden 1991a, 246–253).

The current attempts of the East Bloc of countries to reduce bureaucratic centralism also reveal the many obstacles that reformers have to overcome. The Chinese leadership has been struggling for decades to overcome bureaucratic inertia and corruption. The Soviet leadership ran into every conceivable obstacle in pursuing *uskorenie* (accelerated economic growth), *perestroika* (reconstruction), and *glasnost* (openness). Indeed, the Soviet Union, now the Commonwealth of Independent States, once it began to reform found itself being unravelled, like Yugoslavia after the death of Tito. Reforms were too much for the old-timers and too little for the radicals. Nor has the path been much easier for public sector managerialism and its associated reforms pushed by President Reagan in the United States and Prime Minister Thatcher in the United Kingdom. The Canadians seem to have done better as have the Japanese, Australians, and New Zealanders, but the West Europeans have been much more cautious (Caiden 1991a, 198–239).

Three lessons stand out. First, most government is a given. Politicians inherit much more than they imagine when they take over the reins of government. They find that despite the best will in the world, they cannot change much at all and changing directions (policy) takes more than they bargain for because government organizations are not so much instrumental as institutional (Bjur and Caiden 1978), which is the second lesson they quickly learn. Politicians imagine that all they have to do is give fresh orders and the administration will automatically respond. In reality, government organizations have a will of their own, a life of their own, independent power which can be marshalled against change or against changes that are unacceptable to bureaucratic self-interests and dependents. Such institutions are not easily changed, Third, changes take not only resources, but time, particularly administrative changes which must be reckoned not in months or years but in decades, even generations. What is involved is changing administrative norms, organizational cultures, managerial attitudes, work habits, even social values, and this takes much time, much more time than changing titles, laws, structures, methods, and personnel.

SCHOLARLY REFLECTIONS

Although the world of public management is inhabited by practitioners who rarely have time or inclination to sit back and reflect on what they do, some do share their thoughts and experiences with the academic community. The same is true of administrative reformers. Indeed for several decades administrative reformers have been close with that part of the academic community that has specialized in the study of administrative change, reform, and revitalization—possibly closer than most other areas of public management. They meet often at conferences sponsored by international agencies and confer in reform campaigns. From time to time, they combine efforts to produce manuals or guidelines for potential reformers. The following, given in historical order, are key documents:

1. *Interregional Seminar on Major Administrative Reforms in Developing Countries*, ST/TAO/M/62, United Nations, New York, 1973. This is a collection of 56 papers presented at the first international gathering of administrative reformers held at the Institute for Development Studies, University of Sussex, in 1971. The seminar was chaired by Lord Fulton who had just headed a landmark inquiry into the Civil Service of the United Kingdom and issued the renowned Fulton Commission Report. This seminar defined administrative reform as specifically designed efforts to induce fundamental changes through systemwide reforms or measures to improve key elements (such as structures, personnel, etc.) as distinct from normal and continuing activities for improving administration and management (such as organization and methods, management sciences, etc.). Its aim was to develop greater administrative and managerial capabilities to achieve national objectives. The critical factor was held to be changing attitudes of people both within and outside government.

2. Arne Leemans (ed.), *The Management of Change in Government,* Institute of Social Studies, Martinus Nijhoff, The Hague, 1976. Professor Leemans had been concerned with the behavioral side of administrative reform and edited a special issue of *Development and Change* in 1971 containing essays on this theme. He enlarged the issue into an edited book with additional state-of-the-art essays and rewrote his introduction in which he reorganized the territory of administrative reform into the most comprehensive framework yet. His focus was on the inadequate adaptation of the machinery of government to internal and external needs, demands, and opportunities. So his definition of administrative reform was "constantly induced and directed change in the machinery of government," which included modernization of public sector management, planned organization change, innovations, and increased professionalization of public sector employees to improve government performance, enhance client satisfaction, and heighten the quality of life.

3. G. Stahl and G. Foster, *Improving Public Services,* USAID, Washington, D.C., 1979. The Carter Administration had, so it claimed, brought about the most radical civil service reforms for decades and hosted an International Conference on Improving Public Management and Performance in 1979 to share its experiences and to identify items for future international attention. The focus was on producing better qualified public sector managers and "maintaining an effective, competent, highly motivated, ethically disposed staff of public servants." It did much to set the administrative reform agenda for the 1980s.

4. *Handbook on the Improvement of Administrative Management in Public Administration,* ST/ESA/SER.E/19, United Nations, New York, 1979. This publication, subtitled "measures to enhance the effectiveness of organization and methods services in government," was intended as updating and state-of-the-art regarding organization and management but did include a section on much broader issues and strategies, namely administrative reform. It was also less inclusive and much more management-oriented.

5. Jacob B. Ukeles, *Doing More With Less: Turning Public Management Around,* AMACOM, A Division of American Management Association, New York, 1982. The emphasis on management enhancement as the central concern for administrative reform was continued with the rise of the new managerialism movement which wanted to extend successful business management practices to public sector organizations. Public managers should be encouraged to be their own reformers and judged on their managerial performance. The major objective was to get away from a *rules bound* administration to a *performance bound* administration. Emphasis should be placed on performance, accountability, planning and control, and the latest managerial technology in order to do more with less. This is the business management approach to administrative reform.

6. *Enhancing Capabilities for Administrative Reform in Developing Countries*, ST/ESA/SER.E/31, United Nations, New York, 1983. Its point of departure was concern for the enhancement or creation of reform capabilities rather than the content of the reforms themselves. It is still considered a handbook on administrative reform and a revision of the Leemans' volume with much more of a practical than theoretical slant and a focus on implementing development programs and projects and the delivery of government services.

Over the years, there has been a distinctive shift from the grand designs, the episodic, once and for all reconstructions of public sector administration for much more limited objectives, the continuous improvement of public sector management that would gradually overhaul public sector operations and practices. Revitalization has begun to replace reform. The prospect of wholesale reforms diminishes. The disruption is too costly and the forces that have to be mustered are just too difficult to bring together. Reform is too unwieldy. At least, revitalization is manageable. It is less demanding all around. It is incremental rather than radical, specific not general, and above all "doable," practical, realistic, not dependent on all the pieces fitting together exactly. It is more flexible and accommodating. Different levers can be used at different times. Reforms can be tailormade, culture specific, contextual, situational, activity specific, in short, corresponding much more to the realities of everyday government.

REFORM AND REVITALIZATION

Given the nature of the modern administrative state, both reform and revitalization have their place (Caiden 1982). Some problems are universal and can only be tackled on a systemwide basis. Some public organizations are so inert, so bureaupathologic, so corrupt that shock treatment administered from the outside is the only possible remedy. Some public services just do not possess the administrative and managerial talent and capability to turn themselves around. Reactionary bureaucrats and institutionalized vested interests have to be threatened, forced, and beaten to submission by superior political forces. On the other hand, government leaders can only deal with a small fraction of public business and administrative reform is rarely high on their agenda. Otherwise they are very much in the hands of the bureaucracy and must rely heavily on public administrators and managers to act professionally and improve their own state-of-the-art. Their professional staffs do know the details of government and know what needs to be done to improve government performance. They know how to turn internal resistance into support for change and what levers can be used to change attitudes and behavior. In many cases, there is nobody else to turn to for they are the only people who know anything at all about their specializations, there being no competitors, no rivals, no private counterparts capable of replacing them. They are the only ones who know where stubborn resistance is and the reasons behind opposition to innovation. Self-renewal seems to work in the private sector, so why not in the public?

Revitalization has flaws. It is by nature less idealistic, less perfectionist, less bold, less visionary, and less inclusive. It fails to deal with interorganizational problems and shortcomings that go beyond a single organization. It relies unduly on internal interest, talent, and capability and is restricted to how people within view the world and define their problems. They may be too traditional, too narrow, too rigid, too status conscious, too wary of giving offense, too manipulative altogether, just too timid to do what is required. On the other hand, they do at least attempt change; they practice what they preach. They have organization culture on their side. They have a critical mass going for them, and they can co-opt innovative, enterprising, creative "troublemakers." With proper understanding, they can reduce fears associated with reform. They can take advantage of targets of opportunity. They can create islands of excellence that stand out and have a levelling up effect. It is much easier to form a nucleus of support, manipulate the right levers (political, financial, managerial, personal, external, publicity, etc.), and encourage ripple (or snowball) effects. Above all revitalization is so much more contextual, so less-disturbing and disruptive, and much more attuned to the practitioner's world, the realm of the practical and doable.

More and more it seems that public sector managers will really have to manage on their own and to assume greater responsibilities for improving government performance, devising their own reforms and promoting revitalization. They have available to them many guidelines, lists of "do's and don'ts" based on the experience of administrative reformers. They have access to a growing professional literature on specific reforms and innovations. Every year somewhere around the world international conferences are held to exchange views and experiences related to improving government administrative and managerial performance. There is no lack of interest or information. There is no scarcity of comparison. What still is missing is sufficient real as opposed to superficial research, that is, action research, professional wisdom applicable across cultures, and common acceptance that public sector managers are their own reformers and the only reliable reformers in their particular situation.

REFERENCES

Bjur, W. J., and G. E. Caiden. 1978. "On Reforming Institutional Bureaucracies." *International Review of Administrative Sciences* 46 (4):359–365.

Caiden, G. E. 1982. "Reform or Revitalization." In *Strategies for Administrative Reform*, ed. G. E. Caiden and H. Siedentopf. Lexington, Mass.: D.C. Heath & Co.

_____. 1991a. *Administrative Reform Comes of Age*. Berlin and New York: Walter de Gruyter.

_____. 1991b. "What Really Is Public Maladministration?" *Public Administration Review* 51 (6):486–493.

Caiden, G. E., ed. 1983. *International Handbook of the Ombudsman*. Westport, Conn.: Greenwood Press.

Gandhi, R. 1985. *Speech in Bombay*. New Delhi: Indian Institute of Public Administration.

Smith, R. F. I., and P. Weller, eds. 1978. *Public Service Inquiries in Australia*. St. Lucia: University of Queensland Press.

Woodham-Smith, C. 1955. *Florence Nightingale*. Harmondsworth: Penguin Books.

9

Comparative Perspectives on Public Finance

Larry Schroeder

Decision makers in governments everywhere, from the poorest nations of the Third World to the major industrial powers and from small villages to large cities, face a variety of issues pertaining to *public finance*. Among the questions addressed are: (1) What and how many goods and services are to be provided by the public sector? (2) For whom are these services to be made available? (3) By whom are the goods and services to be produced—public sector employees or private contractors? (4) How are the resources necessary to pay for the goods and services to be mobilized? and (5) Whether one or more governmental organizations are to be involved in the provision and financing of public services? Public finance is the subdiscipline of economics which studies the outcomes of these decisions related to government spending and revenue raising. Of particular interest is analysis of the effects that the outcomes have on individuals and economies.

While the same set of questions arises in all societies, a principal lesson to be gleaned from this chapter is that countries resolve them in different ways. We begin the chapter by discussing the several objectives that are commonly sought from public sector involvement in an economy. The fact that there are alternative objectives helps to explain some of the international differences found in the role that the public sector plays in economies and the sorts of revenue instruments that are used.

We then examine the evidence concerning international differences in the size and composition of government spending. The analysis shows the substantial differences in the roles played by the public sector in various countries and indicates how these roles have also changed over time. The third section focuses on revenues. Again, international comparisons suggest rather substantial variations in the ways in which revenues are mobilized in different countries. We conclude the chapter by raising some additional emerging issues related to the public finance questions listed above. The issues are likely to be faced or have an effect upon public administrators and policymakers everywhere in our increasingly interdependent world.

PUBLIC SECTOR FINANCE AND ITS MULTIPLE OBJECTIVES

Although the specific programs undertaken and the financing methods used are ultimately the result of the budget process (see Chapter 10 in this volume) and political negotiation, public finance economics provides several rationales for involvement of the public sector in an economy. In the case of market-based economies, these arguments for government intervention are generally tied to failures in competitive markets. Basic microeconomic theory emphasizes that, under a set of rather restrictive assumptions, a market system which uses prices to allocate goods and services can yield an allocation of resources such that no one can be made better off without others being made worse off. That is, the allocation of resources is Pareto efficient. Unfortunately, markets do not always function in this manner. Furthermore, Pareto efficiency says nothing about the appropriateness of the distribution of resources nor is there any certainty that the market system will result in an economy where resources are fully employed with prices increasing no faster than does productivity.

These "problems" led Musgrave (1959) in his classic treatise, *The Theory of Public Finance* to argue that there are basically three objectives for public budgets: (1) to allocate resources efficiently; (2) to achieve a desired distribution of income and wealth; and (3) to manage aggregate demand in the economy to ensure that the economy grows sufficiently to keep resources employed without excessive inflation. Public finance economists consider all of these issues.

Students of public finance are aware of the usual arguments given for government intervention into an economy to improve resource allocation. These reasons are tied to "market failures" and include the commonly cited cases of public goods, externalities, natural monopolies, and imperfections or asymmetries in information. Since demographic and social factors vary across nations, differences in these factors can help explain why there are likely to be differences in the role played by the public sector across nations. For example, expenditures on education are generally justified on grounds of the external benefits which an educated labor force and electorate have on society. Thus, one would anticipate that a country with a larger proportion of school age children will spend a greater proportion of its spending on this public service.

In the absence of public policies to the contrary, the distributions of income and wealth may be deemed by the bulk of society to be unfair. In such instances governments may decide to target services to particular groups or individuals or to impose heavier taxes on certain segments of society. For example, even though housing is not a public good, its production is not a natural monopoly, and it does not necessarily yield significant externalities, society may view the provision of adequate housing as a crucial service. Housing subsidies or direct government production of housing can be used to ensure that everyone has a reasonable place to live.

Finally, government expenditure and revenue packages can substantially affect macroeconomic conditions. Current levels of unemployment and inflation, international competitiveness and trade, as well as longer-term economic growth are all affected by public sector decisions and, hence, are topics of public finance analysis.

Multiple objectives and differing circumstances within individual countries can result in substantial variations in the roles played by the public sector across nations as well as in the methods used to finance these roles. The following two sections document some of these differences.

PUBLIC SECTOR ACTIVITIES

Readers familiar with state and local governments within the United States realize that there are both similarities as well as rather substantial differences in the roles that these governments play. Public roads and highways, elementary and secondary schools, and parks and playgrounds are found everywhere. But closer inspection reveals that some communities have invested much more heavily in these facilities than have others. Likewise, some states provide a large number of public colleges and universities, whereas in other states there may only be a few directly supported public universities. Even more substantial differences are observable across countries. This section documents and discusses these differences. But since international comparisons are even harder to make than are interstate or interlocal comparisons, the section begins with a discussion of these analytical difficulties.

Data Issues

There are several reasons why comparative, data-based analyses of public finance issues are difficult. The most important of these difficulties is due to insufficient high quality, timely and comparable data. For a comparative analysis it is necessary that the data be collected in similar ways across all countries and, preferably, released on a timely basis in a common format. Such data are quite accessible for the industrialized countries that are members of the Organization for Economic Cooperation and Development (OECD). Data problems are much more profound when attention is focused on lower-income, developing countries. The two most comprehensive sources that exist are the *Government Finance Statistics* published by the International Monetary Fund and the *System of National Accounts* compiled by the United Nations. However, these two data sources measure the role of the public sector differently and both suffer from quite long lags in the availability of the statistics from at least some countries.

One factor that complicates cross-national comparisons of "the" public sector is the great diversity in the structure of governmental organizations across nations. Public finance students in the United States are familiar with the fact that cross-state comparisons of spending or taxation can be significantly affected by differences in the assignment of service responsibilities. For example, education in some states is provided entirely by local, independent school districts whereas in other states, education services are a part of city budgets. These structural differences are more pronounced across countries. In many countries the central or national government is the principal public sector organization. It raises all or nearly all of public sector revenues and directly oversees the bulk of all expenditures. In other countries, subnational governments such as states or provinces, cities, counties, and special districts carry out a significant amount of this activity. Lack of information concerning the operations of subnational jurisdictions, particularly in developing nations, make internation comparisons especially problematic.

A conceptual issue that arises in attempts to measure government spending (and revenues) concerns what should be included in the measure. For example, should "tax expenditures," provisions in the tax system that lower tax liabilities which otherwise would have to be paid, be included as government spending? In some countries major industries are owned and controlled by the government; should the activities of such state-owned enterprises (sometimes called "parastatals") be included in measures of the public sector? Finally, since transfer payments are simply exchanges of money from one group to another, should such programs be netted out from measures of the size of the public sector?

The IMF data source cited above includes transfer programs but excludes both tax expenditures and public enterprise activities from its measure of government expenditures. Exclusion of state-owned enterprises, particularly in developing countries where they are especially important, has the effect of understating the role of the public sector in these economies.

Size and Composition of Government Expenditure

Table 9.1 illustrates the trends and relative sizes of the public sector in both industrialized and developing countries by reporting government expenditure as a percent of GDP for selected years between 1972 and 1988. Several items stand out in the table. First, the industrialized nations of the Western world have generally spent relatively more of their resources through the public sector than have low-income nations. The only exception to this generalization was in 1975 for nations of the Middle East, which, after the first "oil price shock" of the early 1970s, used a considerable amount of their newly generated funds to build public infrastructure. Second, the table shows an upward trend in the relative importance of public sector spending; the changes were particularly pronounced during the 1970s. Finally, the relative importance of government in the developing economies of Africa is currently much greater than in the developing countries of Asia and Latin America and the Caribbean.

Table 9.1: Public Expenditures as a Percentage of GDP by Region, 1972–1988

	1972	*1975*	*1980*	*1985*	*1988*
Industrial Countries	36.7%	42.1%	46.0%	48.3%	48.9%
Developing Countries	23.8	28.0	30.2	32.7	—
Africa	22.6	25.7	32.6	35.5	35.4[a]
Asia	27.3	24.8	30.3	29.3	27.0[b]
Middle East	32.2	50.7	44.6	43.1	42.7[a]
Western Hemisphere	21.8	24.1	24.6	29.1	30.0

[a]Entry is for 1986.
[b]Entry is for 1987.

Source: Hemming 1991, 23. Entries were based on *IMF Government Finance Statistics Yearbook.*

The data in Table 9.1 mask the considerable intercountry variations in the relative importance of public sector spending. Table 9.2 illustrates the considerable diversity of roles taken on by the public sector in selected OECD countries. Government spending amounts to more than one-half of GDP in several northern European nations. Those who argue that "government" in the United States is too large may be surprised to learn that, among industrialized nations, the public sector in the United States is one of the smallest.

The types of services that governments provide also differ substantially across nations. When spending in the United States is compared with the other four nations, several differences stand out (Table 9.3). One is, of course, the important role played by defense expenditures, at least in 1989. The degree to which this entry can be decreased in response to easing international tensions is a principal policy issue being debated today. The relative importance of education spending is also of interest, particularly in light of much-publicized shortcomings in the quality of the product from the system in the United States. A particularly pronounced difference in the composition of spending in the United States, at least when compared with the European countries, is the considerably smaller proportion spent in the United States on social security and welfare.

Analysis of Spending Patterns

Public finance economists devote considerable effort theorizing and analyzing the differences in spending patterns and their economic implications. We note only

**Table 9.2: Public Expenditures as a Percentage of GDP
in Selected Industrialized Nations, 1988**

Country	General Government Expenditure as Percent of GDP[a]
Australia	36.94
Belgium	53.32
Canada	43.67
Denmark	58.70
France	48.62
Germany (Federal Republic)	47.68
Ireland	51.67
Luxembourg	46.88
The Netherlands	59.54
Norway	58.14
Spain	39.33
Sweden	56.39
United Kingdom	39.51
United States	36.45

[a]General government expenditures include subnational government expenditures.

Source: International Monetary Fund, 1991. *IMF Government Finance Statistics Yearbook*, 108.

**Table 9.3: Composition of General Government Expenditures
by Function, Selected Industrialized Countries[a]**

	France (1985)	Germany (1988)	Canada (1989)	UK (1989)	US (1989)
National Defense	6.1	5.2	9.5	10.3	15.8
Public Services[b]	8.0	6.4	11.0	8.5	10.0
Education	10.1	7.6	11.5	12.2	14.4
Health	20.7	16.5	13.4	12.3	12.5
Soc. Sec. & Welfare	43.5	42.3	27.3	34.7	23.0
Recreation & Culture	1.8	1.7	1.8	1.6	1.0
Economic Affairs	5.0	10.4	11.6	9.3	8.5
Other	5.0	9.8	19.7	11.0	14.8

[a]General government expenditures includes subnational government expenditures.
[b]Includes public safety expenditures.

Source: Computed by author from country tables in International Monetary Fund, 1991. *IMF Government Finance Statistics Yearbook.*

a few of these efforts here. One reason for the differences shown in Table 9.1 is, of course, simply differences in the level of development. These patterns are in line with "Wagner's Law" formulated in the 1880s by the German economist Adolph Wagner which suggested a general increase in the size of government activity in response to economic growth (Musgrave 1969, 73–75). A variety of other social and economic variables that influence either supply or demand conditions have also been hypothesized to explain why there are differing relative sizes of governments across countries (Cullis and Jones 1987, 78–86). The papers by Tait and Heller (1982) and Heller and Diamond (1990) are two attempts to analyze comprehensively international differences in expenditures.

It would be unrealistic, however, to assert that economic reasons alone account for all interventions of government in the economies of the world. Politics also plays an important role (although economic rationalizations may be used by politicians). This is certainly the case as political leaders perceive changes in popular attitudes or in the face of changing international or economic situations.

Finally, there can be important cross-national differences in the appropriate view of the "state." The discussion in this and the preceding section has paralleled that of most market-oriented economists who hold that governments are created by individuals to serve individuals. An alternative, more organic view of the state, holds that the good of the individual is defined according to the good of society. Under this view the state not only has the authority but also the responsibility to define what sorts of goods and services are to be supplied through the public sector.

While the relative or absolute size of government spending is of some interest to public finance economists, greater effort is devoted to the questions of what effects such programs have on economic welfare and on behavioral incentives. For example, current discussions of the efficacy of alternative public health insurance programs in the United States are devoted to questions about their effects on the quality and quantity of care supplied, utilization rates, and overall costs. Since similar programs are already in place in many other countries, cross-national research plays a prominent role in these analyses.

Another public expenditure issue of interest to public finance economists is the income distributional effects of the public sector. While certain programs are often justified on their redistributional grounds, it is likely that, particularly in developing countries, many government programs are pro-wealthy rather than pro-poor. For example, the World Bank (1988, 135) in reviewing government-sponsored education and health programs concludes that "Contrary to policy, the poorest are not only denied a greater share [of service benefits], but they often get less than their proportionate share."

The macroeconomic effects of public expenditures are also important, particularly as they affect international trade. One example of considerable interest today is the effect of government subsidy programs designed to assist particular industries, for example, agriculture. Indeed, Ahmad (1990, 25) concludes that, "the real costs of subsidies in terms of efficiency, welfare, and trade distortions could well be higher than those of trade barriers."

Unemployment is a principal concern in many developing countries where unemployment rates may run as high as 25 or 30 percent. In order to overcome these conditions, particularly in order to try to stabilize the political environment, some countries have attempted to guarantee employment through the use of the public sector as the "employer of last resort." Such policies result in excessive public employment. Furthermore, with a large wage bill but limited public resources they can result in situations where nonlabor expenditures, crucial for public services, for example, textbooks, medicine, or gasoline necessary to transport public employees, are not available.

FINANCING GOVERNMENT EXPENDITURES

Whereas quid-pro-quo payments in return for goods and services constitute the usual transaction mechanism for allocating scarce private goods, this approach is often not feasible nor practical in the case of public sector goods and services. Instead, some alternative resource mobilization mechanism must be used. The most common mechanism is, of course, taxes. Direct user charges can be used to finance at least some services provided by the public sector (but only if exclusion of nonpayers is feasible); however, if income redistribution is also a primary objective, user fees are impractical. A third approach to paying for public services is through debt finance. In this case, most commonly employed to finance capital goods that yield services over a long period of time, taxpayers will have to pay for the services over the life of the debt (which may or may not coincide with the benefits that are being enjoyed from the capital investment).

Tax Revenues

This section focuses primarily on the various taxes used by countries throughout the world (although other forms of finance are certainly not unimportant). Just as states and localities in the United States mobilize tax revenues in a variety of ways, so do other nations. Still, there are relatively few general bases for taxation, with each linked to particular economic decisions. The most common are those linked to the earning of income, to expenditures or to the holding of wealth. The first set includes personal income taxes, payroll taxes, earnings taxes, business profits taxes, taxes on gross receipts of businesses. The second set includes general sales taxes, specific excise taxes on purchases of particular goods or services, and value-added taxes. Taxes on international trade, particularly import duties, are closely related to expenditure-based levies. Finally, property or wealth based taxes can be imposed on the value of land and other real property or even moveable wealth, either tangible or intangible (stocks and bonds etc.).

Table 9.4 shows, by region of the world, the relative importance of different types of taxes in 1985. There are some interesting differences in the composition of taxes in low- and middle-income nations across regions. For example, Latin American and Caribbean countries rely much more heavily on social security taxes than do developing countries in other regions; on the other hand, the other three developing country regions rely much more heavily on business income taxes. Latin American and Asian countries are much heavier users of excise taxes (these are taxes imposed on the consumption of individual goods) than are countries in Africa and the Middle East.

More prominent differences arise when tax structures of the industrialized nations are compared with the developing world. High-income nations rely relatively heavily on personal income and social security taxes. But the greatest difference in tax structures between the developed and developing worlds concerns taxes on international trade, that is, imports and (to a much lesser degree) exports.

It is also useful to compare tax structures of various industrialized nations (Table 9.5). Except for France, the countries exhibited there derive more than one-fifth of their revenues from personal income taxes; and France is the definite outlier in its extremely heavy reliance upon social security taxes (which relates closely to the large proportion of its expenditures made on welfare and social security as shown in Table 9.3). Only a few of the OECD countries, with Japan leading the list,

Table 9.4: Composition of Tax Revenues by Region, 1985
(taxes by type as percent of total taxes)[a]

| | *Region[b]* | | | | |
Type of Tax	*Africa*	*Asia*	*Middle East*	*Western Hemisphere*	*Industrialized*
Personal Income	12	8	13	5	27
Company Income	20	19	19	10	7
Social Security	2	0	8	20	31
Property	1	3	3	2	2
Other Direct Taxes	4	7	13	9	2
Sales, VAT, Turnover	15	14	10	13	17
Excise	9	19	7	17	10
Other Indirect	2	5	4	6	2
International Trade	35	23	22	17	2

[a]Based on a sample of 50 low- and middle-income countries and 17 industrialized countries.
[b]Africa represents sub-Saharan African countries; Northern African countries are included in Middle East.

Source: World Bank, *World Development Report, 1988*, 84.

**Table 9.5: Taxes by Type as Percent of Total Taxes,
Selected Industrialized Countries, 1989**

| Country | Income Taxes | | Social Security | Goods and Services | Other |
	Personal	Corporate			
Australia	44.7	12.6	0.0	28.2	14.5
Belgium	30.7	6.7	31.7	25.5	5.4
Canada	38.4	8.5	12.8	29.5	10.8
Denmark	52.1	4.2	7.9	33.0	8.3
France	11.8	5.5	40.2	28.7	13.7
Germany	29.5	5.5	34.1	25.6	5.3
Ireland	31.7	3.4	13.9	44.3	6.7
Japan	24.7	24.4	24.6	12.6	13.7
Luxembourg	23.4	17.7	24.8	24.4	9.7
The Netherlands	21.1	7.7	35.4	26.1	9.7
Norway	27.4	5.3	26.0	36.3	5.0
Spain	22.9	8.6	32.2	28.7	7.5
Sweden	39.2	3.8	24.9	24.1	8.1
United Kingdom	26.6	12.3	17.0	30.9	13.2
United States	35.7	8.5	28.0	16.2	11.5
OECD Average[a]	29.5	7.8	21.1	30.5	11.0

[a]This is an unweighted average of all 24 OECD countries.

Source: OECD, *OECD in Figures: Statistics on the Member Countries*, 42–43.

rely heavily on taxation of corporate profits. Finally, while reliance upon the personal income tax in the United States is greater than in many of the OECD countries, taxes on goods and services (primarily in the form of retail sales taxes used by states and localities) is considerably less than in most of its counterpart nations.

Evaluation of Revenue Instruments

What might help explain these intercountry differences? For evaluation of revenue instruments, it is useful to add two criteria to the three already mentioned—economic efficiency, equity, and macrostability. One obvious objective is simply that the instrument has the ability to mobilize revenues and that these revenues can grow as the demand for public services grow. This calls for taxes with broad bases which increase as incomes, populations, and prices rise. A second criterion that is most directly related to public administration is that the tax be administered fairly at relatively low cost.

These two criteria go a long way to explaining the preference for trade-based taxes in low-income countries. Direct taxes such as a personal income tax, and even some indirect taxes such as a retail sales tax, can be extremely difficult to collect in a low-income country. There is often considerable illiteracy, significant portions of the economy are not monetized, administrative systems are weak, and accounting practices are not reliable. On the other hand, there are likely to be only a few ports of entry for most goods which makes taxable items much easier to detect and tax; furthermore, many small, low-income countries have to rely heavily on imports, and these imports grow as the economy grows.

These conditions do not mean that taxes on international trade are judged desirable by public finance economists. Such taxes are economically inefficient as they distort relative prices and can act to restrain trade. Where taxes on imports are greater than those imposed on domestic producers, they can encourage inefficient domestic production. Some developing countries also impose taxes on agricultural exports (World Bank 1988, 92). These have the disadvantage of discouraging production for export or shifting production to less efficiently produced crops.

An aspect of Table 9.5 that merits special attention is the relatively heavy use of taxes on goods and services in most industrialized countries. While not explicitly shown in the table, the reason for this is the imposition of value-added taxes (VAT) in the vast majority of countries throughout the world—both developed and developing.

The VAT phenomenon has been one of the most interesting recent developments in the field of public finance. Tait (1988, 3) maintains that "The rise of the value-added tax (VAT) is an unparalleled tax phenomenon. The history of taxation reveals no other tax that has swept the world in some 30 years, from theory to practice, and has carried along with it academics who were once dismissive and countries that once rejected it." Tait (1991, 2–3) lists 56 countries that are using the VAT and 10 more in which its adoption is being discussed (including the United States).

A VAT is sometimes called a national sales tax. It differs, however, from the usual general sales tax that Americans are accustomed to paying whenever they make a purchase of a sales taxable item. The principal way in which the VAT differs from the retail sales tax is that the VAT is imposed at each stage of the production process, but only on the amount of "value added" during that stage. (A turnover tax, another variant on sales taxes, is imposed at each stage of the production process and on the entire value of the product sold.)

The principal arguments favoring the VAT include its revenue-yielding potential, its neutrality, and its efficiency (Tait 1991, 1). There is little doubt that the countries that have imposed the VAT have experienced positive revenue effects from its adoption. Indeed, an argument sometimes given against the VAT is that, since it is an indirect and reasonably "hidden" tax, it will encourage growth in the government sector. If the tax is imposed uniformly across all transactions, it will not encourage the consumption of some items in favor of others.

The efficiency gains from use of a VAT depend very much on what it replaces. For example, the VAT is considered vastly preferable to the previously mentioned turnover tax that has been a commonly used levy in many countries. Similarly, many countries have historically relied upon a long list of excise taxes each with its own specific (rather than ad valorem) rate. Again, the VAT is considered vastly superior. Income taxes, too, have certain nonneutralities that are inefficient. One of these is that the income tax discourages saving (since interest income is taxed) and favors consumption; the VAT would reverse this nonneutrality and favor savings.

Equity issues are commonly raised as a principal objection to the VAT. Multiple rates of different types of goods and services including zero rates on certain items, such as "essential" food, are often advocated and sometimes adopted. Defining what is essential is, of course, problematic. Furthermore, not only do multiple rates complicate the administration of the VAT, they undermine the other economic and revenue advantages of the tax (Tait 1991, 7).

The fact that the VAT has been introduced in a long list of countries, including many low-income nations, suggests that administrative issues are not insurmountable. At the same time, as the several chapters in Tait (1991) illustrate, establishing the necessary administrative apparatus involves a variety of steps. Indeed, Aaron (1981, 9) concludes that the VAT experience in Europe shows that "It creates a host of special problems that give rise to paperwork and more or less arbitrary distinctions." He mentions specifically the treatment of agriculture, nonprofit institutions, secondhand goods sold by dealers, and financial institutions. A final issue that is more political than purely administrative concerns the adoption of a VAT in a federal country such as the United States where states rely heavily on sales taxes.

These and other issues are likely to arise in subsequent policy debates that center on issues of public finance. To close this chapter we consider some of the other public finance issues that have recently emerged or that are likely to be of particular importance during the remainder of this century.

EMERGING ISSUES OF COMPARATIVE PUBLIC FINANCE

While a longer list could certainly have been compiled, we focus here on three sets of issues with public finance implications: economic liberalization, increasing government efficiency, and reforms of tax systems.

Economic Liberalization

The recent liberalization of the economies of Eastern Europe and the former Soviet Union is remarkable. But the change from a socialist to a market-oriented economy also has a variety of public finance implications on both the expenditure and revenue sides of the budget. In their discussion of reforms of socialist tax systems, Gandhi and Mihaljek (1992, 143) argue that tax reform is "a part of a minimum package of reforms that need to be simultaneously implemented in order to launch the transition process." They assert that former tax systems were incompatible with a market-oriented economy, that tax reforms facilitate other aspects of economic restructuring, and that tax reform is essential for macroeconomic stability.

Under the former regimes, a substantial portion of public revenues were derived from the activities of public owned enterprises. The "profits" earned from the enterprises were more closely tied to centralized plans than to what market forces determined. As these enterprises are privatized, the revenue system will need to be rationalized.

On the expenditure side of the ledger, other important changes will have to be implemented. For example, unemployment is likely to be an unwanted side-effect of adopting a market-oriented economy. This will require the creation and funding of a social "safety net" of public programs along with other public-sector initiatives such as developing appropriate education and training programs.

Countries other than those in Eastern Europe are also experiencing changes which have a direct link to public finance issues. For example, throughout much of the developing world, "structural adjustment loans" (often termed SALs) are granted by multilateral lending institutions such as the World Bank. These loans generally contain conditions which require the borrowing countries to adjust the structure of their economies. Such adjustments include liberalizing domestic pricing and international trade policies as well as certain fiscal reforms. Such reforms generally focus on lowering public expenditures but also entail strengthening revenue systems. While the revenue policies usually do not call for substantial increases in tax collections, they do often rely on tax reform packages that lower effective tax rates (to decrease the disincentive effects of taxation) and attempt to "level the playing field."

Efficiency in Government and Privatization

The overall growth in the public sector and particularly the levels of public debt that have been incurred in many nations (both developed and developing) have led to calls for improvements in government efficiency. One particularly widespread phenomenon has been *privatization*. This term has a variety of meanings in different contexts. In the United States, where there never has been substantial direct government involvement in major industries, the policies have either taken the form of deregulation or increased use of private sector contracting to produce services which are provided publicly.

While the bulk of these efforts have focused on services like garbage collection, private production of publicly financed social services is also getting increased attention. For example, there is considerable debate of the merits of privatizing the production of education. Proponents argue that such a policy, which is likely to result in competition among producers, will result in improved quality of education at no greater or, perhaps, even lower costs. Other countries, too, are experiencing considerable privatization. But in many of these countries, the policy has focused on the sale of assets of firms previously owned and operated by the public sector. Again, the expectation behind such policies is that public sector management, since it is generally conducted without substantial competition, is less efficient than is the case for private, for-profit enterprises.

Tax Reforms

The past decade has witnessed a variety of experiences with tax reforms that, very well, may carry on into the end of the decade. As was noted in the previous section, the United States is, at present, one of the few Western nations not to have adopted value-added taxes. It is likely that there will be continuing discussions about adoption of the VAT in this country as well. Furthermore, reforms of the fiscal systems of countries in Eastern Europe will quite likely involve the VAT (Tait 1992).

The widespread and relatively recent adoption of the VAT in many countries is only one aspect of tax reforms that have taken place in many countries throughout the world (Pechman 1988; Tanzi 1987; World Bank 1991). For example, the United States has certainly not been alone in reforming the income tax. Many countries have attempted to change the structure of income taxes by lowering rates and broadening the base, primarily because of the effects which high rates have of discouraging savings, discouraging work effort, and encouraging "underground" transactions. Table 9.6 illustrates these changes for eight industrialized nations.

The changes are quite profound. The highest marginal rates were lowered in each of the eight countries, but in half, the lowest tax rates were either increased or not changed. The implication is, of course, that policymakers are looking less toward the income tax as an income redistributional tool.

Table 9.6: Changes in Highest and Lowest Positive Personal Income Tax Rates Since 1986

Country	Top Income Tax Rate	Lowest Income Tax Rate		
Sweden	Lowered: 50% → 20%	Raised:	4.0% → 20%
United States	Lowered: 50% → 28%	Raised:	11.0% → 15%
United Kingdom	Lowered: 60% → 40%	Lowered:	29.0% → 25%
Japan	Lowered: 70% → 50%	Lowered:	10.5% → 10%
Italy	Lowered: 62% → 50%	Lowered:	12.0% → 10%
France	Lowered: 65% → 57%	No change:	5.0%
Canada	Lowered: 34% → 29%	Raised:	6.0% → 17%
Germany	Lowered: 56% → 53%	Lowered:	22.0% → 19%

Source: Oxley et al., 1990, 36.

Finally, the expanding interdependencies of economies, growth of multinational businesses, and creation of common trading markets all increase the importance of questions about the degree to which taxes need to be coordinated across countries. This is one area of public finance in which there remain many unresolved theoretical as well as empirical questions. For example, fiscal competition, such as often arises between states or localities in the United States, can result in inefficiencies as one jurisdiction attempts to "out-bid" its rivals by providing larger and larger benefit packages (see, for example, Musgrave 1991 and Bovenberg 1991). At the same time, it is argued by some that tax coordination or harmonization will lessen competition between states and result in excessive government budgets (see, for example, Cnossen 1990, who suggests that some coordination efforts are little different than the creation of a cartel).

The issue of international tax competition is an appropriate topic on which to close this chapter because the issue illustrates that many questions of public finance are still being hotly debated. Furthermore, in our ever increasingly interdependent world, the final policy decisions are likely to have implications for everyone.

REFERENCES

Aaron, Henry J. 1981. "Introduction and Summary." In *The Value-Added Tax: Lessons From Europe*, ed. Henry Aaron. Washington D.C.: The Brookings Institution.

Advisory Commission on Intergovernmental Relations. 1990. *Significant Features of Fiscal Federalism*, vol. 2. Revenues and Expenditures. Washington, D.C.: Government Printing Office.

Ahmad, Jaleel. 1990. "Fiscal Subsidies Versus Trade Barriers in OECD Countries—An Analytical Comparison." In *Public Finance, Trade and Development*, ed. Vito Tanzi. Detroit, Mich.: Wayne State University Press.

Balassa, Bela. 1989. "Public Enterprise in Developing Countries: Issues of Privatization." In *Public Finance and Performance of Enterprises*, ed. Manfred Neumann and Karl W. Roskamp. Detroit, Mich.: Wayne State University Press.

Bovenberg, A. Lans. 1991. "The Case for the International Coordination of Commodity and Capital Taxation." In *Public Finance with Several Levels of Government*, ed. Remy Prud'homme. The Hague: Foundation Journal Public Finance.

Cnossen, Sijbren. 1990. "More Tax Competition in the European Community?" In *Public Finance, Trade and Development*, ed. Vito Tanzi. Detroit, Mich.: Wayne State University Press.

Cullis, John G., and Philip R. Jones. 1987. *Micro-Economics and the Public Economy*. New York: Basil Blackwell, Inc.

Gandhi, Ved P., and Dubravko Mihaljek. 1992. "Scope for Reform of Socialist Tax Systems." In *Fiscal Policies in Economies in Transition*, ed. Vito Tanzi. Washington D.C.: International Monetary Fund.

Heller, Peter S., and Jack Diamond. 1990. *International Comparisons of Government Expenditure Revisited: The Developing Countries, 1975–1986*. Occasional Paper No. 69. Washington, D.C.: International Monetary Fund.

Hemming, Richard. 1991. "Public Expenditure and Resource Allocation." In *Public Expenditure Handbook*, ed. Ke-young Chu and Richard Hemming. Washington, D.C.: International Monetary Fund.

International Monetary Fund. 1991. *Government Finance Statistics Yearbook*. Washington, D.C.: International Monetary Fund.

International Monetary Fund, The World Bank, OECD, European Bank for Reconstruction and Development. 1991. *A Study of the Soviet Economy*. Paris: OECD.

Kay, John A., and David Thompson. 1989. "Privatization in the United Kingdom: Regulatory Failure in the Public and Private Sector." In *Public Finance and Performance of Enterprises*, ed. Manfred Neumann and Karl W. Roskamp. Detroit, Mich.: Wayne State University Press.

McLure, Charles E., Jr. 1987. *The Value-Added Tax: Key to Deficit Reduction?* Washington D.C.: American Enterprise Institute.

Musgrave, Peggy. 1991. "Merits and Demerits of Fiscal Competition." In *Public Finance with Several Levels of Government*, ed. Remy Prud'homme. The Hague: Foundation Journal Public Finance.

Musgrave, Richard A. 1959. *The Theory of Public Finance*. New York: McGraw-Hill Book Co.

_____. 1969. *Fiscal Systems*. New Haven, Conn.: Yale University Press.

Organization for Economic Cooperation and Development. 1992. *OECD in Figures: Statistics on the Member Countries* (Supplement to the *OECD Observer*, No. 176, June/July).

Oxley, Howard, Maria Maher, John P. Martin, and Patricia A. Gamo. 1990. "The Public Sector: Issues for the 1990s." OECD Department of Economics and Statistics, Working Paper No. 90. Paris: OECD.

Pechman, Joseph A., ed. 1988. *World Tax Reform: A Progress Report*. Washington D.C.: The Brookings Institution.

Rosen, Harvey S. 1992. *Public Finance*, 3d ed. Homewood, Ill.: Richard D. Irwin Inc.

Smolensky, Eugene, William Hoyt, and Sheldon Danziger. 1987. "A Critical Survey of Efforts to Measure Budget Incidence." In *The Relevance of Public Finance for Policy Making*, ed. Hans M. van de Kar and Barbara Wolfe. Detroit, Mich.: Wayne State University Press.

Tait, Alan A. 1988. *Value Added Tax: International Practice and Problems*. Washington, D.C.: International Monetary Fund.

_____. 1991. "VAT Policy Issues: Structure, Regressivity, Inflation, and Exports." In *Value-Added Tax: Administrative and Policy Issues*, Occasional Paper No. 88, ed. Alan A. Tait. Washington, D.C.: International Monetary Fund.

_____. 1992. "Introducing Value-Added Taxes." In *Fiscal Policies in Economies in Transition*, ed. Vito Tanzi. Washington, D.C.: International Monetary Fund.

_____, and Peter S. Heller. 1982. *International Comparisons of Government Expenditure*. Occasional Paper No. 10. Washington, D.C.: International Monetary Fund.

Tanzi, Vito. 1987. "A Review of Major Tax Policy Missions in Developing Countries." In *The Relevance of Public Finance for Policy Making*, ed. Hans M. van de Kar and Barbara Wolfe. Detroit Mich.: Wayne State University Press.

World Bank. 1988. *World Development Report 1988*. New York: Oxford University Press.

_____. 1991. *Lessons of Tax Reform*. Washington, D.C.: The World Bank.

10

The Management of Public Budgeting

Naomi Caiden

For over a century and a half, public budgeting in Western industrialized countries has been predicted on a model that assumed a high level of resource mobilization for public purposes, strong public accountability, and bureaucratic control. This classical budget model, with its stress on annuality, unity, balance, and a regular budget cycle, replaced a pre-budgetary system based on continuity, decentralization, privatization, and flexibility. Although the pre-budgetary model had persisted for many hundreds of years, the introduction of budgeting was an enormous improvement. It emphasized public accountability against secrecy, democratic decision making against autocracy, regularity and control against opportunism and improvisation, and public norms against institutionalized corruption. Introduced as a tool for the financing and control of public agencies, the potential of the budget process was gradually recognized for other purposes, including planning, policy-making, and management.

Yet even as the success of budgeting made it an unquestioned assumption of modern government, its own assumptions were under stress (Caiden, N. 1982). Whereas once it might have been imagined that public needs were finite and public resources infinite, the opposite now seemed more plausible: public demands were a bottomless pit and the revenues available to meet them were severely limited (Caiden, N. 1981). Moreover, while the budget cycle and its bureaucratic appendages were the accepted means for controlling government finances and maintaining public accountability, this linkage no longer appeared to be effective. By the 1980s, not only did it seem that the promises of public budgeting remained unfulfilled, but it appeared that it was no longer even performing its basic functions effectively. In some respects, it almost seemed that things were going backward, to the bad old days of pre-budgeting.

Was the problem that the accepted budgetary principles, based on notions of tight bureaucratic control, no longer fit the changed circumstances of government?

Many years ago, in constructing a taxonomy of budgetary patterns that extended from feudal times to the present and beyond, I hypothesized that it might be possible to envisage a budget system that achieved a high degree of consonance between available revenues and desired expenditures, as well as high accountability to the public, without relying on accepted bureaucratic methods of budgetary control (see Figure 10.1). Over the past decade, several countries have experimented in this direction, as the extension of a paradigm of public management into the practical world of budgeting. This chapter examines these initiatives from the perspective of budgetary development.

PRE-BUDGETING, CLASSICAL BUDGETING, AND ALL THAT

The abuses of pre-budgeting—admittedly endemic to the system—cloud the mind of the observer to its strengths. The monotonous recounting of pre-nineteenth century budget history numbs the senses to accounts of systematized corruption, out-of-control expenditures, flagrant disregard for equity in taxation, repeated tax riots, persistent plunder of the state, mixing of public and private interests, and archaic and wilfully obfuscating accounting system (Caiden, N. 1978).

Figure 10.1: Theoretical Budgeting Patterns Based on Three Key Variables

Pattern	Resource Mobilization	Administrative Control	Accountability
A	Low	Low	Low
B	High	Low	Low
C	Low	High	Low
D	High	High	Low
E	Low	Low	High
F	High	Low	High
G	Low	High	High
H	High	High	High

The patterns of budgeting discussed in this article are as follows:

B: Pre-budgeting as practiced in absolutist monarchical regimes.
H: Budgeting model in contemporary democratic nations.
F: Management model of budgeting expressed in recent budgetary reforms.

Source: Naomi Caiden, *Patterns of Budgeting: The Experience of France 987–830*, Ph.D. dissertation, School of Public Administration, University of Southern California, 1978, 30.

The persistence of the pre-budgetary model of financial administration, its general acceptance, and its imperviousness to repeated attempts to reform, suggest strengths as well as weaknesses. In an age of poor communications and technology, undeveloped financial institutions, and autocratic government, it served its masters if not well at least tolerably within the constraints they set it, to produce levels of revenue sufficient to support disgracefully opulent standards of living of the ruling classes and to fuel the necessary wars and payoffs of the aggrandizing state.

Details need not concern us here. The archetype of the pre-budgetary model was exemplified in pre-revolutionary France where the system probably reached its zenith. Its major characteristics were decentralization, privatization, continuity, and flexibility. A brief sketch of these features forms a prologue to the transformation brought about by the introduction of budgeting and understanding of the later reforms.

Decentralization

A major impediment to budgeting where communications are virtually nonexistent and monies literally have to be transported is to relate specific revenues and expenditures. A central treasury is less functional than a decentralized system, whereby revenue collectors and payers collect and pay out earmarked revenues on the spot and sometimes are the identical individual. The modern equivalent is a revolving fund.

Privatization

While some financial functions were directly administered, the bulk of monarchical finances were carried out by private individuals, who inherited, bought, or bid for their office. The advantages to these individuals or companies lay in their ability to make profits from the "spread" between the agreed amount they handed over and what they collected, from interest paid to them on advances they provided the state to make timely payments, and from use of idle state money on their own behalf. The state benefited from a guaranteed income, the lack of need to maintain another hungry bureaucracy, and solution of the cash flow problem. Similar benefits are claimed today from privatization of certain government functions.

Continuity

Since accountability, such as it was, need only be internal and not public, annual budgets were not important. Accounts continued without "stipulated closure," all that mattered was maintaining cash flow, and estimated deficits could simply be rolled over. Trust funds operate with a similar continuity.

Flexibility

The pre-budgetary system was extraordinarily ingenious in finding resources. Taxes were imposed in every imaginable way: on windows and carriages; through customs and tolls; on crops and inheritances; through forced ennoblement; on religious communities and foreigners; through fines and forfeits—in short everywhere except where the real wealth and power of the country lay. But this diversity in revenue raising lent the system great flexibility. Governments today are showing a similar ingenuity in imposing all kinds of charges.

Of course after it all collapsed, the defects were all too evident. Decentralization meant lack of control; privatization meant corruption and vast diversion of revenues; continuity meant lack of transparency; and flexibility meant regressive and arbitrary taxation. The system could only be kept in line by the threat of periodic criminal prosecutions, and given the monarch's continued dependence on the very people he was prosecuting, this method was highly ineffective. The time was ripe for quite a different kind of financial administration based on constitutional government, transparency of accounts, and regular control processes. But before we close the door on the pre-budgetary era, it might be noted that in its constituent parts, the system was a highly managed one. The accountants who ran it for their own profit were experts in their field and knew what they were doing. The eventual collapse of the system was not the result of their managerial incapacity.

The classical budget era, presaged by several developments such as the end of tax-farming and establishment of a central treasury in England, may be dated from the statement of Baron Louis, the French minister of finance who took office on the restoration of the monarchy after the Napoleonic Wars. In 1815, he announced a complete break with previous financial disorder, expediency, and corruption:

We are going to present the most exact evaluation of our needs possible, the sums necessary to operate the ministerial departments. Then we shall offer a proposal of the ways and means of meeting them. Each ministry is guaranteed the regular employment of the funds put at its disposal. These funds are in the most rigorous proportion possible to its needs for the services performed. If clarifications are necessary, each minister has to place before you all the elements necessary for you to form your opinion (Caiden, N. 1982).

From this point on, the theory of the budget was quite clear. Classic budgeting embraced four, possibly five, cardinal elements. *Annuality* meant that the budget would be made each year to determine and control expenditures for the coming year, and accounts would be closed and presented for each year in timely fashion. *Unity* meant a central fund or treasury for all revenues, so that choices about expenditures might be made in a centralized way, and that all disbursements had to be made and accounted for from that fund. *Appropriation* meant that no funds could be disbursed except by law, that is, those set out in the annual budget, and thus the legislature had the final word on taxation and expenditures which were *public* in nature and open to public scrutiny. *Audit* meant that all expenditures would be checked regularly against the annual budget to ensure they were made honestly and properly. Finally, to these may be added the element of *balance*: by planning revenues and expenditures in advance (as opposed to just adding them up afterwards), it was possible to ordain a balance between them.

It is difficult to overestimate the influence and utility of this relatively simple mechanism. The idea of the budget, and particularly the notion of executive budgeting, was immensely influential. It was a key element in gaining and maintaining the responsibility of the government to be governed. Although tax revenues grew considerably during the nineteenth century, the tax riot endemic to previous centuries dried out. The budget made possible control of financial administration and the basing of financial decisions on accurate information. It provided capacity for the extension of government into new areas of regulation and welfare and the improvement of older functions. It was an essential foundation for Keynesian fiscal policy. It offered the promise of more analytic decision making by government through a variety of advocated techniques.

Despite these triumphs, budgeting today is a disappointment. Perhaps it was oversold and people expected too much. Perhaps it was a victim of its own success, encouraging claims well beyond the potential for performance. Possibly its real performance is unperceived or underestimated; or it may have been overtaken by events. Whatever the explanation, public budgeting today is seen as a problem, and the theory of classical budgeting and those built upon it, no longer seem sufficient for our time.

THE COMING APART OF BUDGETS AND BUDGET THEORY

Since its inception, public budgeting has been a focus for well-developed, persuasive theories (Caiden, N. 1990). Initial concerns during the nineteenth century with establishing the budget cycle and using it as a framework to forecast revenues and economize expenditures were expanded in the early twentieth century to encompass a more developed concept of the executive budget as a part of a movement toward good government. The executive budget was seen as a key component in achieving efficiency and productivity at all levels of government (Caiden, N. 1987).

Other theories reinforced the centrality of budget processes. Keynesian economic theory, while freeing national budgets from the constraining norm of balance, emphasized the relationship of budget and economy and the importance of aggregate fiscal policy. Efforts were also made to apply welfare economics to the public sector through theories of taxation and public goods. In the United States, a theory of incrementalism related budget processes to the political system, explaining how behavioral norms facilitated decision making and kept expenditures in check (Wildavsky 1966). A sophisticated attempt to revolutionize budgetary decision making under the rubric PPBS (Planning Programming Budgeting Systems) brought the promise of transforming budget routines into analytical techniques (Schick 1966).

Whatever the arguments about the validity or practicality of the theories, and despite inevitable problems caused by wars, recessions, political instability, or constitutional crisis annual budget cycles inexorably succeeded one another. And budgets grew. By mid-century, the expanded role of government into all spheres of life had become an axiom in public administration. Twenty years later, continued growth in public budgets that outstripped available revenues was causing concern. In the 1980s concern progressed to alarm in many quarters as budget growth consistently ran ahead of economic growth. Between 1965 and 1984, general government expenditure as a percentage of GDP in OECD countries grew on average over 20 points. During the same period, the average revenue share grew only 16 points. By 1982, 14 countries were in a deficit position (OECD 1987).

Meanwhile, the composition of public budgets in Western industrialized countries also underwent a dramatic transformation. By 1982, in a selected group of OECD countries, over 52 percent of general government expenditures went for transfer payments (OECD 1987). At the beginning of the 1980s, over three-quarters of the United States federal budget was labelled "relatively uncontrollable," that is, consisting of interest payments, statutory payments of various kinds to individuals, intergovernmental grants, and contracts (Schick 1990). This change in budget composition represented long-term government commitments related to government's role in absorbing risks and stabilizing economic conditions (Schick 1980, 572). But the effect of these commitments was to increase the inflexibility of budgets and contribute to their growth with the expansion of eligibility and the frequent practice of indexing payments to inflation (Bengt-Christer 1982, 7).

Existing budget theory did not really address directly the question of government growth, and the literature investigating its causes was not helpful when it came to considering what ought to be done about it. Classical budget theory was concerned with a year-to-year reckoning and an annual decision process, which coped uneasily with longer-term commitments and made no reference to budget growth.

Incrementalism, though conceptually embracing reductions as well as increases, actually incorporated a theoretically slow but nonetheless upward bias. Whether it was true or not, as theorists argued with increasing irrelevancy, that budgets grew by increments (assuming anyone knew what an increment was), they certainly grew. Incrementalism was also predicted on a year-by-year decision-making process and the institutions and behavioral norms that went with it (Schick 1980, 22–24). To the extent that it acted as a controlling mechanism, it had no influence over the automatic payments that now made up a large part of the budget and were determined more by assumptions about what the economy would do than by detailing horse-trading over individual programs (Wildavsky 1988). By the beginning of the 1970s, in the United States, the political consensus to which incrementalism had contributed was shattered and replaced by a "Seven Years War." Though there might be truces now and then, incrementalism as a normative category had lost its influence, and neither its mirror image, "decrementalism," nor a variety of spending limitation ideas, have replaced it as an organizing concept.

In sharp contrast to incrementalist behavioralist theories of budgeting, what might be called "analytical theories" were deliberately oriented toward reform. Their aim was to transform the routines of budgeting to make them more analytical in nature, so that budget decisions would reflect considerations of efficiency and effectiveness. Budgeting would incorporate elements of control, management, and planning, but emphasis would be on planning. There were a number of variants: performance budgeting emphasized building budgets on the basis of unit costs; program budgeting (PPB) stressed program classifications and data on program effectiveness, which would eventually restructure existing organizational lines; zero base budgeting concentrated on decision packages within existing organizational divisions which would enable ranking of activities relative to priorities and costs.

The extent to which any of these analytical theories found successful implementation is open to debate. Overt failures and abandonment of reform initiatives were common. Program classifications have been employed in many jurisdictions, though they may lack the kind of effectiveness measures, planning orientation, or organizational restructuring envisaged by the theorists. The rhetoric persists, particularly in international aid to developing countries, which are expected to achieve what their counterparts with vastly greater resources have not. Whether the difficulties lay in concept or application, however, the reforms were perceived to have little impact on the main issue of the day: achieving a satisfactory level and balance of public revenues and expenditures.

Keynesianism too came under attack. The efficacy of fiscal policy in dealing with stagflation, or in "fine tuning" the economy, was questioned. Rather than controlling or directing the economy, national budgets seemed prisoners of the economy. There was also a charge that in freeing national governments from necessity to balance their budgets, Keynesian theory encouraged budget growth and endemic deficits.

Finally, applications of microeconomic theories to the governmental sector had little practical effect in constraining public budgets or differentiating legitimate from illegitimate claims on budgets. Public goods theory, externalities, or Pareto optimality, remained textbook exercises that penetrated only weakly the decision-making premises of those grappling with budget making.

By the end of the 1970s, budgeting was overtaken by a perception of crisis. Persistent deficits, taxpayer revolts, sluggish and volatile economies, and ever-expanding claims on budgeting, presaged a need for new approaches. Governments in Western industrialized countries, irrespective of political complexion, initiated "top-down" approaches to take charge of their budgets (Schick 1986). And from the sum of their practical moves combined with the emergence of a revised direction in public administration arose a different approach to public budgeting, which might be called "the management of public budgeting."

THE MANAGEMENT OF PUBLIC BUDGETING

There is, of course, nothing new under the sun, and the management approach to public budgeting traces a respectable lineage—back to Woodrow Wilson who thought of public administration as a business (Wilson 1887), the early days of the municipal management movement in New York (Schick 1966), the Taft Commission on Economy and Efficiency, and the writings of William Willoughby, chief architect of the executive budget in the federal government of the United States (Willoughby 1918). Allen Schick long ago pointed out that all budgets had an element of management, alongside the elements of control and planning (Schick 1966).

The reemergence of public management as a dominant paradigm in public administration is a product of the 1980s. A management emphasis has begun to pervade the discipline, witness the title of the 1991 American Society for Public Administration Conference, "Managing the Transformed Public Service." Public management has been defined as

the part of public administration that overviews the art and science of applied methodologies for public administration program design and organizational restructuring, policy and management planning, resource allocations through budgeting systems, financial management, human resources management, and program evaluation and audit. (Ott, Hyde, and Schfritz 1991, ix)

Public budgeting and financial administration are thus assigned a key position on the public management agenda.

The public management movement in budgeting, however, goes beyond general application of public management theory. It is an identifiable pattern of budgetary management that attempts to combine accountability with efficient resource mobilization and allocation, while dissolving traditional bureaucratic control systems. This model emphasizes similar elements to the old pre-budgeting; however, it goes beyond general application of public management theory. It is an identifiable pattern of budgetary management that attempts to combine accountability with efficient resource mobilization and allocation, while dissolving traditional bureaucratic control systems. This model emphasizes similar elements to the old pre-budgetary model—decentralization, privatization, continuity, and flexibility— but transforms them to apply to a world of advanced information and communications technology, democratic government and administration, and constrained public resources. During the 1980s, several countries have passed legislation intended to transform their budget systems along these lines. The remainder of this section reviews these efforts in Canada, Britain, Australia, New Zealand, and Sweden.

Canada (based on Savoie 1990). One of the earliest attempts to reorient a national budget system was the Canadian Policy and Expenditure Management System (PEMS) introduced in 1979. PEMS grew out of disillusion with the failure of PPB and concern about growth of federal expenditures in general and statutory payments in particular. Its aim was to link policies, programs, and resources through a collective top down decision-making process. The basis for resource allocation was to be planned results within established expenditure limits. A central Cabinet Committee on Priorities and Planning chaired by the prime minister assigned annual and five-year rolling ceilings to different Cabinet committees which were in charge of nine blocks expenditures or envelopes. These envelopes were the distinctive features of the process: within the limits of each envelope activities competed with one another for funds, though several reserves outside the envelopes also existed for their recourse according to circumstances.

A number of shortcomings led to the discrediting of PEMS and its 1989 replacement by an Expenditure Review Committee to centralize expenditure decisions. PEMS was found too bureaucratic; ministers claimed that permanent officials gained too much control over policy. Departments began to bypass the policy committees and deal directly with the Department of Finance. Expenditure reductions tended to be made through capital and maintenance cutbacks rather than, as intended, in programs judged by their results.

The Canadian PEMS example was not really a management model, but it did incorporate some of its aspects. The idea of ceilings based on a government-wide strategic planning process which set broad priorities was one. A second was the idea of envelopes in which decision makers had freedom to reallocate resources.

According to Savoie, "The intent was to place responsibility for saving squarely on the shoulders of those who spent" (Savoie 1990, 67). Third, budget information was to be developed to evaluate program results, effectiveness, and costs, as a means to make decisions.

Britain. The Thatcher government that took office at the end of the 1970s had a much broader and more ambitious agenda: "rolling back the state, restructuring and modernizing the British economy, privatizing public enterprises, extending private ownership, reducing the power of trade unions, and confining the public bureaucracy to managing programs" (Caiden, G. 1991). In 1982, a Financial Management Initiative emphasized the role of management in government. Structural reform would bring about a government administration similar to the Swedish model: a small core of policy making ministries combined with operating agencies held accountable for results according to policies and resource guidelines but with managerial freedom. The government would decide objectives, priorities, targets, and resources; managers of agencies would be responsible for measuring their performance against set objectives, for making the best use of the resources they were allocated, and for ensuring efficiency, productivity, and value for money. The budget process was critical in gaining responsibility and accountability for the achievement of budgetary targets. Information systems would be transformed to incorporate performance assessments of operations and personnel to evaluate efficiency and effectiveness. Budget control systems would be decentralized in departments conceptualized as cost centers, making use of performance indicators, detailed administrative costs, and flexibility in the use of personnel. In 1988, a document entitled "The Next Steps" took the process further to restructure agencies.

Detailed information on the success of the initiatives has been difficult to find. But the outline of the budget management model expressed in them became clearer. Its features may be summarized as:

- an emphasis on efficiency and performance
- decentralized management in which managers have relative freedom to achieve set objectives
- administrative units seen as cost centers operating as self-contained agencies.

Australia. By 1984 there was serious concern in Australia about the state of the lagging economy and the economic future of the country. The Commonwealth (federal) budget was seen both as a key weakness of the current administration and a major tool for reshaping government policy and administration. The Financial Management Improvement Program (FMIP) was initiated to improve accountability and to reverse persistent deficits. It aimed "to improve the productivity of the government sector by giving departmental managers greater freedom and responsibility for developing services within a clear framework of resources and policies" (Preston-Stanley 1990, 1). The FMIP may therefore be viewed from two main perspectives: the central direction or budgetary framework and managerial operations.

At the center, a forward budget provided a tool to assess the financial impact of policy changes and the effects of the incremental costs of investment expenditures. It also formed a stable resource framework to enable departments to plan their budgets. The forward budget was constructed for three years on a current services basis. Each year the estimates were rolled over, and they incorporated forecasts about key economic parameters and how changes in them would affect budget components. The Department of Finance constantly reviewed the forward estimates on the basis of its economic forecasting model, reconciling them with budget estimates (Keating and Rosalsky 1990, 76). Between 1983 and 1989, a tight expenditure planning system based on three-year forward estimates and program retrenchment cut the Commonwealth government's expenditure by 6 percentage points of GDP and resulted in a budget surplus (Preston-Stanley 1990, 2).

In the departments, the tight overall control was matched with flexibility. Managers had increased freedom to determine staffing levels and composition and greater flexibility in procurement. They might carry forward unspent balances up to a limit and also borrow against a limit. They could save proceeds from sales of minor assets and negotiate with the Department of Finance for a percentage of retention of proceeds from major asset sales. But they were required to return a 1.25 percent efficiency dividend each year.

Efforts were made to modernize financial administration. There were regular efficiency scrutinies (departments could keep savings beyond the efficiency dividend); a program format for budgets to encourage departments to pay attention to objectives, costs, and effectiveness; five-year evaluations; and a movement toward performance auditing. Accounting was centralized in the Department of Finance: a Financial Ledger System and Budget Monitoring System allowed consolidated daily updates of the revenue and expenditure position. Detailed information was available to the Ministry of Finance and to departmental managers. All interagency services were costed out and charged for.

The Australian management model operationalized the managerial principles set out in the British blueprint. It conceived government on a corporate model with the Cabinet acting as a corporate executive and ministers as executive directors. The budget system combined:

- a highly developed budget planning process at the center
- a decentralization of management to managers in departments within budgetary limits
- an emphasis on efficiency in operations and "managing for results"
- an integrated information system.

New Zealand (based on Goldman and Brashares, undated). The 1980s found the New Zealand economy in trouble, with a serious balance of payments position and large budget deficits. In 1984, the government began to take action in a series of measures designed toward a more market-oriented competitive economy and a more efficient and effective public sector. Previously, budgets had not been a very effective policy-making or control mechanism since they were passed late in the financial year and regularly augmented by supplementals toward the end of the year. In 1986, the State Owned Enterprise Act separated government commercial operations and incorporated them as state owned enterprises, many of which were privatized and sold to the private sector. In 1988 the State Sector Act restructured the governance of the public sector so that it resembled more closely the private sector. The chief executives of departments were no longer to be permanent, but subject to contract, so that tenure and salary were related to performance. Like private executives, they would have power to hire and fire and set salaries of employees. According to Gerald Caiden, "Public sector managers would have the same freedom to manage as private sector managers but they would also be held strictly accountable for their performance to the government by strengthened central policy and administrative controls and evaluations" (Caiden, G. 1991, 231).

These managerial reforms were quickly followed by financial reforms in the 1989 Public Finance Act. Within two years, departments were to move from a cash- to an accrual-based accounting system, analogous to that of a private company. They would depreciate capital, pay a rate of return or capital charge on departmental assets, and be charged or paid interest on cash balances. Financial performance for each department would be assessed through half yearly and annual financial statements prepared according to GAAP.

Budgetary appropriations would reflect government's roles as purchaser of outputs, funder of transfers, and owner of capital. Appropriations would be essentially output based, with the chief executives of departments given the responsibility to produce a given output at least cost with whatever mix of labor and capital they saw fit. Where departments are providing traditional services to government, Parliament authorizes incurrence of costs for output production, as well as funds for capital and transfer payments. For business type departments, appropriations would be for the value of outputs purchased by the government, and ministers may decide to purchase those outputs elsewhere. Budgetary estimates would include the value of capital assets, balance sheets, cash flow projections, and financial performance goals. Monthly reports would compare budgeted and actual figures.

The New Zealand model appears further-reaching in its scope and implications than those discussed so far. Its major features are:

- reorganization of government
- autonomy of chief executive officers within budgetary policy directives
- operation of departments along private sector lines and extensive privatization
- accrual accounting and GAAP standards of reporting
- budgeting according to outputs.

Sweden. In Sweden, the basic structure of central government is characterized by small policy-making ministries and a large number of agencies that operate relatively autonomously within their own spheres according to written directives. According to Gert Jonsson, "All in all, about 330 government agencies are responsible for their own accounting and prepare their own annual accounts. This type of organization means that central government has long been divided into 'profit centers,' often with a qualified management in charge of accounting and financial management" (Jonsson 1990, 277).

By the beginning of the 1980s, there was considerable discussion of the need for appraisal for central government in the light of high growth of the public sector, the heavy burden of taxation, and the probability of continuing demands on government. It was apparent that changes were required to increase the efficiency, effectiveness and responsiveness of the central government, and recent major proposals are aimed at upgrading the budget process and improving control and accountability.

The new budget process focuses on in-depth reports and analyses by agencies every three years on a rolling three-year schedule. The orientation of each agency, together with financial planning limits, will then be set for the next three years in conjunction with the annual budget appropriation for the next budget year. The aims are to allow greater scope for analysis and priority setting on the basis of information produced by the agencies, and to enable thorough reviews of activities to improve efficiency and effectiveness. In addition, each agency is to present a special report on results and preliminary annual accounts to the government each year, providing concise and clear information on costs, ratios, and productivity trends.

Agencies, which already have considerable autonomy in the Swedish system, will be further freed from detailed controls within the limits of the orientation, anticipated results, and financial limits for the three-year period. Funds will be made available to them in the form of general appropriations, which will not only allow them flexibility to utilize resources in the most efficient and effective manner to achieve their set goals, but also to transfer resources from one year to another over the three-year period.

The new budget process will be backed by more demanding accounting requirements, through a new general model for central government accounting. This model will go beyond accounting for purely financial transactions to enable analysis of information in different ways, such as resource type, organizational criteria, or function (Jonsson 1990, 288). Information systems will be based on uniform concepts of analysis and evaluation, allowing analysis of performance on the basis of relatively simple criteria such as quantity and unity costs. Accounting systems will be "more flexible, up-to-date, and accessible" (Jonsson 1990, 289).

The Swedish model integrates the budgeting and accounting systems and reorients them to enable more informed decision making. Its major elements are:

- decentralization of agency management
- flexibility in the use of resources
- continuous evaluation of agency activities
- sophisticated accounting and information systems
- medium term planning and priority setting.

Do these recent efforts in budget and financial management reform from Canada, Britain, Australia, New Zealand, and Sweden, constitute an identifiable and different direction in public budgeting? Do they represent the wave of the future, a viable step forward in organizing public finances? How should they be judged?

CONTINUITY AND DEPARTURE

The models discussed here are hypotheses: they are too recent to have been properly tested or even in some cases put into operation. At this point, they may be evaluated only in concept and prospective feasibility. Yet even now it is evident that they possess considerable similarities and respond to similar circumstances. They draw on a common background of budget and public administration theory and depart from it in a similar direction.

A marked characteristic of the models is management decentralization within stipulated limits, reminiscent of the pre-budgetary model. Another element that harks back to pre-budgeting is continuity: both Sweden and Australia work within a three-year planning system, but they retain their annual budgets. No country has yet to privatize its revenue collection or financial administration, but there are strong elements of privatization in several countries; perhaps New Zealand goes furthest in this direction.

All the countries retain the major elements of an annual budget system, but have tried to reduce the detailed controls that traditionally typified line item classifications under traditional annual budgeting. Efforts have been made to strengthen the decision-making process through evaluation and information. While only one country (Australia) explicitly invokes program budgeting, familiar elements of analytical techniques are present in emphasis on efficiency and productivity, analysis of programs, and performance indicators. But whereas program budgeting put budget classification and procedures first and restructuring of administration second, the management models construct budget reform upon broader administrative reforms.

The major departure of the public management model is the attempt to integrate budgetary direction at the top with decentralized management in the agencies. The key mechanisms to achieve this integration are, first, information systems that enable calculation of budgetary parameters and continuous monitoring of transactions, and second, holding managers to specific results. Throughout, there is an emphasis on a standard of efficiency in the achievement of set objectives, constant scrutiny of activities, and flexibility in the use of resources. There is a deliberate attempt to introduce the competitiveness, accounting conventions, and assumed managerial practices of the private sector into public financial management.

The elements of the models discussed here are quite consistent with one another, and, drawing from each of them, it is possible to construct an ideal-type or meta-model of public budgeting. According to this model, policies are set at the center related to wider economic trends and adjusted according to economic movements. Agency managers are set objectives and made responsible for achieving them with allotted resources and in the most efficient manner possible at their discretion. The system is held together through the flow of information that transmits data regarding costs and results, enabling impacts to be assessed, priorities to be set, program adjustments to be made, and value-for-money audits to be conducted. Efficiency is achieved *through* managerial flexibility, which rewards managers for results and penalizes them where they fall short. Accountability is improved because of the availability of accurate and relevant information and the capacity to enforce priorities. Resources and activities, income and expenditure, are considered together, as a simultaneous equation, instead of apart, as separate zero sum games.

Will the hypothesis be confirmed? Can public management rescue public budgeting? These questions may only be addressed through empirical detailed research into operations as the systems progress. Meanwhile, several issues may be raised regarding definition of the management budget model, its relevance, and its administrative and ideological implications.

Budgets are all things to all people: thus budget theorists have some trouble even defining what budgeting is. Over 20 years ago, in the first edition of *The Politics of the Budgetary Process*, Aaron Wildavsky set out more than 20 versions of what a budget is or might be. He concluded "Budgets are as varied as the purposes of men" (Wildavsky 1988, 1–51). Irene Rubin and Allen Schick came up with a dozen or so definitions in recent texts and Donald Axelrod provides eight major functions of budgeting (Axelrod 1988; Rubin 1990; Schick 1990). Budget theory is elusive, responding to the focus of interest of the theorist rather than any preconceived agenda. In Allen Schick's words, "It may be more illuminating to examine budgeting as a subset of other fields, than as a field in its own right" (Schick 1988, 68).

The management approach to public budgeting responds to some but not all of the range of budgetary purposes. From a practical perspective, it is concerned with efficiency in government operations and the control of aggregate expenditures. From a disciplinary perspective, it is linked to the public management paradigm, itself hardly a model of clarity. The result is a certain haziness and ignoring of important functions of budget processes. In particular, the management model does not address the policy setting or conflict resolving aspects of budgeting. These functions seem to take place somewhere "outside" or beyond the boundaries of the model, which is concerned only with management or implementation. Fair enough— but we may ask whether it is really possible to set up a barrier between policy and management in this way. The separation of politics and administration has long been found wanting, either as an accurate description of public administration or as a viable precept.

A second question arises regarding the conditions in which the management model of budgeting is applicable. The country experiments discussed here are all drawn from relatively cohesive central administration in rich Western countries with highly developed bureaucracies, strong financial institutions, and a readily available pool of professionals upon which to draw. Despite recent difficulties in adjusting budgetary claims and resources, budget balance now or in the future is not a mirage. There is general agreement regarding the role of government, even if there is disagreement on specific issues or scope. It is not clear whether the model could work in other conditions, particularly in poor countries, with sprawling entrenched bureaucracies, lack of communications, information and financial infrastructure, relatively few trained personnel, chronic shortage of resources relative to needs, chaotic accounting systems, and serious political and social rifts. The potential for enhanced opportunities for corruption in managerial decentralization should also not be overlooked. Further, the management approach seems to be applicable only to a part of government budgets, where a service or commodity is being supplied. It ignores one of the largest problems, that is, transfer payments, and it is unclear how it would be applied to such large areas as defense or contract administration.

Third, concentration on management has its own dangers. Management may simply interpose a new layer of bureaucracy, drawing resources to itself at the expense of line functions. Particularly in budgeting, an emphasis on management may result in a decline in cooperation and participation by line staff, who see themselves without influence in the allocation of funds, and therefore irresponsible in their disbursement. There is also the problem that autonomous managers may set up their own fiefdoms if controls prove inadequate.

Fourth, the assumed neutrality of the managerial model may be spurious. Managerial autonomy is held to be a viable mode of operation only because managers may be held to efficiency in achieving goals. But efficiency is not an objective in itself, but a relationship between resources and objectives, and objectives themselves are hierarchical in nature. In this sense, efficiency stands only as a cover for other values, as the means to an objective becomes an objective in its own right. Managers make decisions on ends at the same time as they make decisions on means, and policy-making is the obverse of managerial autonomy.

But in another sense, efficiency is a value in itself, in the sense that it maximizes use of resources. The private sector does so by allocating resources to the areas that pay the best and not serving those that are unprofitable. If this criterion is to be the controlling factor for public managers, it is important to realize its implications, since in general the public sector takes into account a wide variety of criteria beyond efficiency—equity, public access, environment, community, social well-being, public health, due process—to name only a few. To set efficiency above these is to introduce a definite ideological element that would have serious impacts on budgetary outcomes.

Finally, the managerial models themselves seem to have little self-evaluation built into them. Criteria for evaluation, an agenda for research, or a timetable for assessment of the budget systems themselves seem to be lacking. Since they do appear to mark a departure in direction, embody a remarkable consistency in philosophy, and hold out the possibility for combining accountability with decentralized and hopefully more responsive budget administration, it would be interesting to learn how they fare. Given the level of dissatisfaction with traditional budget administration, the new management of public budgeting has much to offer.

REFERENCES

Axelrod, Donald. 1988. *Budgeting for Modern Government*. New York: St. Martin's Press.
Bengt-Christer, Y., and Ann Robinson. 1982. "The Inflexibility of Contemporary Budgets." *Public Budgeting and Finance* 2:7.
Caiden, Gerald. 1991. *Administrative Reform Comes of Age*. Berlin: De Gruyter.
Caiden, Naomi. 1978. *Patterns of Budgeting: The Experience of France 987–1830*. Ph.D. dissertation for the School of Public Administration, University of Southern California.
_____. 1981. "Public Budgeting Amidst Uncertainty and Instability." *Public Budgeting and Finance* 1 (1):6–19.
_____. 1982. "The Myth of the Annual Budget." *Public Administration Review* 42 (6):516–523.

_____. 1987. "Paradox, Ambiguity and Enigma: The Strange Case of the Executive Budget and the United States Constitution." *Public Administration Review* 47 (1):84–92.

_____. 1990. "Public Budgeting in the United States." In *Public Administration: State of the Discipline*, ed. Naomi B. Lynn and Aaron Wildavsky. Chatham, N.J.: Chatham House.

Goldman, Frances, and Edith Brashares. Undated. *Performance and Accountability: Budget Reform in New Zealand.*

Jonsson, Gert. 1990. "Government Accounting in Sweden." In *Government Financial Management: Issues and Country Studies*, ed. A. Premchand. Washington: International Monetary Fund.

Keating, Michael, and David Rosalky. 1990. "Rolling Expenditure Plans: Australian Experience and Prognosis." In *Government Financial Management: Issues and Country Studies*, ed. A. Premchand. Washington: International Monetary Fund.

OECD. 1987. *The Control and Management of Government Expenditures*. OECD: Paris.

Ott, Steven, Albert. C. Hyde, and Jay M. Schfritz. 1991. *Public Management: The Essential Readings*. Chicago: Lyceum Books.

Preston-Stanley, Tony. 1990. *Public Expenditure Management in Australia: The Financial Management Improvement Program*. Unpublished paper written for the World Bank.

Rubin, Irene. 1990. *The Politics of Public Budgeting*. Chatham, N.J.: Chatham House.

Savoie, Donald, J. 1990. "Reforming the Expenditure Budget Process: The Canadian Experience." *Public Budgeting and Finance* 10 (3):63–78.

Schick, Allen. 1966. "The Road to PPB: The Stages of Budget Reform." *Public Administration Review* 26 (2):243–258.

_____. 1980. *Congress and Your Money*. Washington: Urban Institute.

_____. 1986. "Macrobudgetary Adaptations to Fiscal Stress in Industrialized Democracies." *Public Administration Review* 46 (2):124–134

_____. 1988. "An Inquiry into the Possibility of a Budget Theory." In *New Directions in Budget Theory*, ed. Irene Rubin. Albany, N.Y.: State University of New York Press.

_____. 1990. *The Capacity to Budget*. Washington: Urban Institute.

Wildavsky, Aaron. 1966. *The Politics of the Budgetary Process*. Boston: Little Brown.

Willoughby, William. 1918. *The Problem of a National Budget*. New York: Appleton.

Wilson, Woodrow. 1887. "The Study of Administration." *Political Science Quarterly* 80 (1).

11

Projects, Plans, and Programs

Steven H. Arnold and E. Philip Morgan

Translating public policy into concrete action is at the heart of public management. Once policy goals have been chosen and directions set, it is up to the managers to plan and organize the work needed to change policy into practice, by specifying the tasks to be done, how they are to be carried out, how resources will be allocated to achieve them, and who is responsible. This typically involves such activities as the drafting of specific procedures, standards, and guidelines; recruiting and supervising personnel; and establishing monitoring and evaluation mechanisms. One of the key issues is the establishment of an appropriate organizational framework that enables the managers to be as effective as possible in carrying out their duties.

PROJECTS AND PROGRAMS AS OPERATIONAL STRATEGIES

Complex organizations have become essential for enabling the manager to administer public policies. Ideally, an effective organization provides a rational way to divide the tasks involved into discrete activities (specialization), as well as a way to tie these activities back together into a unified whole (coordination) (Mintzberg 1979, 1–16). While such organizations may seem bewilderingly complicated, this is often due to the wide variety of needs and interests to be served. For example, the U.S. Department of Agriculture has become a highly complex bureaucracy because the interests of large farmers are different from those of small ones; cattle ranchers from sheep herders; grain farmers from vegetable farmers, etc. These different "interests" include farming conditions, prices and marketing concerns, access to resources (such as land or research), and loans for equipment purchases.

Because of their size and inertia, complex organizations tend to be most successful when dealing with routine, unchanging tasks. They are much less able to deal effectively with *new* problems, particularly where the appropriate action might be uncertain, and the new proposed tasks cut across the existing responsibilities and lines of authority in the present bureaucratic structure. For example, a government with a ministry of health and a ministry of agriculture may find it difficult to deal with an intersectoral problem such as increased illness resulting from chemical fertilizer runoff into urban ground water. While both ministries would be good at specifying routine, recurring tasks and responsibilities in objective, nonpersonalistic ways within their own traditional areas of responsibility, they would have much more difficulty dealing with these new demands (mediating between the need for clean water and a need for productive agriculture) that do not fit within the preestablished organizational system of either ministry. A typical but often ineffective bureaucratic response is to take the path of least resistance, in which each ministry creates a new department that corresponds to the demands of the new constituency or problem. But this approach of "administration by addition" makes public organizations unnecessarily complex and costly, leading to redundancy, inflexibility, and resistance to change. Furthermore, it is also unlikely to succeed, since it has not dealt with the problem of bringing together all of the relevant parts of the bureaucracy that have an impact on the problem. For example, one bureau or department in the ministry of agriculture cannot "solve" the problem of groundwater pollution, since it also needs the cooperation of the relevant parts of the ministry of health.

A second, more radical strategy is to attempt a major bureaucratic reorganization when a new problem does not fit neatly into ongoing routines and hierarchies. But while reorganization may help to deal with the new problem more effectively, it may be inadvisable for at least three reasons. First, it is exceptionally costly. Putting a large organization together takes a great deal of time and effort, and reorganization can be very expensive in time lost, designing of new routines, and the ironing out of all the bugs in the system that inevitably accompany major change. Second, such reorganization may not be politically feasible, as it may be strongly resisted both internally and by outside supporters of the existing system. Third, and perhaps most important, complex organizations are expected to achieve many goals simultaneously that are more or less mutually compatible. In essence, the design of an organization often represents a sort of compromise among various goals. Thus, a single-minded reorganization to increase the capacity to deal with only one problem or goal may in fact *reduce* the capacity to deal with the others. This may be acceptable if the new task is so important that it overrides all of the others, but this is a rare event. More typically, this new task is seen as one to be added on to other tasks, rather than replacing them. For example, while urban ground water pollution is a serious problem, it probably is unrealistic to see it as so overwhelming as to warrant a reorganization of both the ministry of health and ministry of agriculture to make this the top priority for both ministries. More likely, this problem would be considered to be an additional task, to be accomplished along side all other traditional duties.

Given this situation, the creation of special projects and programs can be seen as a specific organizational strategy to meet the particular needs of dealing with a new policy problem while allowing the existing bureaucratic structures to remain relatively intact. Projects and programs take a variety of forms, but their defining element is that they are a bounded set of activities with the expressed purpose of addressing a specified problem. Actual examples include the World War II Manhattan Project (to build the first nuclear weapon) and the National Aeronautics and Space Administration (NASA), which initially had the goal of landing the first man on the moon. These projects involved basic scientific research, materials development, and other advanced engineering technologies which did not exist at the time the policy goals were fixed. In both cases, the core organization was only the focus for the thousands of interagency and contracting transactions that were necessary to the success of the respective projects, which could not have been carried out successfully by any existing agency within the normal bureaucratic structure.

CHARACTERISTICS OF PROJECTS AND PROGRAMS

A variety of organizational techniques have been used to increase the capacity of a bureaucracy to focus on a specific problem without undergoing major structural reorganization. Special study commissions, task forces, and coordinating committees of various types have been created to plan and even carry out strategies. But these are normally considered as ad hoc and short-term measures, and do not create a very strong institutional base from which to operate.

A *project* is typically considered to be a much more formalized arrangement. It tends to focus attention on a problem and provide an integrated approach to solving it by creating a new organization. The new arrangement will have its own identity apart from the existing bureaucratic structures, often including its own personnel, specific legal status, and access to special resources. The Tennessee Valley Authority represents such a project with its own enabling legislation, autonomy, and authority to undertake negotiations with state and local governments, and contracts with the Army Corps of Engineers and dozens of other agencies and private firms to do its work (building dams, power plants, fisheries, recreation areas, etc.). TVA, in many ways the ultimate project, has become an institution in American public affairs.

The term *program* has been used similarly, as well as differently. Some professional observers see programs as coordinating devices to bring clusters of projects together, ensuring that all the pieces are working toward a larger goal (Bryant and White 1982, 110). For example, the Philippines has a national irrigation program that is an umbrella over many small local irrigation projects. Another theoretical example would be a local community with a health program that links projects to build a health clinic, nutrition services, and secure potable water (White 1987, 10). Alternatively, programs are also defined in terms of ongoing activities that are more closely integrated into the established bureaucracy, administered by the existing staff, with limited, if any, claims to special budgetary support. In this view, programs tend to be contrasted with projects by suggesting that, while they do have specific goals, these tend to be broader than for projects, with rather longer time lines or larger, more geographically (or demographically) dispersed spans of application. Brinkerhoff (1992, 488) suggests that these distinctions are important at the margins perhaps, with the differences best understood as on a continuum between operating and strategic tasks (see Figure 11.1). From this perspective, program managers are a bit more preoccupied with strategic tasks and functions, for example, finding allies or collaborators and mobilizing resources, while project managers are more fully engaged in the details: roles, responsibilities, schedules, etc.

While such efforts at conceptual distinctions between projects and programs abound in the academic literature, in practice the actual terms "project" and "program" are used in much looser and even contradictory ways. Despite NASA's being one of the defining enterprises in the world of project management, throughout its history we have been treated to references to the "Mercury Program," the "Apollo Program"—which were clearly subactivities to the project goal of getting to the moon! Furthermore, in one careful study of what are referred to as successful

Figure 11.1: A Continuum of Project and Program Management Tasks and Functions

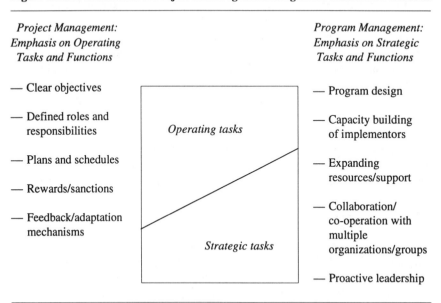

Project Management:
Emphasis on Operating
Tasks and Functions

— Clear objectives

— Defined roles and
   responsibilities

— Plans and schedules

— Rewards/sanctions

— Feedback/adaptation
   mechanisms

Operating tasks

Strategic tasks

Program Management:
Emphasis on Strategic
Tasks and Functions

— Program design

— Capacity building
   of implementors

— Expanding
   resources/support

— Collaboration/
   co-operation with
   multiple
   organizations/groups

— Proactive leadership

Source: From Derek W. Brinkerhoff, *Improving Development Program Performance: Guidelines for Managers.* Copyright © 1991 by Lynne Rienner Publishers, Inc. Used with permission of the publisher.

development programs, Paul suggests that three key elements of success include an initial focus on a single goal or service, some measure of organizational autonomy, and flexible selection of personnel and training processes (1982, 229), all of which appear to fit the academic definition of project characteristics. This apparent confusion reflects not only the vagueness of language, but also the fact that real-world organizations have unique or idiosyncratic features which might only roughly approximate the ideal type that academics, who are looking for consistency, might call a program or project.

The effort to distinguish precisely between the two appears somewhat artificial given the frequency with which one encounters organizational arrangements that appear to mix both types of characteristics in varying ways. Focusing on the supposed differences takes attention away from the commonalities, which appear far more significant. Regardless of whether an intervention is referred to as a project or program, the essential characteristic is that it is defined by its *task*, which tends to be relatively specific and unitary, rather than by its place in an organization. Its advantage is that it serves as the organizational focus for a concerted attack on a specific problem or set of problems, less constrained by the requirements and organizational patterns of the ongoing bureaucracies. Some projects and programs have specifically earmarked budgets, while some do not; some have separate staffs, while some rely on existing organizations; some have a specific time frame, while others are ongoing; some are independent, while others are embedded in existing organizations. But in all cases, they represent a strategy to integrate key resources in a new way to deal more effectively with a problem while respecting the integrity of the ongoing bureaucracy. To summarize, both projects and programs represent an organizational strategy that has the following characteristics: a focus around a specific task; a scope that cuts across existing lines of bureaucratic authority and responsibility; and a goal of being more institutionalized than ad hoc efforts such as coordinating committees. In all cases, then, projects and programs represent institutionalized organizational efforts to deal more effectively with a problem by integrating key resources in a new way without having to deal with the costs and problems inherent in reorganization.

STRATEGIC CHALLENGES

The actual design of projects and programs depends on a number of strategic questions. Three of the most important challenges are the following, which are considered below:

1. What type of vision should dominate the design of the project?
2. To what extent should the project or program be separate from, or integrated into, the existing bureaucratic system?
3. How can the sustainability of the project or program be assured?

Organizing Vision

Many consider that the design of projects and programs should be informed by an engineering metaphor that is derived from the scientific and engineering experience of Western industrialized countries. Public works engineering is the imagery contained in the minds of planners, economists, policy analysts, and managers when conceptualizing what goes into accomplishing a complex goal. At the risk of oversimplification, the basic elements of this engineering vision include the following, at least in theory:

1. disciplined conceptual disaggregation of complex, or ill-defined problems into discrete tasks for which resources can be mobilized and targeted;
2. specific time boundaries within which projects begin and end according to a funding schedule and work plan;
3. preprogrammed activities in which the resources, contracting, procurement, training, and anticipated outcomes are all planned or "designed";
4. applied economic and systems analysis employed to appraise a project idea to determine whether it is economically viable or rational according to other technical criteria;
5. standardized reporting procedures for monitoring, control, and evaluation. (Morgan 1983, 330)

The essence of the engineering approach, then, is the faith that problems can indeed be solved, plus an elaboration of procedures that show how to specify the problem, break it down into manageable components, choose rationally among alternative courses of action, and devise indicators to tell if the goals are being achieved.

In essence, the "task" focus of projects and programs, plus the confidence that complex problems can be understood and solved through carefully designed interventions, provides a strong rationale to support this engineering mentality, encouraging policymakers to devise strategies and to build support in ways that can be key levers for change. But the virtues of this approach are also its limitations. The confidence of the engineering metaphor may be quite appropriate in situations where the problem is relatively straightforward and the technologies known, for example, construction. Its appropriateness becomes less certain, however, when the problem is in the domain of social policy, where the situation is typically more complex and less well understood—for example, designing an effective family planning program or an education project to reach the bored or estranged. How then can one cope with the limitations of the engineering models in dealing with highly complex and uncertain problems?

Many factors must be taken into account when designing projects and programs. One of the most important is the extent to which the nature of the problem itself is clear (Siffin 1991, 10). In some cases, the nature of the problem is relatively clear-cut, for example, getting to the moon was enormously complex, but essentially a problem of "big science." Even the horrendous cost was muted by the cold war rivalry with the USSR and the benefits to constituencies nationwide as new aerospace subcontractors emerged to service NASA. But if a pattern of illness appears to be coming from toxins in groundwater traced to runoff from nearby farm land, what is the problem to be solved—an inadequate water treatment process, poor management of agro-industrial versus residential land use, or chemical fertilizer use? Or, more likely, some unique combination of all three.

Simplifying, there are two different types of uncertainties lurking in this "problem": those having to do with facts and those reflecting values. The cause of ill health can be traced factually to a source such as chemical fertilizer runoff seeping into groundwater. This is a matter of fact, or information, or knowledge. But when we take up the choices for remedial action, we evoke value conflicts: those willing to go with a technological solution in the water treatment process versus those arguing for reduction in the use of chemical fertilizers. In a constituency highly dependent on agriculture, there is great uncertainty as well as conflict in vigorous regulation of chemical fertilizer use, so the path of least resistance is to create a water treatment project. Moreover, we know how to use the engineering vision to design water treatment, so that is often what gets done. The weakness of the engineering vision is that too often a solution is chosen before the uncertainties are fully diagnosed. It can also be used to provide a scientific cover for justifying a solution that provides a feasible path that avoids facing costs that would be unacceptable to the political community or its representatives. This tendency to act as if a problem is subject to a technical cure without the political pain of changing behavior is called "premature programming" (Landau 1979).

Furthermore, the separate, "projectized" focus can encourage a very narrow view of the problem, which will not provide a long-term solution. In fact, searching for the realistic and "feasible" solution may reduce incentives to look for a more systemic strategy that in the long term could be more effective. We know well that the effect of more and wider expressways to relieve traffic congestion only attracts more vehicles, viz. Los Angeles. So, if the independent project uses an engineering vision that focuses only on road-building, it stands little chance of dealing effectively with the problem of traffic congestion. In Lusaka, Zambia, a similar problem arose with regard to a project that focused on providing housing for the poor migrating to the capital. The exclusive focus on housing availability served only to attract more migrants. Focusing on housing alone, therefore, faces the same problem as focusing only on road-building as the "solution." In each case, the problem is much broader, but the narrow focus limits the capacity to achieve or even conceptualize an effective strategy. So simply "projectizing" the most feasible option can become part of the problem.

In contrast to the engineering approach, some advocate a "social learning" strategy, far more experimental in its outlook, stressing that only during the actual process of implementation does one begin to understand the problems fully and begin to be able to design a system that works (Korten 1980). For social programs and other highly complex problems, this vision can be a healthy antidote to the confident certainty of the engineering approach, encouraging the project or program manager to carefully test all assumptions at each step along the way, and constantly revise the design of a project or program to take advantage of the new information that is generated in the implementation process. Such an approach has been highly successful in designing creative solutions to difficult problems, ranging from providing effective irrigation systems to small farmers to providing credit to the poor.

Separate vs. Integrated Organizations

Projects and programs hold considerable promise as ways to mobilize resources to get things done, but they often have an uneasy relationship with the rest of the bureaucracy. Some projects, because of their size and support, may be free standing and long term (such as NASA, TVA and other regional resource management institutions). However, if this becomes the standard pattern, the country ends up with a "bypass model" in which existing public agencies charged with similar responsibilities are essentially ignored and are displaced by the new projects or programs.

Bypassing functional departments by creating multi-sectoral project authorities has yielded two nearly universal consequences. Special projects with special authority and special claims on resources tend to create a hostile institutional environment around them as neighboring political and administrative jurisdictions see competition rather than collaboration. Second, complex, multidimensional projects or programs often involve contracting different parts to different vendors (or in the case of development assistance, to different donors). The upshot is a set of discrete activities which, despite the original intent to achieve synergy through functional integration, are extremely difficult to bring together into an operating whole (incompatible technologies, different financial management systems, etc. In addition, discontinuities occur in information management. Data resulting from agricultural experiments at one time are not available at another when comparison could be very important. It is as if each project starts from scratch, with no sense of history or context. Furthermore, the regular institutions within the country that might try to pull this together are weakened, not strengthened by the programmatic focus. The irony of this situation, of course, is that the very effort to "get things going" that motivates the project and program approach, may in fact have the long-term impact of reducing, rather than improving, overall administrative capacity.

To avoid the problems of the bypass approach, some advocate that projects and programs should be more fully integrated into the existing bureaucratic institutions, with less independent control of staff, budgets, and policies. While this holds the promise of being more supportive to the existing system, it also raises the obvious problem that the new initiative could become swallowed up in existing routines and procedures, dramatically reducing its impact to combine resources in a new way to deal with the problem it is trying to solve. One possible way around this is to search the bureaucracy for the most effective existing organizations and make them responsible for the new project or program. While attractive in theory, however, these "good" organizations can be asked to take on so many projects and programs that their staff can quickly become overwhelmed, in effect undermining the organization that should be supported.

One way in which many countries are attempting to deal with this is by establishing formal or tacit agreements with various nongovernmental organizations to provide services the government is unable to deliver. This is a particularly attractive strategy in an era in which government budgets are becoming tighter while needs get greater. One of the most well-known examples is the Grameen Bank in Bangladesh, which is now one of many microsavings and credit schemes around the world using private money, some outside funding, and local savings (and a functional equivalent of "sweat equity") to provide working capital to the poor. Largely freed from government procedures and regulations, this nongovernmental organization has successfully experimented with new approaches to lending and works in areas that the government cannot afford to, or simply does not, reach. Such experiments are not confined to financial services. In Kenya the research and start-up costs for a cook stove project were underwritten jointly by the Kenya government and the U.S. Agency for International Development. Once off the ground, the stoves were sold in the private marketplace. Larger production runs were then financed privately with proceeds from sales, and no further government institutional or financial support was provided or required.

An alternative approach is to use the project or program as a way of reforming the bureaucracy so that it can carry out its tasks more effectively. Here the goal is often to begin with the project largely independent of most of the ongoing bureaucratic structure, but with the intention of integrating it into the existing system once the experiment is complete, successful, and ready to replicate. The key to success is to be sure that government officials essential to the program's long-term success have a hand in the experimenting from the begininning, so that they can see its advantages and have an interest in making the changes that will be needed to incorporate this project into the existing bureaucratic system. One well-known example is the creation of a major irrigation program for poor farmers in the Philippines. In effect, the project began as an independently funded experiment involving key operating personnel and decision makers in the National Irrigation Authority in a process to discover more effective methods of canal construction and maintenance, ultimately leading to a process of reorganization so that it could carry out this mandate more effectively. The strategy for carrying this out was complex, but it is an example of a successful effort to combine the energy and innovation of an independent effort while simultaneously integrating it into the ongoing bureaucratic structure (Korten 1980).

Sustainability: Getting Support—And Keeping It

One obvious theoretical advantage of a project or program is that it provides a mechanism to focus attention on a systemic issue, working across hierarchies to pull together resources for a concerted and sustained attack. This can be seen as a way to increase the capacity of the public sector to solve problems.

But it is also possible that the project or program can be seen as threatening ongoing functions rather than enhancing overall bureaucratic capacity. For some the advantage of the project or program is that it provides focus; but for others, this becomes a narrowness of perspective, oblivious to opportunity costs, in which project success becomes paramount even if it damages other goals. For example, in an effort to ensure that its projects succeed, a donor organization providing the loan or grant often specifies the inclusion of particular, highly talented local personnel. While this considerably enhances the success of that project, a consequence might be the neglect or displacement of other activities that these individuals were previously supervising. This illustrates the dilemma of scarce resources: how to enhance the chance of project success without weakening other existing institutions? What makes this all the more problematic is that the measures for project and program success (which provide both the information for policymakers and the incentives for the officials involved) rarely if ever take into account the problems they are creating elsewhere by shifting personnel and other resources to the project. This is true even if you give responsibility to an existing institution—as this can so overload that institution and its staff that it is faced with a choice of doing its regular business or the add-on project (Gow and Morss 1988, 1403).

A second issue addresses the tendency for focused programs to have relatively short time horizons and to focus on the high visibility issue of capital costs, while giving much less attention to the even more critical long-term issues of recurring costs and maintenance. This of course is not just a problem of projects and programs—political visibility (hence support) is always high for the building of a road, school, or clinic, including the highly publicized ribbon-cutting ceremony that gives the impression that the task is "completed." But projects and programs often compound this problem by going out of business at this point, handing over to "someone else" the responsibility for upkeep. But "upkeep" in the sense of recurring costs is essential for project and program success and often requires extensive resources: for schools, for example, this includes building maintenance, salaries for personnel, books, and equipment. By not having maintenance considerations as part of the frame of reference for the project, project managers may focus on what gets built most quickly or cheaply, rather than what, in the long term, is most cost-effective to maintain and will make a longer term contribution to education.

The key is to focus on the *institutional* infrastructure necessary for dealing with recurring costs, as well as the creation of the more visible physical infrastructure. This includes a focus on institutional learning and capacity building, as well as a concern with reaching physical targets. The capacity to mobilize resources and achieve objectives are embodied in institutions. Such learning institutions might already exist in a community (age sets, school or occupation-based cohorts), or they might be new, special purpose organizations. In any case, they are a source of energy, ideas, and demands that can keep a bureaucracy from closing up, helping it adapt (especially if these external influences are reinforced by reorienting the internal workforce) as occurred in the National Irrigation Administration in the Philippines (Korten 1980). In this vein, Gow and Morss recommend three basic changes in project design: switch primary emphasis from production increases to performance improvements; examine potential side effects on local institutional capacity; and take account of the existing "institutional landscape" (Gow and Morss 1988, 1402–1403).

Other solutions to recurring costs include: securing maintenance budgets in advance (although this is problematic due to annual budget decisions, inflation, etc.); user fees (e.g., toll roads, licenses, etc.); "sweat equity"—maintenance and improvement by people themselves—for example, urban homesteading, sites and services projects where standpipes and sewage infrastructure are provided but individuals build on their own plots. The main drawback of any of these self-help approaches is the assumption that people have plenty of free time. This is particularly misleading when considering women whose current economic activity, though extensive, is not formally measured and therefore is seriously undercounted. In all cases, the key is to ensure that the project/program includes a long-term perspective in order to calculate the total cost of the project (building and maintenance). Otherwise, the tendency will be to build as quickly and cheaply as possible and assume that maintenance is "someone else's problem."

CONCLUSIONS

Translating policies into action is not easy, particularly if it involves new initiatives that cut across the existing bureaucratic hierarchies. The use of projects and programs is one organizational strategy for carrying this out that offers the promise of encouraging the energy and initiative of a focused and integrated approach, while at the same time respecting the integrity of the existing organizational structure and avoiding the high costs of major reorganization. While there is some lack of clarity about the differences between projects and programs (or even whether such a distinction is meaningful in the practical world of management), both projects and programs generally tend to exhibit, the following general characteristics: (1) they draw their identity from their task, rather than their place in the organization; (2) they serve as the locus for coordinating an integrated effort that goes across existing lines of bureaucratic authority and responsibility; and (3) they are more institutionalized and operationally focused than ad hoc arrangements such as coordinating committees or advisory panels, yet they do not require major reorganization of the existing system.

To be effective, projects and programs need to face a number of strategic challenges: deciding the most appropriate "vision" to provide guidance; calculating the advantages and disadvantages of integration or independence; and ensuring sustainability of project and program efforts. Different projects and programs employ different strategies to meet these challenges, illustrating the point that most of these strategies represent the need to consider tradeoffs rather than perfect solutions to problems.

Nevertheless, the use of projects and programs are common organizational devices employed by project managers worldwide. While the results have been mixed, experience suggests that a careful consideration of the dilemmas and tradeoffs outlined above can substantially improve their effectiveness and enable them to be an effective tool in the imperfect world of public management.

REFERENCES AND SUGGESTED READINGS

Baker, R. 1989. "Institutional Innovation, Development and Environmental Management: An 'Administrative Trap' Revisited." *Public Administration and Development*, Part I: 9 (1):29–47, Part II: 9 (2):159–167.

Baum, Warren. 1982. *The Project Cycle*. Washington, D.C.: The World Bank.

Brinkerhoff, Derick W. 1992. "Looking Out, Looking In, Looking Ahead: Guidelines for Managing Development Programs." *International Review of Administrative Sciences* 58:483–503.

Bryant, Coralie, and Louise White. 1982. *Managing Development in the Third World*. Boulder, Colo.: Westview Press.

Gow, David, and Elliott Morss. 1988. "The Notorious Nine: Critical Problems in Project Implementation." *World Development* 16 (12):1399–1418.

Honadle, George, and Jay Rosengard. 1983. "Putting 'Projectized' Development in Perspective." *Public Administration and Development* 3:299–305.

Korten, David C. 1980. "Community Organization and Rural Development: A Learning Process Approach." *Public Administration Review* 40:480–511.

Landau, Martin, and Russell Stout, Jr. 1979. "To Manage is Not to Control: Or, the Folly of Type II Errors." *Public Administration Review* 39:148–156.

Mintzberg, Henry. 1979. *The Structuring of Organizations*. Englewood Cliffs, N.J.: Prentice-Hall.

Morgan, E. Philip. 1983. "The Project Orthodoxy in Development: Re-evaluating the 'Cutting Edge.'" *Public Administration and Development* 3:329–339.

Paul, Samuel. 1982. *Implementing Development Programs: The Lessons of Success*. Boulder, Colo.: Westview Press.

Selznick, Philip. 1949 and 1980. *TVA and the Grass Roots: A Study in the Sociology of Formal Organization*. Berkeley, Cal.: University of California Press.

Siffin, William J. 1991. "The Problem of Development Administration." In *Handbook of Comparative and Development Public Administration*, ed. A. Farazmand. New York: Marcel Dekker.

Webb, James. 1969. *Space Age Management*. New York: McGraw-Hill.

White, Louise G. 1987. *Creating Opportunities for Change: Approaches to Managing Development Programs*. Boulder, Colo.: Lynne Rienner.

12

Comparative Intergovernmental Relations

Robert Agranoff

Although interest in the intergovernmental relations of nations has emerged only recently, such practices no doubt reach back to antiquity. Was not imperial taxation and provision of "defense" from outsiders between Rome and their subject provinces a form of intergovernmental relations? Clearly, the visibility of current relationships is a result of the frequency and intensity of interunit transactions, sometimes becoming highly visible events. The volatility of such interconnections is sometimes system defining or threatening, such as the crisis in Canadian federalism, the break up of Czechoslovakia, and the status of Hong Kong and Macau as self-governing autonomous communities of the People's Republic of China. Americans, Nigerians, Spaniards, Yugoslavs, and others who have experienced civil wars know that such relationships can be, to paraphrase Clausewitz, intergovernmental relations by other means. Nevertheless, these connections are more likely to involve routine policy and program issues faced by politicians and administrators as a result of the increasing interdependence of governments within nations.

Although many Americans tend to think of such routines as uniquely a result of their federal system, the practice is widespread in most Western or Western-style democratic political systems, even so-called unitary systems. The experience, as Vincent Ostrom (1985) maintains, is that no democracy rests all the prerogatives of government within a single entity. Processes of government are mediated through multiple decision structures, implying multi-organizational arrangements. Contacts between these units have become more regular, particularly through welfare state programs (i.e., in broad conception of social protection and promotion). The component units become part of a national system of governance, or "nation wide government" as Rose (1985) suggests. Such governmental systems are characterized by: (1) linkages that arise from the functional imperatives of program coordination, (2) multiple institutions (public and private) that are used in the same programs, (3) national government statutory authority and financial responsibility that needs to be blended with local delivery concern, and (4) involvement of subnational governments in national programs that is encouraged because of the desire to allow communities to share in decision making and adaptation. In addition, many experts believe that the spread of democratization, industrialization, and urbanization have contributed to this policy and program interdependence (Ashford 1982, 1986; Dente and Kjellberg 1988; Kjellberg and Tuene 1980; Sharpe 1988). The resulting multiple institutional connections involve territorial authority and functional responsibilities. "Policy unites what constitutions divide," suggests Rose (1985, 22).

INTERGOVERNMENTAL RELATIONS DEFINED

In its most basic sense, intergovernmental relations (IGR) follows William Anderson's (1960, 3) definition as, "an important body of activities or interactions occurring between governmental units of all types and levels." Anderson's reference is to the United States federal system, since the term appears to have originated in the United States in the 1930s. The concept is best understood in terms of the five distinctive features identified by Wright (1988, 15–24) in relation to the United States, but appears applicable in many other national contexts and governmental systems: (1) transcendence of constitutionally recognized patterns of governmental involvement to include varieties of relationships, including national-local, regional-local, national-regional, interlocal, as well as quasi-governmental organizations and private organizations; (2) a human element or the activities and attitudes of persons occupying official positions in the units of government under consideration; (3) relationships between officials involved in their continuous contacts and exchanges of information and views; (4) involvement of all types of public officials—legislators, judges, administrators—at different levels of government as potential or actual participants in decision-making processes; and (5) a policy dimension, involving interactions of actors across boundaries surrounding the formulation, implementation, and evaluation of policy. IGR involves an approach that focuses on the location of decision making, on what basis, whose values are being served, and the consequences of those actions (Edner 1976).

Elazar (1987a, 16–17) explains that IGR has not caught on in most other nations because of the U.S. tie to federalism as self-rule and shared rule, in which federal theory holds that the people delegate powers to different governments serving different arenas for different purposes. Unless the American usage has gained currency in other federal systems, the accepted theory of the state in Europe and the Old World holds sovereignty to be indivisible, with the state as the exclusive source of power, with all other bodies exercising powers to be merely authorities and instrumentalities. Thus, on a strict legal basis there can be no IGR within systems. Practice, however, suggests otherwise.

The concept of IGR transcends constitutional-legal approaches to divisions of government and their respective powers and duties. It is not a replacement for such historical concepts as federalism and the structure of unitary systems, but a supplement allowing for the growing realities of politics and administration as governments have expanded (Elazar 1987a, 15). IGR is, however, distinctively nonlegal in orientation. The tradition in central/subnational government research has been legalistic, with its emphasis on constitutional structures and procedural rules. Intergovernmental approaches are more nonlegal, involving a variety of organizations, behaviors, and patterns. As Wright (1981, 10) has suggested, perhaps an asset of IGR in this respect is "that it does not ignore or depreciate legal/ constitutional analyses but attempts to overcome the potential limits of the strong justice tradition inherent in federalism." Wright (1981) also suggests that as a relatively new approach, IGR does not carry the political baggage that has sometimes accompanied systems of government such as federalism. This apolitical connotation increases its analytic utility, helps preserve its precision, and fosters accumulation of knowledge that adds to understanding.

MULTI-ORGANIZATIONAL GOVERNANCE IN FEDERAL AND UNITARY SYSTEMS

Scholars increasingly maintain that it makes less difference whether a system is federal or unitary, despite legal differences. Patterns of operation show similar trends. Nevertheless, because constitutional frameworks make one difference some important distinctions need to be maintained. Federal systems unite smaller polities within an overarching political system by distributing and guaranteeing power between the general and constituent governments in a manner designed to protect the existence and authority of both national and subnational systems (Elazar 1987b). Unitary states, on the other hand, place dominant authority in their central or national governments; constitutional grants of power to subnational governments are a direct function of national authority. However, many practices, such as subnational elected bodies, division of functions, sharing of taxes, and political balances, exist in both systems. Thus, it appears useful to examine the forces of convergence that affect IGR.

Multi-organizational governing systems in fact blur the legal edges of federal and unitary systems. Despite the constitutional supremacy of national governments in unitary systems, many modifying forces exist. Multiple decision structures at national and subnational levels, such as cabinet ministries (with subnational structures), provincial councils, and provincial committees provide one such force. Other forces include nationalist movements, nationality groups, religious interests, and language groups that seek political recognition. In some nations, ideological and/or partisan forces promote subnational interests, such as regional autonomy, decentralization, local autonomy, or even federative alternatives. Fiscal practices such as tax sharing, general grants, and dedicated grants also modify the "unitary" nature of systems. Recent trends of administrative decentralization, devolution of national functions, and co-government, that is, joint program implementation among levels of government, have also moved unitary systems to shared power models. Of course, political bargaining pervades all of these forces.

Similar trends, although usually in reverse, have moved federal systems into more national control modes. Sharing of programs has led to greater involvement by national governments in subnational affairs. Clearly the role of national grants attached to programs has put national governments in more of a supervisory position than they otherwise would be, as conditions have been attached to subventions. In addition to program conditions, national regulations have been imposed on subnational governments, sometimes as financial aid conditions, but also as a means of protecting and guaranteeing rights on a nationwide basis. Much of this nationalization has also been made possible by the increasing tax superiority of national governments in federal systems, and when tax revenues are shared there have often been national attempts at controlling overspending. In addition, national governments have increasingly assumed previously subnational functions, such as social welfare programs, and have undertaken shared roles in subnational functions, such as education, highways, and aviation. Of course, federal systems contain ideological and partisan forces that support national over subnational interests, particularly to ensure that particular benefits, rights, or values are guaranteed across nations. Finally, political bargaining between subnational and national interests is pervasive and as likely to "centralize" federal systems as it is to decentralize them.

Certain IGR patterns thus seem to make federal systems increasingly display centralizing and national control tendencies without making them unitary. The converse is also true. Unitary systems increasingly display decentralization and devolution tendencies without necessarily becoming federal. These IGR patterns suggest that there are few pure types.

INSTRUMENTS OF INTERGOVERNMENTAL RELATIONS

The foregoing suggests that IGR is conducted by many different means. A more focused look at some transactional approaches will demonstrate the international character of these instruments. Following the major categories of study that characterize U.S. IGR, the overview will include intergovernmental fiscal relations, grants and program subventions, intergovernmental regulation, subnational governmental structures, political forces, and bureaucratic actions. The review will also raise some questions relating to the comparative research of intergovernmental instruments.

Intergovernmental Fiscal Relationships

Some analysts view fiscal relations as the essence of IGR. While there is no doubt that the fiscal tie is a basic one, it will be demonstrated that political and managerial determinations also formulate important means of understanding IGR.

Intergovernmental fiscal relationships do, however, help determine the parameters of interdependent systems.

In virtually every Western nation the central government is the primary tax recipient, later distributing revenue through various means. Moreover, in most nations, accounting for income transfers are usually central functions, regardless of whether nations administer programs nationally or subnationally (Page and Goldsmith 1987). While there have been some experiments with tax decentralization, the results are inconclusive (Aten 1990; Groenewegen 1990; King 1984). The revenue-raising powers of subnational powers is thus subordinate. It is also variable. Rose's (1984) analysis reveals that the range is from 46 percent and 41 percent of taxes raised by local and intermediate governments in Canada and Switzerland respectively, to 1 percent in the Netherlands and Italy. In federal systems, subnational governments raise 32 percent of taxes whereas in unitary systems only 14 percent of taxes are *not* raised by national governments. However, Rose also reports that there was virtually no correlation between total tax as a share of the national product and the share of tax raised by state and local government. He thus concludes that there is no need to complicate matters by examining differences between federal and unitary systems. Clearly what is more important is the revenue predominance of national governments and the intergovernmental ties they create with fund subventions.

The chief fiscal vehicles for subventions in most nations have been through grants. Three major forms of grants are used: (1) unrestricted transfers of money for general subnational government operation; (2) broad purpose or block grants, which do not detail expenditures but are required to be used in specified general areas; and (3) categorical or restricted purpose grants that specify expenditure areas and are subject to strict legal controls. The growth of national grants to support subnational governments appears to be a widespread corollary of the expanding welfare state (King 1984). In the United States, for example, national grants as a percentage of state-local receipts from government sources grew from 10 percent in 1955 to 26.5 percent in 1978, its high-water mark. In dollars, the growth was from $3.2 billion to $77.9 billion. Spending in 1990 reached $133.8 billion (ACIR 1990).

Another critical fiscal consideration is expenditure controls placed by higher levels of government on lower levels. In unitary nations and in unitary relationships, such as those of many U.S. states and their local governments, controls may come by direct limit of revenue/expenditure levels. They may also come in the form of program standards or fiscal expenditure rules, which are subject to later audits. In some areas, such as social services in Britain, grantees negotiate program budgets, which in turn are related to negotiated forward planning and priorities. Another popular device for subvention is either a contract for the delivery of specific services at a fixed rate or the outright purchase of services for negotiated fees. In some nations, funding agencies offer loans, loan sanctions, or cash advances as means of fiscal transfer. Finally, many nations, centrally or by second tier governments, "fiscally supervise" the financial operations of subnational governments, including the handling of regional and local government monies raised and expended locally.

Supervision comes in many forms, ranging from verifying the propriety of expenditures to training of local fiscal officers.

Intergovernmental Grants

Two of the three types of grants—categorical and bloc—are "conditional" and cement greater interdependence. Some work has been done that examines the type of grants to subnational governments and the types of program and policy ties they create, but they tend to be studies that focus on single countries (Dente and Kjellberg 1988; Galligan and Walsh 1990; Page and Goldsmith 1987). Other studies have comparatively examined the budgetary impact of intergovernmental grants (Gramlich 1987). Unfortunately, more cross-national analyses have been conducted on areas of government spending and growth (Rose 1984) than on grant systems.

A literature on the economic impact of intergovernmental grants exists (e.g., King 1984; Oates 1972) that suggest that grants: (1) subsidize programs where benefits accrue outside of the jurisdiction, (2) serve as efficient and sometimes equitable resource transfer mechanisms, and (3) can equalize fiscal "capacity across jurisdictions." Others (Inman 1989) have questioned the economic benefit of grants, pointing to more political explanations. Another issue is the stimulative effect of subnational grants: do they induce increases in budgets? Research on the "fly paper effect" (Oates 1990) suggests that unconditional grant money is not usually passed on in the form of lower taxes but "sticks where it hits!" On the other hand, there is evidence from the United States that in the face of budget cuts (Gramlich 1987; Mirando 1990), and even the elimination of national general grants, local governments do fill the gaps by increasing taxes and replacing lost grant funds, suggesting that the fly paper effect may only work in one direction.

A number of political factors relating to grants also raise important research questions regarding IGR processes, including the: (1) impact of grants on subnational government policy agendas; (2) impact on subnational choices among competing claims; (3) impact on the role and influence of program specialists versus program generalists; (4) consequences of national officials' powers of review, oversight, and approval of subnational actions; (5) impact of choices relating to programming; and (6) role of grant generated conflict and cooperation (Wright 1988, 265–267). Many of these issues will be elaborated on in subsequent sections. Although very few of these concerns have been investigated outside of the United States, they cut across national boundaries, and thus there is much to be learned by comparing grant programs.

Intergovernmental Regulation

Regulatory activity, that is actions of central or higher level governments exerting rules designed to affect the behavior of subnational/subordinate governments, constitutes yet another widely used instrument. Although it is a fairly universal political concern, regulation has been more of an analytical concern in the United States where regulations come in many forms: (1) total or partial preemption of previous subnational regulatory activity; (2) program requirements that are attached to grants; (3) crossover regulations, that make a related action a condition of receiving national financial assistance; (4) requirements that a subnational government not engage in certain activities; and (5) requirements for the provision of services that are considered "custom and culture" but not written in laws.

Although many of these types of regulation also appear in other national contexts, there appears to be less concern over the growing "power" of central government regulators in other contexts. This may be explained somewhat by the shared power and limited government tradition in the United States. By contrast, European unitary states have a longer tradition of the imposition of requirements by a legally all-powerful centre. To a degree, this may be a function of greater political bargaining than goes on in other systems, to blunt the impact of increased requirements through such means as negotiating compensatory concessions, for example, through revenue raising powers. This appears to be the case in France (Ashford 1982).

Since regulation is so universal, several comparative research issues appear to be relevant. The most commonly asked question in intergovernmental regulation relates to "unfunded mandates" or subnational financial costs associated with meeting compliance (Stenberg 1992). What is the intergovernmental fiscal burden placed on subnational governments with a given regulatory effort? Another issue that appears central to IGR is a locational question, that is, should regulation be a central government function or should standards vary across jurisdictions in accordance with local circumstances? Another related question would be, should standard-setting be national, local, or negotiated in some form? The arguments for and against are both economic and political (Oates 1990, 53–54). Two other issues relate to the examination of regulations as IGR instruments. First, what is the degree to which central governments use regulations or mandates as instruments of national policy priorities, and how successful are these approaches? Second, to what extent are regulations imposed on subnational governments really instruments imposed to solve national fiscal problems by shifting financial burdens (Kettl 1987, 178; Walker 1991)?

As the foregoing suggests, analyses of IGR regulation must not only include economic foci, but questions of political feasibility. Any effective regulatory program is based on political as well as economic criteria. A regulatory program is said to require adequate support—be based on a sound theory identifying principal factors and causal linkages affecting policy objectives. It should also contain legislative structuring of implementation that involves assignment to sympathetic and supporting agencies, and also possesses the capacity to operate and interact with supporters (Mazmanian and Sabatier 1987, 41–43; Reagan 1987, 194).

Governmental Structures

Why be concerned about structure? Because, as James March and Johan Olsen (1984) maintain, government institutions are important for structuring patterns of interaction in society. As a result, a host of comparative studies have examined the structures of executive departments, patterns of governing systems (party systems, executives, distribution of power), and the machinery of government (bureaucratic capabilities, institutional environment of planning, social characteristics related to governance). The framework of Peters (1988) appears to be most useful. It focuses on extensiveness, centralization, hierarchy, and participation as major categories of analysis.

This increased interest in the structures of government as predictors of behavior and public policy have obvious IGR implications. One of the earliest and best-known government structure studies, *Democracies*, by Arend Lijphart (1984) examines 21 systems with two broad classifications: the majoritarian (Westminister) and consensual (consociational) models. Among other characteristics, the former is defined by its unitary and centralized structures, whereas the latter ordinarily is decentralized and federal. Jean Blondell's (1982) classification scheme is based on two major dimensions, the more traditional unified versus divided governments and the emergent hierarchial versus collective decision making. He suggests that as multilevel governments are becoming more numerous, we are witnessing the gradual development of this second dimension. This is particularly important as more groups demand political representation, particularly with the emergence of a strong bureaucracy whose weight often tends to divide governments.

The clearest manifestation of multilevel government is the emergence of regional or second level governments in nonfederal systems. France, Italy, Spain and Japan are all cases where regionalization has been strengthened in the past few decades. Sweden is in the process of strengthening its regional structures, that is, its consolidated counties, particularly in the areas of planning and development. In cases where regional bodies have constitutional status, elected representative bodies, and legislative powers, such as that of Spain, regional governments are becoming federal in "arrangements" (Elazar 1987a) and considerably more powerful than mere decentralized authorities. They are becoming similar to intermediate governments in federal systems (Agranoff 1992; Monreal 1986). Study of intermediate governments in unitary states suggests that the rise of these structures is attributed to a number of factors: administrative efficiency and the need for regional planning as means of dealing with ethnic subnational grievances of the periphery and to enhance democratization (Rousseau and Zariski 1987, 270–271). Emergent regional structures in all nations affect the patterns of IGR, introducing new levels of contact and interaction.

Two additional prevalent organizational changes are the consolidation of local government organizations and the increasing use of nongovernmental organizations to administer programs. Contrary to the practice in the United States, where the number of local government units has steadily increased (Wright 1988), in many nations local general purpose governments (municipalities and counties, or their equivalent) have been consolidated, thereby reducing their numbers. This has been particularly true in Northern Europe (Dente and Kjellberg 1988; Page and Goldsmith 1987). The reason for this consolidation has been to create greater administrative efficiencies in administering welfare state programs, thereby eliminating small villages or rural counties that did not have the machinery to carry out large national programs on a local basis. The other move, greater reliance on nonprofit and for-profit organizations for the delivery of programs, is partially accountable to the desire for greater efficiency, but also reflects less reliance on the public sector to deal with public problems (Bennet 1990).

As a result of these trends, four comparative areas of inquiry appear to be challenging: (1) the role and impact of local government reorganization, including consolidation of units as well as boundary changes; (2) creation of regional or intermediate bodies that plan and operate programs, as well as serve representational and decision-making purposes; (3) the apparent increasing use of quasi-governmental organizations and nongovernmental organizations as intergovernmental partners in expanding government functions; and (4) welfare state generated expansion of the number and type of national cabinet ministries with extensive subnational interactions.

Political Forces

Many political forces obviously influence IGR. Officials' actions are as likely to be political as they are economic or administrative. Thus, factors such as use of elected position, political ideology, political parties, military, or business role, and ethnic subnational movements could be important factors in understanding the IGR of a particular country. One interesting framework for political analysis is that of R. A. W. Rhodes and Vincent Wright (1987). They refer to this category as the comparison of national government environments, indicating that, while difficult to generalize across nations, they were able to identify three important unifying political factors: institutional structure, ideology of central elites, and the party system.

In regard to institutional structure (Rhodes and Wright 1987, 13), "the centre sets the boundaries to subcentral actions. This power has its roots in the centre's constitutional and legislative resources, and to ignore such factors is to impoverish analysis. Legal institutions do not constitute the whole of comparative analysis but they remain an essential component." The position of local authorities to operate within a federal system differs from those of nonfederal systems, as do differences in nations with written and unmodified constitutions. Constitutionally reserved powers at subnational levels restrain central powers in both unitary and federal systems. The importance of institutional structure on IGR behavior has also been suggested in other frameworks (Peters 1988).

Elite ideologies also affect IGR. Following Tarrow's (1977, 33-35) framework, Rhodes and Wright suggest that normative equality, technocratic reformism, and distributive welfare constitute different ways of responding. France has moved from technocratic reformism in the 1960s and 1970s to democraticization in the 1980s. Regional reform in Italy has shifted elite behavior from equality and welfare to more technocratic systems in which "effective coordination" became the cry of the 1980s. The revival of 19th century liberalism is another ideological position that has altered IGR, as less government and privatization becomes the hallmark of behavior (see also Bennet 1990). In a number of nations, this ideology has led to other "off-loading" or financial participation by local governments and the nongovernmental sector (Walker 1991).

Political parties in the Rhodes and Wright (1987, 14) framework are the primary vehicles for ideologies and alternative actions. Strong central parties in the United Kingdom are obviously linked to "strong executive fostered unilateral action and the adoption of a command territorial operating code by the centre." In the Federal Republic of Germany, by contrast, demand for participation and keen party competition has led to greater bargaining and center accommodation, constraining centralizing strategies. Regionalism in Italy has been a product of center and left party strategies for some time. However, they also point to cross-national forces of party *convergence*; welfare state expansion led to substantial subnational responsibility and discretion; recession-generated resource squeezes led to subnational cost sharing and privatization, often shaking the foundations of welfare-state generated IGR; program platforms that lead to subnational grants in turn stabilize relationships between governments; success in subnationalism that in turn has led to "politicization" of territorial relations, such as nationalist movements (see also Sharpe 1979, 1986). Thus, party systems have shaped IGR, and the reverse, in a reciprocal political fashion. Together, the three components of the Rhodes and Wright scheme offer one useful way to think about comparative IGR political behavior.

Bureaucratic Actions and Intergovernmental Communications

Since the predominant IGR actions are those of officials attempting to work out policy, it is these behaviors that have become the central foci. Anderson (1960, 3) suggests: "it is human beings clothed with office who are the real determiners of what relations between units of government will be. Consequently the concept of intergovernmental relations has to be formulated largely in terms of human relations and human behavior."

Patterns of access of local officials to central governments have been studied comparatively in Western Europe (Page and Goldsmith 1987). Contacts to national governments were channeled through a variety of means: national interest groups of local authorities; political party channels, particularly when the local and national parties were the same; "administrative entrepreneurship" or brokering and representing on behalf of local government; through functional professional channels, a type of politics of expertise; and by direct contacts by local elites to national officials. The emphasis on these channels varied somewhat by nation, with the southern countries—France, Italy, and Spain—relying more on local elites and direct administrative channels, and the northern nations of Britain, Sweden, Norway, and Denmark showing a tendency to rely more on associations, professional channels, and political parties (see also Ashford 1982; Tarrow 1977).

Technical roles of central government officials in IGR represent patterned actions. Fesler (1962) has traced the evolution of the field agent from political generalist to that of a specialist administrator. Specialists are said to have three primary roles: responsibility for overall policy and standards, coordination of programs, and control over expenditure (Webb and Wistow 1980, 209). What have been characterized as "trust relationships or trust ties" hold IGR actors together bureaucratically (Breton and Wintrobe 1982; Dupuy 1985). These functional links are said to be nurtured by: (1) common values and vocabulary; (2) relative departmental autonomy at central government levels to make key intergovernmental decisions; (3) trust relationships nurtured by continuous contact; (4) distributive effects of grants that expand program activity, enhance bureaucratic careers and "lock-in" promises of resources or other considerations; and (5) special interest representation through associational ties of departmental officials.

Policy guidance roles, such as the idealized framework identified by Webb and Wistow (1980, 70) in regard to British personal social services, provide useful means for understanding the type of national controls that bureaucrats often impose:

professional and service objectives; current theories and knowledge about social problems; the implications of such theories for the choice of service outputs and professional practice; professional standards; the reconciliation of resource scarcity with the exercise of public accountability (primarily through enquiries into mistakes and disasters); priorities between client groups (not least because of the demographic pressure from the elderly population); priorities between types of service provision and intervention; the local compatibility of personal social services with health service planning (over which the DHSS has direct control, nominally at least); the compatibility with other statutory services (e.g, housing and education) and with voluntary and informal provision. (Webb and Wistow 1980, 70–71)

They believe in this case that the national Ministry of Health and Social Services must provide guidance relating to these concerns due to uncertainty over goals and priorities and increasing interdependence.

The prefectural system in France illustrates processes of generalist interactive guidance. For example, commune level managerial assistance is regularly offered by national civil servants, who often serve in dual roles as paid consultants and national officials. Thoenig (1978, 179–180) uses the example of the *subdivisionnaire des Ponts et Chaussées* (subprefects), who determine major public works policies and watch over municipal budgets. These state bureaucrats coordinate and integrate the actions of various communes within their area and gain in the support of local political leadership for their objectives, which is said to lead to sound management. The French decentralist reforms are said to be a recognition of the evolution of the prefectural system from one that emphasized the right of *tutelle* (Ashford 1982), to one of the monitoring local authorities. Despite French intergovernmental reforms, which Dupuy (1985, 144–43) maintains actually confirmed ongoing decentral practices of officials, the prefects' successors—*commissaires*—retain critical roles. They have been shifted from local government executives to IGR representatives of the state within networks of officials. Thus, there appears to be two interactive models of IGR administrative contact worthy of examination, one of a more functional specialist nature and one of a generalist nature.

INTERGOVERNMENTAL MANAGEMENT

Managing affairs between governments on a daily basis is a rapidly ascendent component of IGR. Hesse (1987), for example, refers to the West German system as not only involving extensive entanglement and interdependence but operating through processes of cooperation and coordination. Agranoff's (1986) U.S. study focuses on the importance of routines as officials work at the margins of their governments, making adjustments as they attempt to make programs work. The prevalence of such behaviors has led observers to ask whether the present is not an era of intergovernmental management (IGM), an emergent phase of IGR (Wright 1984).

IGM refers to the daily transactional or "working out of relationships" between component governmental elements in a system of governments. As a function of IGR, it emphasizes the goal achievement process, since management is a *process* by which cooperating officials direct action toward goals. Deil Wright (1984) attributes three special qualities to IGM: (1) a problem-solving focus, that is, "an action oriented process that allows administrators at all levels the wherewithal to do something constructive" (Mandell 1979); (2) a means of understanding and coping with the system *as it is*, including strategic perspectives that address how and why interjurisdictional changes occur, as well as guidance on how to cope with the system; and (3) an emphasis on contacts and the development of communication networks. Agranoff and Lindsay (1983) conclude that IGM involves parties developing joint solutions while recognizing the importance of, and making accommodations among, the jurisdictional-legal/political and technical questions involved. IGM is therefore depicted as a complex and involved process of joint action, searching for feasible courses of joint management activity.

The significance of these managerial activities has been identified in many national contexts. In an introduction to a symposium on "Interorganizational Policy Making" in Western nations, Hanf (1978) identifies the authors' focus on the interorganizational characteristics of government problem-solving, involving a myriad of government levels and private agencies. Divisions of responsibilities, decision frameworks, and divergent interests lead to the need for "serving coordinated policy actions through networks of separate but interdependent organizations where the collective capabilities of a number of participants are essential for efficient problem solving, or where the activities of individual units are to be guided by more general policy considerations." Hanf, Hjern, and Porter's (1979) study of labor market training networks in Germany demonstrates the complexity of these network arrangements: multiple power centers, many resource suppliers, diffused responsibilities, overlapping divisions of labor, high potential for poor coordination, and the need for massive information exchanges. The study of networks in implementation of intergovernmental policy has led to increased focus on IGM as an approach in solving problems through contacts and communications. It has even led to the identification of new units of analysis, that of implementation structures (Hjern and Porter 1981; Mandell 1990).

In a more focused way, Rhodes' (1985) assessment of IGR in the United Kingdom identifies a series of "rules of the game" that were characteristically played by units of government during the 1970s and early 1980s. The long list includes pragmatism, consensus, fairness, accommodation, territoriality, and so on. More important, he identifies a series of managerial strategies: bureaucratic use of resources, co-optation of local authorities into central decision processes, consultation with local authorities, bargaining and exchange of resources, confrontation over nonconformity, finding allies by penetrating the other government, avoidance by each unit of government pursuing its own policy, offering financial inducements, creation of professional domains, and simplification by dividing problems.

Deil Wright (1984) refers to the present as an IGM era for three major reasons, all of which can be linked to the growth and complexity in intergovernmental arrangements: (1) increased *calculation*, for example, the need to weigh the costs and benefits of federal grants, to play the game of who benefits by formula distribution of funds, and to assess the risk of noncompliance with regulatory requirements versus the cost of compliance; (2) the game of *fungibility*, or the ability to shift or exchange resources received for one purpose in order to accomplish another purpose; and (3) *overload*, leading to excessive cost, ineffectiveness, and overregulation. These conditions, explains Wright, have highlighted the roles of public managers. Increasing complexity, interdependency, uncertainty, and risk have all enhanced the status of actors with experience, expertise, and knowledge— attributes that appointed managers generally possess in substantial measure.

Many different techniques and approaches to IGM have emerged. Agranoff (1988, 1989) has organized the literature on managerial processes into a dozen categories: (1) *planning* or the use of grant expansion to effectuate national purposes through subnational governments and nongovernment organizations; (2) *grants-manship* or the acquisition and administration of grants; (3) *regulation* management by attempts on the part of one government to influence the actions of other governments; (4) *structural-legal reform* altering the program framework of IGR, for example, grant requirement standardization or the enactment of block grants;

(5) *process revision*, that is, smoothing grants management through managerial process changes, such as joint applications and reviews or waiver of requirements; (6) *capacity development* or improved ability to anticipate and influence program changes, make informed and intelligent policy decisions, attract, absorb, and manage resources, and, evaluate current activities in order to guide future action; (7) *program management* or actions taken by managers to ensure that a program is developed and administered within the needs of a jurisdiction's perspective; (8) *policy management* or managing multiple categorical programs into combined efforts toward jurisdictional ends, such as redevelopment, economic growth, or frail elderly policies; (9) *bargaining and negotiations* or settlement of differences through formal or informal mechanisms in which managers use their respective positions to recognize both conflicting and common interests, but focus on one party's gain is perceived to be tied to another's loss; (10) *problem solving* or mutual adjustment, when inherent differences are not apparent and the formats of adjustment are less formalized; (11) *cooperative management* or mutual agreements by governmental parties to provide services, procure services, exchange services, or form mutual purpose organizations or compacts; and (12) *political games*, that is, the use of day-to-day politics as a managerial weapon, such as making contacts, seeking information, lobbying or influencing, and forming super government associations for the purpose of engaging in intergovernmental politics. As more complex interdependencies between governmental units develop, managers must learn to undertake these IGM approaches. As the basics of IGR are worked out, the stage becomes increasingly routine and managerial. There remain games to be played.

ISSUES AND CONCERNS IN IGR RESEARCH

A comparative study of IGR is emerging. The largest body of research examines the intergovernmental relations of single nations. That is understandable, inasmuch as the main reason why analysts and officials have an interest in IGR is to enhance the understanding and operation of governance within particular systems, requiring a focus on relationships within their contexts. The works of Ashford (1982), Rhodes (1981), and Wright (1988) are exemplary in this regard. Nevertheless, useful cross-national work is needed and is emerging, due to discovery of similarly occurring phenomena in multiple national contexts, and because of the broader practical interest in dealing with in-country interdependencies. Comparison of abstract processes such as IGR and IGM is obviously difficult because of these varied contexts, so that many comparative studies to date are compendia of single country analyses bound into volumes with introductory essays. Nevertheless, these studies are useful because primary linking concepts, such as patterns of national government access, revenue disparities, or subnational extension of welfare state programs are emerging as research foci.

Comparative research in related areas is also building useful knowledge. This research comes from five different traditions. First, studies involving centre-periphery relations or territorial politics, particularly subnational governance arrangements that recognize the maintenance of economic, cultural, social, ethnic, and even psychological differences (Mény and Wright 1985; Rhodes and Wright 1987; Rousseau and Zariski 1987). Second, policy implementation research through complex horizontal and vertical networks of multi-organizational arrangements (Hanf and Scharf 1978; Hanf and Toonen 1985; Kaufman, Majone, and Ostrom 1986). Third, studies of central-local government relations that focus on patterns of interaction, centralization-decentralization studies, strategies of accessing different levels of government, and national versus subnational allocations of powers (Ashford 1982; Bennet 1990; Elander and Montin 1990; Goldsmith 1986; Page and Goldsmith 1987; Picard and Zariski 1987; Rhodes 1981; Smith 1985; Wright 1988). Fourth, studies of local or regional government change and reform, which inevitably deal with national-local and often intermediate level government connections (Dente and Kjellberg 1988; Kjellberg and Teune 1980; Rousseau and Zariski 1987; Sharpe 1979). Fifth, cross-national governmental structures research, which focuses partially on unit connections, both legal and operational (Blondell 1982; Campbell and Peters 1988; Lijphart 1984; Rose 1984). These studies also make it possible to analyze IGR beyond the context of one nation.

To conclude, the most fruitful avenues of research in comparative IGR appear to be those which attempt to analyze patterns of interactions involving government officials, program structures, policy implementation, or policy processes. If one thinks in terms of the five features of IGR—variety of governmental units, multiple official involvements, actions of officials, patterns of contact among officials, and pursuit of policy development and implementation—a logic of research emerges. Perhaps this view may help clarify why comparing older categories of analysis, such as law and respective governmental powers and functions, as well as contextual forces are of more limited utility. Each of the latter contributes to a level of understanding about the framework of how governmental systems operate, but focuses less on the *transactional* nature of governmental systems. The growing interdependencies among national systems makes IGR an ever present component of study and practice in public administration.

REFERENCES

Agranoff, Robert. 1986. *Intergovernmental Management: Human Services Problem-Solving in Six Metropolitan Areas*. Albany, N.Y.: State University of New York Press.

_____. 1988. "Directions in Intergovernmental Management." *International Journal of Public Administration* 11:357–391.

_____. 1989. "Managing Intergovernmental Processes." In *Handbook of Public Administration*, ed. James L. Perry. San Francisco: Jossey-Bass.

_____. 1991. "Examining the IGM Approaches of National Governments: A Comparative Perspective." Paper presented at annual meeting of the American Society for Public Administration, April 1991, Washington, D.C.

_____. 1992. "Redesigning Spain's Intergovernmental System: An Experiment in Federal Arrangements." Paper presented at 8th Annual Roundtable, Committee on Federalism and Federation, International Political Science Association, September 1992, Muskoka, Ontario, Canada.

_____, and Valerie A. Lindsay. 1983. "Intergovernmental Management: Perspectives from Human Services Problem-Solving at the Local Level." *Public Administration Review* 43:227–237.

Advisory Commission on Intergovernmental Relations. 1990. *Significant Features of Fiscal Federalism*, vol. 12. Washington, D.C.: ACIR.

Anderson, William. 1960. *Intergovernmental Relations in Review*. Minneapolis: University of Minnesota Press.

Ashford, Douglas E. 1982. *British Dogmatism and French Pragmatism: Central-Local Policymaking in the Welfare State*. London: George Allen and Unwin.

_____. 1986. *The Emergence of the Welfare States*. Oxford: Basil Blackwell.

Aten, Robert H. 1990. "Accountability and Equity in British Local Finance: The Poll Tax." In *Decentralization, Local Governments and Markets*, ed. Robert J. Bennet. Oxford: Clarendon.

Bennet, Robert J., ed. 1990. *Decentralization, Local Governments, and Markets: Towards a Post-Welfare Agenda*. Oxford: Clarendon.

Blondell, Jean. 1982. *The Organization of Governments*. London: Sage.

Breton, Albert, and Ronald Wintrobe. 1982. *The Logic of Bureaucratic Conduct*. Cambridge: Cambridge University Press.

Campbell, Colin, and B. Guy Peters. 1988. *Organizing Governance: Governing Organizations*. Pittsburgh: University of Pittsburgh Press.

Dente, Bruno, and Francesco Kjellberg, eds. 1988. *The Dynamics of Institutional Change: Local Government Reorganization in Western Democracies*. London: Sage.

Dupuy, François. 1985. "The Politico-Administrative System of the Department in France." In *Centre-Periphery Relations in Western Europe*, ed. Yves Mény and Vincent Wright. London: George Allen and Unwin.

Edner, Sheldon. 1976. "Intergovernmental Policy Development: The Importance of Problem Definition." In *Public Policy Making in a Federal System*, ed. Charles O. Jones and Robert D. Thomas. Beverly Hills, Cal.: Sage.

Elander, Ingemar, and Stig Montin. 1990. "Decentralization and Control: Central-Local Government Relations in Sweden." *Policy and Politics* 18 (3):165–180.

Elazar, Daniel J. 1987a. *Exploring Federalism*. Tuscaloosa, Ala.: University of Alabama Press.

_____. 1987b. "Federalism, Intergovernmental Relations, and Changing Models of the Polity." In *Subnational Politics in the 1980s,* ed. Louis A. Picard and Rafael Zariski. New York: Praeger.

Fesler, James W. 1962. "The Political Role of Field Administration." In *Papers in Comparative Public Administration*, ed. Ferrel Heady and Sybil L. Stokes. Ann Arbor: Institute of Public Administration, University of Michigan.

Galligan, Brian, and Cliff Walsh. 1990. "Australian Federalism: Developments and Prospects." *PUBLIUS: The Journal of Federalism* 20:1–18.

Goldsmith, Michael J. 1986. *New Research in Central-Local Relations*. Aldershot: Gower.

Gramlich, Edward. 1987. "Federalism and the Federal Deficit Reduction." *National Tax Journal* 40:299-313.

Groenewegen, Peter. 1990. "Taxation and Decentralization: A Reconsideration of the Costs and Benefits of a Decentralized Tax System." In *Decentralization, Local Governments, and Markets*, ed. Robert J. Bennet. Oxford: Clarendon.

Hanf, Kenneth. 1978. Introduction to *Interorganizational Policy Making: Limits to Coordination and Central Control*, ed. Kenneth Hanf and Fritz W. Scharpf. London: Sage.

_____, and Fritz W. Scharpf, eds. 1978. *Interorganizational Policy Making: Limits to Coordination and Central Control*. London: Sage.

_____, Benny Hjern, and David O. Porter. 1978. "Local Networks of Manpower Training in the Federal Republic of Germany and Sweden." In *Interorganizational Policy-Making: Limits to Coordination and Central Control*, ed. Kenneth Hanf and Fritz W. Scharpf. London: Sage.

_____, and Theo A. J. Toonen. 1985. *Policy Implementation in Federal and Unitary Systems*. Dordrecht: Martinus Nijhoff.

Hesse, Joachim Hans. 1987. "The Federal Republic of Germany: From Cooperative Federalism to Joint Policy-Making." *West European Politics* 10:70–87.

Hjern, Benny, and David O. Porter. 1981. "Implementation Structures: A New Unit of Administrative Analysis." *Organization Studies* 2 (36):211–227.

Inman, Robert. 1989. "Federal Assistance and Local Services in the United States." In *Fiscal Federalism*, ed. Harvey Rosen. Chicago: University of Chicago Press.

Kaufman, Franz-Xavier, Giandomenico Majone, and Vincent Ostrom, eds. 1986. *Guidance, Control and Evaluation in the Public Sector*. Berlin: Walter de Gryter.

Kettl, Donald F. 1987. *The Regulation of American Federalism*. Baltimore: Johns Hopkins.

King, David. 1984. *Fiscal Tiers: The Economics of Multi-Level Government*. London: Allen and Unwin.

Kjellberg, Francesco, and Henry Tuene. 1980. "Introduction." *International Political Science Review* 1 (2):137–142.

Lijphart, Arend. 1984. *Democracies: Patterns of Majoritarian and Consensus Government*. New Haven: Yale University Press.

Mandell, Myrna P. 1979. "Letters to the Editor: Intergovernmental Management." *Public Administration Times* 15:2, 6.

_____. 1990. "Network Management: Strategic Behavior in the Public Sector." In *The Evolution of Strategies and Networks: The Politics of Intergovernmental Relations for the Future*, ed. Robert Gage and Myrna P. Mandell. New York: Praeger.

March, James G., and Johan P. Olsen. 1984. "The New Institutionalization: Organization Factors in Political Life." *American Political Science Review* 78:742–754.

Mazmanian, Daniel A., and Paul A. Sabatier. 1987. *Implementation and Public Policy*. Glenview, Ill.: Scott, Foresman.

Mény, Yves. 1984. "The Politics of Decentralization of the French Socialist Government." *West European Politics* 7:61–73.

_____, and Vincent Wright. 1985. *Centre-Periphery Relations in Western Europe*. London: George Allen and Unwin.

Mirando, Vincent L. 1990. "General Revenue Sharing: Termination and City Response." *State and Local Government Review* 22:98–107.

Monreal, Antoni. 1986. "The New Spanish State Structure." In *Federalism and Federation in Western Europe*, ed. Michael Burgess. London: Croom Helm.

Oates, Wallace E. 1972. *Fiscal Federalism*. New York: Harcourt Brace Jovanovich.

_____. 1990. "Decentralization of the Public Sector." In *Decentralization, Local Governments and Markets*, ed. Robert J. Bennet. Oxford: Clarendon.

Ostrom, Vincent. 1985. "Multi-organizational Arrangements in the Governance of Unitary and Federal Systems." In *Policy Implementation in Federal and Unitary Systems*, ed. Kenneth Hanf and Theo A. J. Toonen. Dordrecht: Martinus Nijhoff.

Page, Edward C., and Michael J. Goldsmith. 1987. *Central and Local Government Relations: A Comparative Analysis of Western European Unitary States*. London: Sage.

Peters, B. Guy. 1988. "The Machinery of Government." In *Organizing Governance: Governing Organizations*, ed. Colin Campbell and B. Guy Peters. Pittsburgh: University of Pittsburgh Press.

Picard, Louis A., and Rafael Zariski. 1987. *Subnational Politics in the 1980s*. New York: Praeger.

Reagan, Michael D. 1987. *Regulation: The Politics of Policy*. Boston: Little, Brown.

Rhodes, R. A. W. 1981. *Control and Power in Central-Local Government Relations*. Aldershot: Gower.

Rhodes, R. A. W. 1985. "Intergovernmental Relations in the United Kingdom." In *Center-Periphery Relations in Western Europe*, ed. Yves Mény and Vincent Wright. London: George Allen and Unwin.

_____, and Vincent Wright, eds. 1987. Introduction to *Tensions in the Territorial Politics of Western Europe*. London: Frank Cass.

Rose, Richard. 1984. *Understanding Big Government*. London: Sage.

_____. 1985. "From Government at the Centre to Nationwide Government." In *Centre-Periphery Relations in Western Europe*, ed. Yves Mény and Vincent Wright. London: George Allen and Unwin.

Rousseau, Mark O., and Raphael L. Zariski. 1987. *Regionalism and Regional Devolution in Comparative Perspective*. New York: Praeger.

Sharpe, Laurence J., ed. 1979. *Decentralist Trends in Western Democracies*. London: Sage.

_____. 1986. "Intergovernmental Policy-Making: The Limits of Subnational Autonomy." In *Guidance, Control and Evaluation in the Public Sector*, ed. Franz-Xaver Kaufman, Giandomencio Majone, and Vincent Ostrom. Berlin: Walter de Gruyter.

_____. 1988. "The Growth and Decentralization of the Modern Democratic State." *European Journal of Political Research* 16 (3):365–380.

Smith, B. C. 1985. *Decentralization: The Territorial Dimension of the State*. London: George Allen & Unwin.

Stenberg, Carl W. 1992. "The Deregulation Decade: Debate, Delusion, Dilemma." Paper presented at Conference on Transitions in Public Administration, June 1992, Örebro University, Grythyttan, Sweden.

Tarrow, Sidney. 1977. *Between Center and Periphery*. New Haven: Yale University Press.

Thoenig, Jean-Claude. 1978. "State Bureaucracies and Local Government in France." In *Interorganizational Policy Making: Limits to Coordination and Central Control*, ed. Kenneth Hanf and Fritz W. Scharpf. London: Sage.

Walker, David B. 1991. "Decentralization: Recent Trends and Prospects from a Comparative Governmental Perspective." *International Review of Administrative Sciences* 57:113–129.

Webb, Adrian, and Gerald Wistow. 1980. "Implementation, Central-Local Relations and the Personal Social Services." In *New Approaches to the Study of Central-Local Government Relationships*, ed. George W. Jones. Westmead, Farnborough: Gower.

Wright, Deil S. 1981. "The Concept of Intergovernmental Relations: Assets and Liabilities." Paper presented at the annual meeting of the American Political Science Association, September 1981, New York, New York.

_____. 1984. "Managing the Intergovernmental Scene: The Changing Dramas of Federalism, Intergovernmental Relations and Intergovernmental Management." In *Handbook of Organization Management*, ed. William B. Eddy. New York: Marcel Dekker.

_____. 1988. *Understanding Intergovernmental Relations*. Belmont, Cal.: Brooks/Cole.

13

Central Issues in Comparative Analysis of Criminal Justice Systems and Criminal Policy: The Need for a Comparative Approach

Wolfgang Deichsel

CRIMINAL POLICY AS CRIMINAL JUSTICE OR SOCIAL POLICY?

Crime policy in the United States and Germany, as well as in other countries, follows a mixture of diffuse, unstructured responses to crime lacking both internal coherence and external evidence of a rigorous design concept. There is no theory of criminal policy, but instead a conceptual and practical patchwork. But there are two different patterns around which such policy is organized: (1) the conservative model, proposing increasing penalties on criminals to reduce crime, and (2) the liberal approach, proposing social programs aimed primarily at reducing crime by reducing poverty and alienation (Donnelly 1989, 457). The debate between conservatives and liberals has become personalized by the confrontation of quite opposite theoretical perspectives associated with two American criminologists and their work.

In 1985 James Q. Wilson published the second edition of *Thinking about Crime*; in 1985 Elliott Currie wrote *Confronting Crime*. These two books provide alternative ways of examining and dealing with the problem of street crime in the United States. Wilson argues for a focus on a policy perspective that is largely independent of traditional social scientific theories of crime. His analysis and recommendations center primarily on the criminal justice system. He examines the effects on crime of various traditional and innovative strategies in policing, sentencing, and correctional programs. Wilson also challenges social scientists to conduct better research on what programs will affect crime rates (see Donnelly 1989, 457).

Wilson's causal analysis model of crime, which underlines his criminal policy perspective, is individualizing causes of crime—locating them in the individual (Wilson 1985, 46). Currie, on the other hand, calls for changes beyond the reform of the criminal justice system, aiming at the broader society by dealing with inequality, unemployment, poverty, and family problems, which for him are the important causes of crime.

Criminal Policy as Criminal Justice Policy from Arrest to Prison

There is no better test for evaluating the state of democracy and freedom in a country than by looking at the state of its criminal justice system. It reflects the specific culture of the country, with national characteristics of a legal culture (Ehrmann 1976) being demonstrated in the criminal justice system. However, criminal justice systems around the world are confronted with similar questions as instruments of dealing with, and—special irony as a consequence of its reverse, and often neglected, side—"causing" delinquency by selecting it out of the field of hidden crime, by naming and prosecuting it. Both the Wilson and Currie perspectives share the following common goals based on the individualistic model targeting criminal behavior: apprehending and visiting harm upon the guilty (punishment); making offenders more virtuous, or at least more law-abiding (rehabilitation); dissuading would-be offenders from criminal pursuits (deterrence); protecting innocent citizens from being victimized by convicted criminals (incapacitation); inviting most convicted criminals to return as productive citizens to the bosom of free community (reintegration).

These multiple ends in a "crime control model," emphasizing the need to repress crime by maximizing the effort to locate, apprehend, and convict offenders, have to be pursued by complying with the "due process model," protecting the individual against the state's unwarranted intrusion, unreliable judgments, and harsh penalties. There is a growing consensus in Western modernized countries about the failure of the criminal justice system to integrate and achieve the crime control and due process goals. "In its most direct contacts with crime—prevention, detection, apprehension, conviction and correction—the system of criminal justice fails miserably" (Clark 1970, 117). Deterrence and incapacitation through criminal justice, as central tenets of an anti-crime policy, have turned out to be false promises and shattered hopes, or have at least not been scientifically confirmed. Research data about deterrence of potential young offenders in Germany show that what Cesare Beccaria called the "promptness of punishment" may have some slight effects on the future behavior of juveniles, but the same can not be said for the severity of sanctions. A classical American study about deterrence is very careful in its conclusions because different sanctions are imposed on different types of persons who may react differentially to the experience of punishment. "We can offer only some tentative suggestions. There is no doubt that the 'actual experience' of punishment is, in some sense, 'much stronger than the theoretical knowledge' and that even apprehension and investigation alone may in some cases have a 'dramatic impact'" (Zimring and Hawkins 1973, 246).

As with the deterrence research, so the research about the rehabilitative effects of social programs substituting for, or supplementing, criminal sanctions have not turned out to show great results. However, no longer does the all-or-nothing attitude of "nothing works," in which the conclusions from the evaluation of rehabilitation programs were much stronger than the data warranted, prevail. A new and better generation of studies in the 1980s demonstrated that some types of criminal rehabilitation programs worked under some conditions (Rotman 1990).

The most recent trends in all modernized societies are the growing market of control industries and the application of the broad range of new technologies in the criminal justice system, especially as regards investigation and identification, decision making, correctional supervision, treatment, information processing, and communications (Roberts 1988). The application of new technologies in penal justice revolutionizes the criminal justice system as a whole, and only the speed of this revolutionary reform is comparatively different in the various modern countries as an international conference (the 38th International Course in Criminology of the International Society of Criminology: New Technologies and Penal Justice, Montreal 1988) has demonstrated.

To varying degrees the systems apply devices to verify the identity of persons seeking access to controlled or classified data or secured areas (GEN-Analysis, DNA-Fingerprints, or other biometric devices), use parole, sentencing, and bail guidelines to bring structure, rationality, and consistency to correctional and judicial decision making, electronically monitor the geographic location of parolees and probationers, or try to gain "prosecutorial power" by storing large amounts of data or by information processing (e.g., through mobile digital terminals installed into police cars). As the police gain ready access to the major technological resources, these turn the position of the police from servant to the master of the criminal justice system, unbalancing the principle of equality of power between prosecution and defense.

But there is another convergence of policing in modern Western countries; this concerns the public demand in the form of individual requests for assistance versus decisions about priorities in police work (Bayley 1985, 30). Police work becomes more proactive and less reactive, operating beyond the phone number "911." New forms of crime and the construction of so-called organized crime as an alleged threat to public order in modern countries have pushed this process of organizational specialization into police units for secret investigation (e.g., by undercover agents) and militaristic forms of intervention. While these secret police strategies (which have European origins) try to avoid public gaze, the actions contrast with the other key goal in modern patterns of policing—seeking transparence and cooperation by police and public. However, police work in developed countries differs in its distribution between crime control and servicing.

With the exception of the United States, the richer and more developed the region, the more likely it is in both rural and urban areas that the police will handle a larger proportion of non-crime situations. Conversely, the poorer a country is, the more likely it is that the police will deal more exclusively with crime-related matters. . . . This is true for Europe in relation to

South Asia and Singapore as well as for South Asia in relation to Singapore. The United States provides the anomalous case. Although there are significant differences in the composition of police work between the United States and each of the other regions, encounters in the United States are proportionately more crime related. (Bayley 1985, 149)

How deeply national legal cultures are rooted and the degree to which they are prevented from cross-cultural learning brings up another key issue in police work: the principle of legality. In Germany, creating an obligation to prosecute and rejecting all attempts to make the system more flexible is one practical example of the role of cultural specificity. The "opportunity principle," giving more discretion in the decision whether a prosecution is launched or not, as practiced in the United States and the Netherlands, would be more practical in dealing with different forms of petty crime, especially concerning drug consumers.

Comparing criminal courts in various industrialized countries shows us that there are also common distinguishable trends like the overload of cases they have to deal with, and in consequence, the often enormous length of time it takes from arrest to adjudication. This is not primarily a managerial task of better handling this overburden, though of course the application of organizational models out of the private business sector in the bureaucratic court administration could contribute to a more effective operation of the justice system. The inordinate delays result from a tendency in penal legislation to use criminal laws as an "anti-poison" against the growing amount of so-called social risks and an increasing influx of criminal cases into the system by more and more litigious populations (even in Japan) while at the same time the courts are understaffed.

Other central issues of the court system are particular to certain legal cultures and traditions, such as the jury of the American criminal justice system, which derived from the English common law tradition ("No man can be convicted or imprisoned except by the lawful judgement of his peers"), stands permanently on trial (as demonstrated by the Rodney King decision in Los Angeles), and can be considered as a key element of the organization of the American justice system (Neubauer 1992). As noted by Alexis de Tocqueville in *Democracy in America*, the character of the jury system is disclosed only with difficulty to foreigners. This is also true for cross-examination, the confrontation of prosecutor and defense, and for plea bargaining as an American way of justice (though movement in other legal cultures toward these tendencies is discernible). Forms of "deals," though foreign to the formal German criminal justice system and to the statutory continental law tradition, have started to prevail in that country. Courts—like the police—do more than just enforce or evolve new norms through the accretion of decisions; they also create new norms through conscious policy-making (Jacob 1984, 35). This is especially the case for the Supreme Court in the United States, which has a substantial impact on the political and legal balance between federal and state courts. The *Bundesverfassungsgericht*, the constitutional court in Germany, appears more and more to be on the road to becoming a "second legislator." A common field of criminal law in which the highest courts of United States and Germany have exercised their legislative power is the question of abortion. The dividing line between law enforcement and policy-making is also not clear in the work of public prosecutors. They have the selective power to direct resources to specific forms of crimes, for example, to prosecute against petty or economic crime.

The crucial questions in the politics of punishment are (1) are prisons necessary at all, and (2) are lifelong imprisonment and capital punishment justifiable? It is highly disputed that prisons are indispensable, especially because according to criminological research, their deterrent effect is estimated to be low, and it is argued that the stability of society rests on internalized values and ideology and not on severe punishment. Three positions are identifiable in the criminal policy debate about imprisonment. Supporters of a radical position ("abolitionists") want to abolish prisons completely. Liberal reformers maintain that probation programs, community service orders, and community-based treatment and corrections programs can replace prisons entirely if they are combined with constructive job-training programs and other forms of social action. A conservative "just desserts position" argues that prisons demonstrate that crime doesn't pay, that those who commit serious crimes have to get what they deserve, and that society can't abandon prisons. While the abolitionist perspective is the permanent stimulus, the real politics of imprisonment is characterized by conjunctures and waves between the conservative and liberal positions. Prison populations initially moved downward in the 1960s and then upward in the 1970s and 1980s in America (Zimring and Hawkins 1991, 220) and Europe (the United Kingdom, the Netherlands, and Germany). "In 1977 the incarceration rate in federal and state prisons in the United States was 208 per 100,000. At the opposite extreme . . . the Dutch rate was about 22 per 100,000. In between these extremes lay most of the rest of the world's industrial societies, many clustered toward the lower end of the scale: Japan—44, Norway—45, Sweden—40, West Germany—60, Denmark—54, France—56, and Great Britain—84" (Beirne and Messerschmidt 1991, 616–617).

Overcrowdedness, with a fourfold increase in U.S. state and federal prisoners between 1925 (ca. 100,000) and 1985 (481,616) (Beirne and Messerschmidt 1991, 619), is a permanent feature of American prisons, and such is the construction debate about new prisons, (Zimring and Hawkins 1991, 205–220) though the levels of imprisonment in the United States vary widely both over time and from state to state. "Both Democratic and Republican parties are dependent upon funding from the very rich, who tend strongly to see their interests served by a repressive criminal justice system. Many politicians have built their careers on condemning 'softness on communism' or 'coddling of criminals'" (Wright 1973, 262). Apart from this dependence on the shifting sands of public opinion, there are various other more sophisticated cause-effect relationships of correctional policy, for example with regard to the degree of tolerance in a country, the punitive attitudes of the criminal justice agents and available space in prisons.

The core of the debate about the scale of imprisonment is the idea of incapacitation, probably the issue of most public concern. The need for incapacitation is always voiced by politicians or the public after atrocious crimes to isolate "the few" dangerous offenders to save "the many" and to deter others from committing such crimes. The concept of incapacitation is based on the rediscovery of the positivistic criminology, especially of Cesare Lombroso, dividing offenders into types according to the frequency with which they commit criminal acts. Crime control means to identify and incapacitate those highly heavily, and repeatedly, involved in crime. The most obvious and cruel forms of incapacitation are the life prison terms in Western European penal justice systems and the death penalty in America. Thirty-seven states have passed legislation allowing the death penalty within the guidelines prescribed by the U.S. Supreme Court. A 1976 Supreme Court decision ended a virtual moratorium on executions for capital offenses in the United States, ruling that "the death penalty does not invariably violate the Cruel and Unusual Punishment Clause of the Eighth Amendment" (van den Haag and Conrad 1983, v). In strong contrast to the ever-increasing use of the death penalty in America stand the rising number of European countries abolishing the death penalty; human rights movements like Amnesty International, which demonstrate how inhumane ("flawed executions") and socially as well as racially discriminating the death penalty really is (Amnesty International, *Todesstrafe in den USA*, February 1987); and findings of criminological research. Thorsten Sellin demonstrates the fallacy of the arguments for the deterrent and retributive value of the death penalty. He argues cogently and passionately for the body of evidence showing that abolitionist states suffer no more capital crime than do the others, and that retribution is neither swift, certain, nor equitable (Sellin 1980).

Looking for the potential reform of the criminal justice machinery from arrest to imprisonment (Jacob 1974) and strengthening the policies and strategies of the criminal justice agencies are attempts to try to cope with the challenges to criminal justice system. "In the past two decades, the four major innovations I examine (bail reform, pretrial diversion, sentence reform, and speedy trial rules), have been tried repeatedly in order to overcome some of the problems alluded to above" (Feeley 1983, 7).

Alternative strategies for coping with crime, such as community programs, reconciliation and compensation, probation, etc., are easy to conceive of for juvenile status offenders; they are tested in depth by substituting imprisonment and they are challenged the most by the attempt to drive back incapacitation strategies. Here it is most obvious how transgressions of the boundaries of different policies, and an integral approach combining various strategies, are indispensable for giving a complex answer to such a complex social phenomenon as crime.

Criminal Policy, Social Policy, Other Policies

The program for criminal policy as social policy is at the same time an attack on the conservative model limiting criminal policy to criminal justice policy. If we are serious about attacking the roots of this American affliction we must build a society that is less unequal, less depriving, less insecure, less disruptive of family and community ties, less corrosive of cooperative values. In short, we must begin to take on the enormous task of creating the conditions of community life in which individuals can live together in compassionate and cooperative ways. (Currie 1985, 226)

A profound diagnosis—the first step to this proposed cure—is offered for American society by the 1990 study of Wesley G. Skogan, "Disorder and Decline," which by describing the unique American situation also depicts actual or future perspectives of developments in other modern industrialized countries. Skogan shows that disorder, always a natural and even necessary part of urban life—a condition and a consequence of the maximized individual freedom that cities have always offered—can undermine the social fabric on which neighborhood stability depends when such a disorder goes too far. Such urban disorder cannot effectively be policed because it is not covered by criminal statute. The explosive events in Los Angeles following the Rodney King court decision bring out not only the chasm between the two separate hostile and unequal "nations" of the black and the white, but also bring the erosion of community life and urban violence into clear focus.

The best criminal policy against disorder and decline of communities is not only social policy but the consideration of crime aspects in policies as diverse as city planning, architecture, media policy (e.g., against marketing crime and stigmatizing reports), economic policy, foreign policy, etc. Dealing with crime is too important and its "governmentality" (a discussion concerning modern states initiated by the French philosopher Michel Foucault in his later works) too much questioned to be diverted by arguments about disciplinary boundaries of policies and politics.

But in all modern industrial societies there is still an ever-growing reliance on criminal law and criminal justice enforcement. For the modern penal law the leading "ultima ratio principle: criminal law as the last resort," turns into the principle: *nullum crimen sine periculo sociali.* Social risks as diverse as environmental destruction, growing right-wing movements, social protests, bio- and computer-technology, AIDS, (child) pornography, insider trading, and so on, have become the target of criminal legislation often having only symbolic and not instrumental functions and scraping only the surface of their structural problem dimensions. Within the context of the existing criminal laws and of conflicting criminal justice priorities, criminal policing and jurisdiction are still overwhelmingly concerned with petty thieves, vandals, and violence by young males. Diversion strategies, diverting young people from the criminal justice system (in the United States: deinstitutionalizing offenders), are still the hallmark of juvenile justice policy in all Western industrial countries. Their decriminalizing effects, however, which free resources for more serious crimes, are endangered in Germany by the widespread drug problem among juveniles, and in America by a conservative shift in criminal policy as well as by the drug situation.

National juvenile justice trends reveal a system growing more formal, restrictive, and punitive. Juvenile correctional facilities are increasingly filled with black and Hispanic youth. These changes are occurring even as the youth population and juvenile arrests are declining. Moreover, the changing nature of our juvenile justice system is occurring amidst an intense ideological debate over the value of previous reform efforts. It is apparent that the liberal reform thrust of the early 1970s has been replaced by a more conservative agenda. This watershed period provides a unique opportunity for policymakers, practitioners, and child advocates to examine and benefit from lessons learned from the earlier reform era. (Krisberg et al. 1986, 28)

The significance of a multidisciplinary (criminal) policy approach can be easily and convincingly demonstrated in the fields of crime prevention and drug policy. The preeminent role of the communities in the development of crime corresponds with their significance in the prevention of crime (see Reiss and Tonry 1986). The European and North-American Conference on Urban Security and the Prevention of Crime, held in Montreal (1989) and Paris (1991), brought the mayors of municipalities of different continents together to discuss measures of situational and social prevention. To confront the disorder and decline of communities, Wesley Skogan suggests pursuing multiple strategies at the same time. These could be community policing, community organizing tactics aimed at stimulating residents' participation in local problem-solving, changing the political economy of the community by substantial political and economical "designing out" (environmental designs) disorder by changing those physical features that are related to crime (e.g., the design of buildings, the use of streets and parks, lighting, landscaping, and other land use factors) and by specific regulations (e.g., concerning littering, vandalism, "zoning out" threatening activities), and changing from the criminalization of drug use and institutionalization of the mentally ill to more care- and treatment-oriented approaches (Skogan 1990, 159–186).

The idea of community policing and of the National Crime Prevention Council, founded in 1980 with many suborganizations and strong support for Neighborhood Watch Programs, was exported from the United States to European countries such as the Netherlands, the United Kingdom, France, and Germany. Crime prevention commissions of the Ministries of Interior and Justice in the Netherlands, the Crime Prevention Unit and the Crime Prevention Center of the Home Office in England, the *Conseil National de Prévention de la Délinquance* since 1983 in France, the first *Rat für Kriminalitätsverhütung* in Germany/ Schleswig-Holstein, and the already existing (since 1974) National Council for Crime Prevention in Sweden pursue different strategies and combinations of the many elements in the community policing package.

Community policing in this substantial sense is very much alive around the world and appears to be growing rapidly. Examining experiences on four continents, we have found four programmatic elements occurring again and again under the banner of community policing: (1) community based crime prevention, (2) reorientation of patrol activities to emphasize nonemergency servicing, (3) increased accountability to the public, and (4) decentralization of command, including, under certain circumstances, civilization. (Skolnick and Bayley 1988, 5)

As, and insofar as, state preventive measures do not guarantee sufficient protection, private individuals and business firms have turned to forms of private policing (Shearing and Stenning 1987) and invested heavily in self-protection and have otherwise changed their behavior to decrease the likelihood of their own victimization. Citizens, not relying entirely upon state protection, take additional measures (as is documented by the exploding security industry market in all industrialized countries [see the "Hallcrest Report": Cunningham 1988]), ranging from simple door locks to sophisticated security systems, from such practices as leaving houselights and radios operating in the inhabitant's absence to installation of window bars and security screens.

Drug policy is presently the most challenging topic for criminal policy (see National Drug Control Strategy 1989; *Nationaler Rauschgiftbekämpfungsplan* 1990) with consequences for other criminal justice issues such as the widespread concern with organized crime, undercover strategies, and criminal legislation. By the end of 1980 most of the European Economic Community (EEC) states had passed legislation providing for the forfeiture of drug trafficking assets and have passed or are considering legislation to criminalize money laundering. The American drug policy model has been behind these legislative endeavors (Beke-Bramkamp 1992). The drug policy demonstrates in a special manner the necessity of criminal policy as an interdisciplinary policy approach. Drug policy is part of public health policy; social policy (also in the sense of enabling unconventional forms of life); educational, economic, and foreign policy; etc. The drug legalization debate (Inciardi 1991), fought with engagement and at a highly argumentative level (as demonstrated by the discussion at the congress of the American Society of Criminology, October 1990, between Ethan A. Nadelmann and James B. Jacobs) in the United States as well as in all European countries, has to be understood as an attempt to free the drug problem from the severe grip of criminal justice policy. The secondary effects created by the criminalization of drug users (increased health problems for drug users, crime to get money for drugs, corruption, criminal justice costs) are mostly more harmful than those of the drug use itself. The proposal is to shift the drug problem to the competence of different policy arenas (e.g., maintenance programs, normalization of drug use, "accepting social work" concerning drugs, controlled distribution of hard drugs to junkies). Therefore, there is a recognizable disarmament in the "war on drugs," fought in all Western industrialized countries, having been continually "declared" in the United States by Presidents Nixon (1971) and Reagan (1982). The opposition to the war on drugs as the "tyranny of the status quo" (Friedman and Friedman 1985), ranging between normalization and legalization, transcends the split between the conservatives, having advocated strict law enforcement, and liberals, having been identified with a permissive approach to the drug issue. Losing the war on drugs has led to breaking the impasse in the war on drugs (Wisotsky 1990), though the National Drug Control Strategy

(The White House 1989) and the German *Nationaler Rauschgiftbekämpfungsplan* (Der Bundesminister 1990) are still relying mostly on the conventional strategies of the criminal justice system.

THE FRAME OF ANALYSIS OF CRIMINAL JUSTICE AND CRIMINAL POLICY

Criminal justice and criminal policy in a specific country are highly dependent on various contextual conditions that can only be sketched here but should not be left unmentioned, especially since their recognition saves us from drawing false conclusions in a comparative public administration and policy approach.

Tolerance or intervention—permissiveness or social control? Everybody who goes to Hyde Park Corner in London can convince themselves of the proverbial tolerance of the English people toward any kind of "spleen" and deviant behavior. So can a visitor to any part of the Netherlands experience the meaning of "leven en leven laten" (live and let live). "Both Britain and the Netherlands lay claim to a culture of tolerance, notably in the expression of opinions and ideology. In relation to deviant behavior, however, the Dutch have fashioned a culture of tolerance that seeks to accommodate it, wherever possible, to a greater extent than in Britain" (Downes 1988, 204). Policy-making in the criminal justice field is responding to tolerant or repressive attitudes in public opinion that differ very much culturally as cross-cultural studies show.

Newman constructed a "deviance control scale" based on answers to questions about how seriously illegal each act was and how punitive a reaction seemed appropriate to the respondent. The samples from Iran, Yugoslavia, and Indonesia tilted toward stricter "deviance control," while the Indians and the Americans tilted toward leniency. Italy was at about the average over all samples. (Wilson and Herrnstein 1985, 449)

Less-educated and rural people favored strict control when compared with more-educated and urban respondents. In her study, Brown (1952) demonstrated that every known society has a range of approved or at least tolerated sexual practices and another range of practices subject to taboos. From these different punitive perspectives and taboo zones within and across countries, states are judged with respect to their crime control policy as being either too lenient or too repressive with subsequent leaning toward an intervening or a "hands-off" policy.

How (Not) to Lie with Crime Statistics

Crime statistics in Western urban, industrialized countries are annually released provoking the same old question addressed to the politicians—how will they react to increasing crime rates, which are taken as being a correct reflection of reality.

Crime statistics have a central pivotal position in criminal justice and criminal policy: they are at the same time a mirror of law enforcement interventions, reflecting the extent of the activities of the criminal justice agents, as well as their basis and legitimation, determining the allocation of federal, state, and local funds and influencing criminal law legislation. While they are on one side an important tool of measurement of crime for criminal policy purposes (as is actually demonstrated by their absence and their necessity for penal law considerations within the emerging market economies of the former socialist countries), they are on the other hand a constructed phenomenon with a large potential for errors, needing to be contrasted with other sources of information about crime. Victimization surveys, for example by anonymous questionnaires, are regarded as offering more reliable indicators of crime than the national police statistics, as is the case in the United States with the Uniform Crime Reports (UCR).

One of the greatest obstacles to comparative criminology is the lack of reliable cross-national data. Most existing data ignore national differences in the legal definitions of crime as well as the variety of ways in which crimes are reported by the public and accepted and recorded by the police. These problems plague the data of Interpol, the World Health Organization, the World Crime Survey, and Amnesty International. Accordingly, much of these data are inadequate for rigorous comparisons. Scholars acknowledge that the best available data are provided by the United Nations, and by Archer and Gartner (1984) in their Comparative Crime Data File. (Beirne and Messerschmidt 1991, 585)

Criminal Justice and Criminal Policy Evaluation

Evaluation of the criminal justice and criminal policy field and behind the surface of raw statistical material is a reaction to the question: "what works?" "What works" conferences for workers within the criminal justice system and those conducting research projects (Martinson 1974) circle around this challenge to any existing conventional or experimental criminal policy strategies. Evaluation and funding of projects trying to prevent or to deal with crime are closely linked. This is especially true in the United States where the most sophisticated research strategies for the process and outcome evaluation of criminal justice programs have been elaborated (Klein and Teilmann 1980). Evaluation studies—for example, of the Youth Authority in Sacramento, evaluating the Community Treatment Program (CTP) in California in the 1960s and 1970s—demonstrate that the "what works" question is more complicated than it may seem at first sight. Some educational programs may work for some types of offenders in certain specific life situations, and yet may be neutral or even harmful for others not matching these criteria for intervention, so that multiple (non)intervention strategies could and should be pursued. Evaluation of criminal justice and policy programs, though a difficult business, is mandatory for more effectively confronting the challenge of crime in a certain country, for (re)integration of the offender into society, for cost containment, for disclosing the paradoxical effect of assessing the state's contribution to crime (by laws and intervention strategies) itself, and for showing the limits of criminal (justice) policy and the necessity of a structural-ecological (social) policy turn.

Such evaluation studies, on which a vast body of literature already exists about the diverse approaches to criminal (justice) policy mentioned above—for example, criminal justice legislation, correctional systems, deterrence effects, community policing (Rosenbaum 1986), drug policy, neighborhood watch programs (Bennett 1990), and new forms of social control as electronic monitoring (see the diverse comparative evaluation studies in Klein and Teilmann 1980)—are of special value for comparative research and the exchange of ideas, models, and programs between countries. This is even more true if the evaluation study reflects the local, state, and national frame, distinguishing it from structural dimensions that are, and could be, also true for decision makers in other public policy and administration contexts. Thus the degree of transferability and dissemination of evaluation research data into the international exchange network is enhanced.

Benefit-Cost Analyses

The rational choice model in criminology sees criminals as calculators of the possible costs and benefits they may expect from criminal acts they consider committing. "Does crime pay?" is the question they pose to themselves. The state, however, has to ask whether nonintervention or intervention "pays" and, if so, what kind of intervention? Does incapacitating the recalcitrant offender really help to reduce crime rates? And what are the possible side effects and unintended consequences of such a policy for a due and human justice model? The final context for policy formulation is that of limits, and that is to a large extent a question of resources. Resources are limited in the criminal (justice) policy field, since there are many other pressing problems on the agenda and the public is not always willing to allocate funds to fight crime.

Crime in the United States today imposes a very heavy economic burden upon both the community as a whole and individual members of it. Risks and responses cannot be judged with maximum effectiveness until the full extent of economical loss has been ascertained. Researchers, policy-makers, and operating agencies should know which crimes cause the greatest economic loss, which the least, on whom the costs of crime fall; and what the costs are to prevent or protect against it; whether a particular or general crime situation warrants further expenditures for control or prevention and, if so, what expenditures are likely to have the greatest impact. (President's Commission in Law Enforcement and Administration of Justice, Task Force 1967)

Total U.S. criminal justice system expenditures at local, state, and federal levels for police protection, judicial, prosecution, legal services, indigent defense, corrections, victim compensation, and related services have nearly doubled between 1971 ($10.5 billion) and 1976 (more than $19.5 billion) (see U.S. Department of

Justice 1978). This trend of increasing economic costs of crime and of the criminal justice system has led—more commonly in the United States than in Europe—to benefit-cost analyses of specific criminal policy measures. Opportunity costs are not only seen as an utilization of resources that could be used for other fields of politics but also for other and more effective fashions within crime and social policy itself. By releasing juveniles from the prison system—such was the request in the Hamburg debate about diversion in the juvenile justice system—money saved on the cost of expensive prison cells could be used for social work and educational programs. It costs more to keep a young man behind bars for a year than to send him to Princeton University for the same time period.

The increasing "costs of crime" (Gray 1979) have also led to the introduction of an American experience into the debate in Britain: the privatization of the penal system by having private firms run prisons or deliver prison services under the assumption that they have a greater productive efficiency, saving tax money from being spent for "loss-making state industries" (Ryan and Ward 1989). The promise of privatization in the criminal justice system has not been verified yet, at least not in England, and may serve as an example of transatlantic misunderstanding or of the dangers of transferring criminal justice models from one cultural context to another.

But one final word of caution—a warning we might say, against the dangers of American criminological imperialism. The more this study progressed the more we were struck by the differences between the penal systems we were considering and between the contexts in which they operated: how, for example, the balance between the public and the private sector varied and how within each of these sectors penal arrangements were constrained by different political and legal frameworks, not to mention the cultural legacy of history which has a powerful impact on the way policy makers respond to demands for change. For all these reasons, both the threat posed by the profit making private sector and the potential of the voluntary or non-profit sector as a site for radical intervention, are likely to vary from country to country. (Ryan and Ward 1989, 114)

Economic costs of crime and of criminal justice systems are not to be divorced from external costs, such as political costs, by delegating substantial parts of the "res publica" to private enterprise; social costs, reducing the aggregate well being or welfare in a society; and moral costs, shattering the confidence of the population in its sense of justice, its confidence in the norm, and its value system.

The Institutional Context of Criminal (Justice) Policy

Each country has a different distribution of tasks in the field of criminal (justice) policy among local, state, and federal governments, which creates problems not only for national coordination of a loose administrative confederation of an array of agencies, operating under specific political, legal, and budgetary constraints, but also in international cooperation. In modern countries there are two opposite identifiable trends: decentralization to the communities, for example by community policing, and centralization of functions by the federal government, supported by new dimensions of (organized) crime with special accents in Europe and the United States (Fijnaut 1990) and by the need for the internationalization of crime control. In the United States federal influence in crime policy is exerted by government and police agencies, by national institutes and councils, by presidential or national commissions (like the President's Commission on Organized Crime 1986), and anti-crime programs. The Federal Bureau of Investigation (FBI) as well as the *Bundeskriminalamt* in Germany, and other similar national police forces are the best technologically equipped crime-fighting institutions, sometimes competing with secret services, which after the end of the Cold War are searching for reorientation. The Law Enforcement Assistance Administration (LEAA) was proposed by the President's Commission on Law Enforcement and the Administration of Justice in 1967, launched by President Johnson as the strongest instrument in the first "war on crime and poverty" (1967–1980), giving federal support to state and local law enforcement agencies—up to 8 billion dollars in total by 1980. It was finally phased out in 1982 by the Reagan administration. The Drug Enforcement Administration (DEA) is combatting drug trafficking together with a dozen of other federal agencies such as the FBI, the Customs Service, and the U.S. Coast Guard, coordinating state and local forces on the field of drug policy and playing an important role in trying to establish an international bulwark against crime. The National Institute on Drug Abuse (NIDA) and the National Crime Prevention Council are permanent federal organizations specializing in important segments of criminal policy.

Probably the most influential commission in the field of criminal policy, with 200 recommendations, has been the President's Commission on Law Enforcement and the Administration of Justice, also known as the Katzenbach Commission (after its chair, Attorney General Katzenbach). It issued its final report, "The Challenge of Crime in a Free Society," in 1967, flanked by nine detailed task force documents on topics ranging from juvenile delinquency to organized crime. The Kerner Commission was an immediate response to the race riots of the mid-sixties, while the Violence Commission was a clear reaction to the assassination of Robert Kennedy. The latter also served as a model for the French government commission's *Réponses à la Violence* and for the German *Gewaltkommission*, established in 1987. The "National Drug Control Strategy," issued by the White House in 1989, has shaped the German *Nationaler Rauschgiftbekämpfungsplan* of 1990 as the national platform for drug policy. Similar national commissions and crime control programs in the United States, Germany, and other countries show how comparable crime situations have led to comparative research and crime policy strategies. Finally the federal influence is also strong in legislation and jurisdiction. "Since the creation of the U.S. Children's Bureau in 1912, the federal government has attempted to play an increasingly active role in juvenile justice policy" (Krisberg et al. 1986, 29). The controversial debate about abortion has been brought before the Supreme Court in the United States, as well as before the *Bundesverfassungsgericht* in Germany. But as the European Convention on Human Rights has gained in status and authority since the 1950s, the ruling of the European Court and the European Commission have assumed greater influence over the criminal justice policies of the member-states.

However, despite the growing federal presence in the United States as well as in European countries, criminal policy, such as juvenile justice policy, is still made at the state and local levels. The bulk of the growth of criminal justice expenditures—also as result of federal legislation the state and the local communities have to implement—has to be financed by the dwindling budgets of the communities. This is well characterized by the realities of Reagan's "New Federalism."

Each country also has different ways of coordinating criminal policy of so many different actors besides the criminal justice systems, dependent of course upon the size of the particular country. A strong contrast to the complex network of criminal policy actors in the United States is the English "Home Office," with a strong concentration of government, coordination, programming, and research tasks. Linking policy and criminological research has been achieved in national crime commissions, but is often still lacking in the exertion of criminal justice and policy functions on local, state, and federal levels. The Home Office in England and the *Kriminologische Zentralstelle* in Wiesbaden, Germany, with significant research staff fill part of this gap of enabling research data to become practical and useful. On the international level, remarkable progress in this field has been made by the European Community (e.g., the European Committee on Crime Problems) and the United Nations in compliance with Article 55 ("promotion of international welfare") of the United Nations Charter, though it is still very much in a state of infancy.

INTERNATIONALIZATION OF CRIME AND CRIME CONTROL

The "Pizza Connection," "Chinese Connection," "Balkan Route," and other groups are symbolic of a worldwide joint-venture in crime and are taken as alarm signals for new dimensions in crime. Therefore, not the local policemen as "street corner politicians" nor even the national police alone are supposed to have the power to confront this situation appropriately; international interagency actions and transgovernmental relations are demanded. This is not a new phenomenon, for the statutes of the intergovernmental organization Interpol date from 1956; 146 countries were members in 1988. Its predecessor organization, the International Crime Police Commission (ICPC) was established in Vienna in 1923. However, the growing internationalization and specialization of crime, and the political events following the breakdown of the East European communist countries, the impoverishment of many developing countries, the opening up of national borders, the introduction of the single market by the European Community in 1992, and the virtual abolition of internal frontier controls between France, the Benelux states, and Germany, have required a new horizon.

International forms of crime, such as drug-trafficking and other criminal economic activities, terrorism, transfrontier right-wing movements, and even soccer hooliganism, cannot be controlled within state boundaries. As a result, the doctrine of sovereignty is questioned in its last bastion of police and criminal justice. There is a noticeable convergence of methods of policing in the highly industrialized democracies.

Police co-operation has a variety of forms—the exchange of intelligence about crimes and criminals, joint or coordinated surveillance of suspects, investigation of crimes, as well as provision of training facilities and exchange of information about police techniques. These activities take place on a multilateral and bilateral basis and at the global, regional, and local levels. (Anderson 1989, 1)

A significant example of bilateral police cooperation has been the assistance of officials of the American Drug Enforcement Administration (DEA), with its representatives in some sixty foreign cities around the world, to their French colleagues in the fight against the "French Connection," which has become a model for other agreements involving DEA presence in other countries (Anderson 1989, 153). Multilateral approaches to international policy-making in the field of social control are regional cooperative networks within the Interpol (e.g., South American Interpol, African Regional Conference of Interpol) or are being set up outside of Interpol as regional organizations or intergovernmental coordination such as ASEAN (Association of South East Asian Nations) or TREVI (terrorism, radicalism, extremism, and international violence). TREVI was founded at a European ministerial meeting in 1975, establishing a secure communication system for sensitive information about terrorism between the governments of the member-states. Perhaps the greatest challenge confronting European police was the elimination of border controls in 1992, in effect extending the Nordic and Benelux arrangements to all members of the European Community. In anticipation of 1992, the governments of France, Germany, and the Benelux states agreed in a treaty signed in Schengen, Luxembourg, on June 14, 1985 (Schengen I) (postponed, however, in 1989 and renewed in 1990 [Schengen II]), to move toward the elimination of border controls for both persons and goods along their mutual borders by 1990; included in the treaty were extended possibilities of better immobilizing transnational criminals by identifying, tracing, seizing, and forfeiting their assets.

On an even more global level—taking a further step from transnational organizations to international organizations—since 1946, the United Nations has evolved a criminal policy mainly through the Committee on Crime Prevention and Control, international congresses every five years, the United Nations Crime Prevention and Criminal Justice Branch in Vienna, and four U.N. institutes for training, information, documentation, and research (Lopez-Rey 1985). The United Nations Development Program (UNDP) and the United Nations Crime Prevention and Criminal Justice Branch have sponsored and coordinated drug enforcement and related training programs among their other activities. While at first the U.N. crime policy was aiming at prevention of crime and the treatment of offenders centered around social defense, the support of economic and technical developments in crime-ridden countries in cooperation with the Economic and Social Council (ECOSOC) became more and more predominant on its priority agenda. Criminal policy as development policy starts from a systematic view, considering the increasingly complex and multidimensional interdependence of states and societies, the international division of labor in committing crimes (for example, among segments of the illegal drug trade: financiers, growers, producers, transporters, distributors, consumers, money launderers, etc.). As long as a nation's economy rests to a large extent upon the production and export of drugs, like that of Bolivia on the plantation of coca plants, only alternative models of national economic and international support for the attempts of realizing this economic transformation will have an effect on the criminal policy goal of limiting cocaine consumption. The United Nations is also weak in the criminal policy field insofar as it lacks executive powers. The United States has partially filled this vacuum. As global prohibitions against drugs and the enforcement thereof has changed over the past two decades, the nature and scope of American involvement have also changed, not only in the evolution of norms in international society but also in international law enforcement activities.

The United States government has responded to the internationalization of crime and law enforcement in a variety of ways. It has enacted new laws and amended old ones to expand United States jurisdiction over transnational criminal activity and to reduce some of the obstacles to effective cooperation in international law enforcement matters. It has dramatically increased the financial and human resources devoted to this area both at home and abroad. It has negotiated a multitude of extradition, mutual legal assistance, and other international law enforcement treaties and agreements. It has sponsored multilateral conventions and prodded international organizations to expand their efforts against transnational crime. It has raised the profile of international law enforcement concerns in its diplomatic relations and public rhetoric. And it has not shied away from using coercive methods to induce greater cooperation from foreign governments, particularly those hesitant to relax their secrecy laws. Certainly the most distinctive feature of United States involvement in international law enforcement has been its strikingly high level of activity and initiative (Nadelmann 1990, 74–75).

Globalizing policing across national borders is inseparable from social control technologies, which have a strong impact on the internationalization of social control and are themselves shaped by this process. Technological developments in transportation, telecommunications, and information processing have dramatically enhanced the capacity of both transnational criminals and law enforcers to pursue their efforts across national borders. Yet to be discovered are the repercussions of such global international strategies of social control—becoming a branch of foreign policy—on the national criminal justice jurisdictions. Different legal traditions and cultures with substantial disparities in criminal justice jurisdictions led to conflicts between different criminal justice norms and frictions of the criminal justice agents applying them. Harmonization of criminal justice systems, both as a global homogenization of criminal laws and a mutual accommodation of criminal procedures, is the most probable consequence of the internationalization of law enforcement as a response to the proliferation of transnational criminal activities. And it is not improbable that harmonization means Americanization of foreign criminal justice systems, which change or have changed in response to American requests, pressures, and successful criminal policy models.

CONCLUSIONS FOR A STRUCTURAL APPROACH TO COMPARATIVE CRIMINAL (JUSTICE) POLICY ANALYSIS

The search for scientific insights into deviance and crime and for creative and effective means of dealing with it requires comparative analyses as well as reformers willing to examine what other states are doing. While criminology is committed to science, criminal justice is committed to law, and criminal policy has to cope with the tension between science and law, for example by alleviating the pressures on the criminal justice system through scientifically based crime prevention. The purposes of criminologists committed to such comparative and multidisciplinary syntheses should be the refinement of theoretical understanding instead of having their goals dictated—as is often the case—by practical correctional objectives. Independent basic criminological research institutions are needed.

The example of modern Western countries with low crime rates, such as Japan, Ireland, and Switzerland, which have always occupied the minds of criminologists working comparatively, can teach us a lesson only when deep theoretical groundwork is done. Refined criminological work discovered that the Switzerland is no longer "as white as snow" (Balvig 1988). Clinard (1978) had found this out in his study about crime in Switzerland 10 years earlier and derived the "Swiss model" policy recommendations for the United States, such as restricting city size to a maximum of 250,000–500,000, greater political decentralization and citizen responsibility for obedience to laws and crime control, integration of youth and adults into common pursuits and activities, greater use of noncustodial sanctions, and rigid control of guns and other lethal weapons (Clinard 1978, 155–158). Wealth and misery, money laundering through Swiss banks, and the needle exchange programs in "Needle Park" at Platzspitz-Zurich are not only close and connected but also the expression of a hidden reality of crime. "Balvig suggests that because Clinard was not a Swiss (or even a European) criminologist, he was therefore not privy to information that the reticent Swiss prefer to keep to themselves" (Beirne and Messerschmidt 1991, 607). Crime policy and its transference into other countries have therefore to be based on criminological research, combining ethnographic studies (integrating the "insider view") with more global trend analyses of the development of crime in different countries to distinguish the genuine particularistic characteristics of a certain country from cross-cultural traits and to demonstrate how general trends are refracted by the features of a certain culture. For example, the trend in modern industrial countries toward property crime with a simultaneous reduction of violent crime is not true in the United States for various reasons.

There is no evidence that the first war on crime (1967–1980), which was committed to liberal anti-crime programs, nor the second war on crime (1980–1992), which was based on penal sanctions, had convincingly succeeded in dealing with or reducing crime in America. The complex nature of crime can only be confronted by an equally complex multidisciplinary approach.

Even if successful, all these suggested structural transformations and support programs would not eliminate crime and violence, which are to a certain degree inextinguishable and even necessary for the cohesion of society, but only reduce or stabilize it to a supportable level. Specific interests and the degree of tolerance in the population and among the politicians in a certain country decide what deviant acts are criminalized and which are not (e.g., by transference to civil law regulation), and if criminalized, how the sanctions against those who committed these crimes are realized or avoided.

Evaluation of criminal policy has, in compliance with the change of paradigm in criminological theory away from the narrow view on the individual criminal to the sociostructural aspects of crime, consequently shifted to the evaluation of the success of crime programs and criminal policy instead of measuring the effects of (non)intervention on criminal behavior patterns. Policy evaluation like that of the Drug Policy Foundation, which had been initiated by law professor Arnold Trebach in Washington to evaluate from an external view the successes and failures of public anti-drug campaigns, seems to indicate a promising trend of evaluation research. Evaluating crime prevention measures is also a very important task in criminal policy evaluation. Successful crime prevention would do away with high costs of crime, overcrowded criminal courts, police brutality, civil rights violations, a victimized public, and a criminal population suffering at the hands of a revengeful public. The evaluation of benefit-cost relations is an outstanding instrument for shaping the definition of crime and the subsequent criminal policy, which can be demonstrated in the drug policy in all modern industrialized countries. In the United States the expenditures of the communities, the states, and the federal government in the war on crime have, in the estimation of Milton Friedman (*Der Spiegel* 1992), risen from one billion dollars at the beginning of the 1980s to an amount now 20 or 30 times larger; in addition, 40 to 50 percent of all prisoners are addicted to drugs.

The institutional network of criminal policy in modern industrialized countries follows two opposite orientations: on the one hand, a trend toward decentralization (e.g., federations of municipalities and mayors around the world committed to preventive programs or "community policing"), and on the other a trend toward centralization at the level of the federal government, which is to a high degree because of the organizing and internationalization of crime and crime control.

There are three main models of international criminal policy: police cooperation within and without Interpol, regional transnational organizations and intergovernmental coordination, and international criminal policy by the United Nations and—compensating for its lack of executive power—by the United States. It is in Western and Central Europe that the bilateral and multilateral dimensions of transnational policing (toward Europol) and law enforcement have proceeded the furthest.

REFERENCES

Amnesty International. 1987. *Todesstrafe in den USA, Ein Kurzbericht von Amnesty International.* Bonn: Amnesty International.

Anderson, M. 1989. *Policing the World.* Oxford: Clarendon Press.

Archer, D., and R. Gartner. 1984. *Violence and Crime in Cross-National Perspective.* New Haven and London: Yale University Press.

Balvig, R. 1988. *The Snow-White Image: The Hidden Reality of Crime in Switzerland.* Oslo: Norwegian University Press.

Bayley, D. H. 1985. *Patterns of Policing: A Comparative International Analysis.* New Brunswick, N.J.: Rutgers University Press.

Beirne, P., and J. Messerschmidt. 1991. *Criminology.* San Diego: Harcourt Brace Jovanovich Publishers.

Beke-Bramkamp, R. 1992. *Die Drogenpolitik der USA, 1969–1990.* Baden-Baden: Nomos.

Bennett, T. 1990. *Evaluating Neighborhood Watch.* Aldershot: Gower.

Brown, J. S. 1952. "A Comparative Study of Deviations from Sexual Mores." *American Sociological Review* 17:135–146.

Der Bundesminister für Jugend, Familie, Frauen und Gesundheit (BJFFG) and Der Bundesminister des Inneren (BI), eds. 1990. *Nationaler Rausch-giftbekämpfungsplan.* Bonn: BJFFG and BI.

Clark, R. 1970. *Crime in America. Observations on its Nature, Causes, Prevention and Control.* New York: Simon and Schuster.

Clinard, M. B. 1978. *Cities with Little Crime: The Case of Switzerland.* Cambridge: Cambridge University Press.

_____, and D. J. Abbott. 1983. *Crime in Developing Countries: A Comparative Perspective.* New York: S. John Wiley.

Cunningham, W. C. 1988. "An Overview of the Hallcrest Report: A Study of Private Security and Police Resources and Relationships in the United States." In *New Technologies and Penal Justice,* ed. Centre International de Criminologie Comparée. Montreal: University of Montreal.

Currie, E. 1985. *Confronting Crime: An American Challenge.* New York: Pantheon Books.

Donnelly, P. 1989. "Book Review Essay—Alternative Perspectives on Crime and Crime Prevention: The Wilson-Currie Debate." *Justice Quarterly* 6:457–455.

Downes, D. 1988. *Contrasts in Tolerance: Post-War Penal Policy in the Netherlands and England and Wales.* Oxford: Clarendon Press.

Ehrmann, H. 1976. *Comparative Legal Cultures.* New York: Prentice-Hall.

Feeley, M. M. 1983. *Court Reform on Trial: Why Simple Solutions Fail.* New York: Basic Books.

Fijnaut, C. 1990. "Organized Crime: A Comparison Between the United States of America and Western Europe." *British Journal of Criminology* 30:321–340.

Friedman, M. 1992. *Der Spiegel.* 34:123.

_____ , and R. Friedman. 1985. *Die Tyrannei des Status Quo.* Munich: Verlag Langen-Müller.

Gray, C. M. 1979. *The Costs of Crime.* Beverly Hills, Cal., and London: Sage.

Inciardi, J. A., ed. 1991. *The Drug Legalization Debate.* Newbury Park, Cal.: Sage.

Jacob, H. 1984. *Justice in America. Courts, Lawyers and the Judicial Process,* 4th ed. Boston and Toronto: Little, Brown and Company.

_____ , ed., 1974. *The Potential for Reform of Criminal Justice.* Beverly Hills, Cal., and London: Sage.

Klein, M. W., and K. S. Teilmann, eds. 1980. *Handbook of Criminal Justice Evaluation.* Beverly Hills, Cal., and London: Sage.

Krisberg, B., I. M. Schwartz, P. Litsky, and J. Austin. 1986. "The Watershed of Juvenile Justice Reform." *Crime and Delinquency* 32:5–37.

Lopez-Rey, M. 1985. *A Guide to United Nations Criminal Policy.* Aldershot and Brookfield: Gower Publishing Company.

Martinson, R. 1974. "What Works: Questions and Answers about Prison Reform." *Public Interest* Spring:22–54.

Nadelmann, E. A. 1990. "The Role of the United States in the International Enforcement of Criminal Law." *Harvard International Law Journal* 31:37–76.

Neubauer, D. W. 1992. *America's Courts and the Criminal Justice System.* Pacific Grove, Cal.: Brooks/Cole Publishing Company.

President's Commission on Law Enforcement and Administration of Justice. 1967. *The Challenge of Crime in a Free Society.* Washington, D.C.: Government Printing Office.

_____ . 1967. *Task Force Report.* Washington D.C.: Government Printing Office.

Reiss, A. J., Jr., and M. Tonry, eds. 1986. *Communities and Crime.* Chicago and London: University of Chicago Press.

Roberts, D. J. 1988. "New Technologies in Criminal Justice: An Overview." In *New Technologies and Penal Justice,* ed. Centre International de Criminologie Comparée. Montreal: University of Montreal.

Rosenbaum, D. P., ed., 1986. *Community Crime Prevention: Does It Work?* Beverly Hills, Cal.: Sage.

Rotman, E. 1990. *Beyond Punishment: A New View on the Rehabilitation of Criminal Offenders.* Westport, Conn.: Greenwood Press.

Ryan, M., and T. Ward. 1989. *Privatization and the Penal System: The American Experience and the Debate in Britain.* Milton Keynes: Open University Press.

Sellin, T. 1980. *The Penalty of Death.* Beverly Hills, Cal., and London: Sage.

Shearing, C. D., and P. C. Stenning, eds. 1987. *Private Policing.* Newbury Park, Cal.: Sage.

Skogan, W. G. 1990. *Disorder and Decline: Crime and the Spiral of Decay in American Neighborhoods.* New York: The Free Press.

Skolnick, J., and D. H. Bayley, eds. 1986. *The New Blue Line: Police Innovation In Six American Cities.* New York and London: The Free Press.

Tocqueville, Alexis de. 1840. *De la Democratie en Amerique.* Paris: Charles Gosselin.

van den Haag, E., and J. P. Conrad. 1983. *The Death Penalty: A Debate Pro-Con.* New York and London: Plenum Press.

The White House, ed., 1989. *National Drug Control Strategy*. Washington, D.C.: The White House.

Wilson, J. Q. 1985. *Thinking about Crime*. New York: Vintage Books.

_____ , and R. J. Herrnstein. 1985. *Crime and Human Nature*. New York: Simon and Schuster.

Wisotsky, S. 1990. *Beyond the War on Drugs: Overcoming a Failed Public Policy*. Buffalo and New York: Prometheus Books.

Wright, E. O. 1973. *The Politics of Punishment. A Critical Analysis of Prisons in America*. New York: Harper and Row.

Zimring, F. E., and G. J. Hawkins. 1973. *Deterrence: The Legal Threat in Crime Control*. Chicago and London: University of Chicago Press.

_____ . 1991. *The Scale of Imprisonment*. Chicago and London: University of Chicago Press.

14

Human Resources Management

Lois R. Wise

INTRODUCTION

The current global transition in public management is closely connected with changes in human resource management structures (Peters, forthcoming). Civil service systems in general, and civil service pay systems in particular, have been the targets of reformists. A global movement toward more flexible market-oriented practices in public sector compensation policy is apparent throughout Anglo-American systems as it is in the European Community (EC). The personnel process has become more decentralized, and new instruments of pay administration have been introduced. Decentralization increases the significance of personnel management rules as determinants of the amount of flexibility managers have in assigning and utilizing human resources. Efforts toward more decentralized and discretionary management systems are in sharp contrast with rigid and highly structured personnel management rules and wage-setting practices that exist in many national civil service systems. Existing organizational rules and policies may undermine management reforms and send conflicting signals to employees about what behavior or which attributes are valued in public organizations.

In counterpoint to national decentralization activities, a pattern of integration is evident on the European continent. As part of the drive toward a European community, as well as a condition of global competitiveness in an increasingly interdependent community of nations, a transition toward greater harmony in personnel policies is evident in Europe. European integration has the potential for making a profound impact on the structure of labor markets in Europe and the policies affecting human resource management (Sedel 1989). EC directives regarding working hours and other human resource management policies may alter the composition and character of European public service systems. Similarly, the growth of the international civil service in Brussels and the opportunities it provides national public servants in temporary assignments has an impact on the demand for public servants. Changes in employment policies within nations are inevitable as governments attempt to compete for qualified staff within the new labor market boundaries.

Within this environment preferential and restrictive hiring practices come under increasing scrutiny (Krislov 1989). Restrictive practices may disqualify candidates from certain groups (raising an issue of democratic representativeness) or candidates with certain types of training (raising an issue of professional bias). Sakamoto (1991), for example, describes how the Japanese civil service favors people with legal training and graduates of Tokyo University. The U.S. national civil service prohibits hiring of noncitizens (excluding excepted positions), but other national systems are less restrictive. Canada, for example, hires noncitizens into all job categories, although it gives first preference to Canadian citizens. Similarly, another Anglo-American system, Australia, hires noncitizens into temporary positions with the condition that they apply for citizenship. A recent report by the U.S. Merit System Protection Board (USMSPB) (1992) has recommended the United States consider revising its policy. Canadian managers believe a less restrictive system gives them greater flexibility in staffing hard-to-fill positions and finding people who will serve in less desirable locations (USMSPB 1992, 16).

A related transition under way in the United States is the growing popularity of the philosophy of managing for diversity. This approach offers a clear challenge to the legalistic environment of human resource management that has characterized the American scene (Newland 1976; Sayre 1948), but discussion of the impact of a culturally diverse workforce is not limited to the United States (Boyle 1991; Orr 1989). The philosophy of managing for diversity goes beyond the protection of individual rights and the goal of neutral treatment in that it seeks to recognize and capitalize on individual variations in abilities and orientations. Managing for diversity emphasizes the efficiency and profitability of an operation using the flexibility and discretion available to management rather than focusing on protecting the rights of particular employees and preventing the opportunity for or appearance of discrimination. A continent's rich cultural diversity offers an advantage for future development. Managing for diversity has relevance for nations or regions composed of people from different social groups.

This chapter discusses the current trends in how people are managed in public organizations. It identifies four major personnel systems found in different public sector organizations that can exist simultaneously within a nation's public service. The discussion then examines three key functions of classification, staffing, and compensation within the context of the transitions of decentralization and flexibility in public management. The chapter concludes with a discussion of the implications of these changes for the public service.

PERSONNEL SYSTEMS

Numerous attempts have been made to develop a typology of personnel systems in government. Distinctions can be clearly drawn among four different categories. *Merit systems,* which rely on competitive tests and formal entry requirements, represent one type of system that usually emphasizes career development, job security, and fair treatment. Although prominent in the West, efforts toward establishing merit systems have not been fully successful in other regions, such as Latin America (Ruffing-Hilliard 1991). A second category involves *career systems*, which are based on individual skills and potential. Rank or status is attached to the employee rather than the position as is typical of merit systems. *Political appointee* systems represent a third category of public employees who hold position without job security but based on the ability of a political party to maintain control of the executive office. Such systems often devalue employee development and training activities since they assume employment in government is short term. About ten percent of all federal Senior Executive Service employees in the United States hold noncareer and mainly political appointments, but many governments restrict executive positions to members of the competitive career service. Although both Germany and Sweden provide for two categories of political appointees, the principle in most West European nations is to separate politics and administration and to assume that top civil servants are neutral agents. As Leemans (1987) forcefully argues, the integrity of this assumption has been steadily undermined by a growing politicization of top-level posts throughout Western Europe. The same concerns have been raised for Australia and New Zealand (Mascarenhas 1990).

Finally, *collective bargaining* systems are found in many public organizations and can involve both blue- and white-collar employees. In the U.S. case, collective bargaining systems are particularly significant at the state and local levels of government. For federal employees, collective bargaining over working conditions and wages is limited to postal and blue collar workers. In these systems, through their trade union representatives, employees have the right to negotiate wages, benefits, and working conditions collectively. In Canada, almost all nonmanagerial national public employees are covered by a bargaining unit. In the Scandinavian countries, even managers are trade union members.

Administrative policies and practices that determine the way human resources are used within an organization are often distinct in public sector organizations. A traditional assumption is that policies should be uniform throughout a political jurisdiction, but this notion is clearly challenged in the current environment of management reform. Stewart and Walsh (1992), for example, interpret government reforms in the United Kingdom as an attempt to change the culture of the public service and the assumption of standardization in staffing is one notion being undermined.

Oversight commissions and boards to monitor adherence to stated policies and regulations are typical of government. The responsibility for federal personnel policy in the United States, for example, resides in the Office of Personnel Management (OPM). It is an independent agency reporting to the president. The Office of Management and Budget (OMB) has substantial executive branch authority over personnel policy and practice in that it controls the flow of funds for salary and determines staffing levels. The integrity of the merit system is monitored by the Merit System Protection Board and the Office of Special Counsel, an independent agency. As an agent of the legislative branch, the General Accounting Office (GAO) pursues special studies of personnel practices and policies.

The structure for personnel policy differs sharply in other countries. In Canada, for example, two separate organizations, the cabinet-level Treasury Board (TB) and the Public Service Commission (PSC), have central authority for public personnel policy. The Secretary of the Treasury Board promulgates personnel policies and procedures and represents the government in negotiation. The Public Service Commission has the responsibility for staffing and monitoring the merit system (USMSPB 1992).

COMPONENTS OF THE PERSONNEL SYSTEM

Organizational rules and regulations establish the conditions and terms of employment within an organization, as well as the opportunity structure for groups of workers. Three key functions of human resource management reviewed here are job evaluation, staffing, and compensation systems.

Job Evaluation Systems and Classification

The hierarchy of jobs within an organization is determined by the job evaluation system. It plays a significant role in defining the boundaries among work areas. To the extent that job evaluation standards are used to establish the criteria for hiring, placing, evaluating, and rewarding employees, they form the underpinnings of personnel management. Efforts to achieve uniformity across a jurisdiction in job titles, rankings, and standards are common in many countries, including the United States. Position classification systems in the United States typically organize jobs into four or five broad categories and establish a set of ranking factors for each category of work that are standardized throughout a political jurisdiction or government. In systems patterned after the French civil service, work in each ministry is organized into cadres that establish their own rules for recruitment and promotion that are sensitive to the needs of the ministry and the conditions of the relevant profession.

Position-based classification systems, which establish job worth without regard to the skills and knowledge of the incumbent employee, are typical of merit systems in the United States. These systems gained popularity at the beginning of the twentieth century as part of the scientific management movement which promoted efficiency in task performance over other aspects of work. Within government organizations, position-based job classification plans have been a popular method of job evaluation because they are seen as impartial and therefore less likely to provide opportunities for nepotism or political patronage.

In recent years, however, career service or rank-in-person systems have gained popularity not only because they are less rigid and therefore easier to work with, but also because they put more emphasis on the potential and real contributions of individual workers. In the United States, a rank-in-person system for top-level civil servants and political appointees was established in 1978 at the federal level, and many states followed suit by setting up senior executive services for top state employees. Rank-in-person systems for senior executives can be found in other national governments including Canada, Australia, and New Zealand. One of the most comprehensive shifts toward a career service occurred in 1990 when Sweden eliminated position classification grades for all white-collar national civil servants.

Staffing

Placement and mobility within an organization are determined by rules affecting recruitment and career advancement, as well as by an organization's policies for and investments in staff training and development. Opportunities for promotion and job training can be seen as part of an organization's culture and the extent to which it is willing to invest in its current workforce. Thus merit systems or career service systems with a norm of lifetime employment are more likely to invest in existing human resources.

Recruitment. Recruitment is a powerful instrument for organizational change and renewal, but public organizations often underutilize this tool by relying on passive, ineffective, or elitist recruitment practices. The rules concerning recruitment may in themselves serve as barriers to organizational entry when they require extensive testing and processing delays. In the U.S. case, civil service managers have limited flexibility in the selection process. The "rule of three," for example, which limits the hiring choice to the top three candidates, is in sharp contrast with the Canadian system which gives managers substantial authority in both setting job qualifications and assessing how well a particular candidate meets them.

Some organizations take a very traditional approach to recruitment focusing on an organization's staffing requirements and attempting to find and recruit employees with the needed skills. An alternative, more individualized approach to recruitment is to attempt to match organizational staffing requirements and reward structures with the abilities and human needs of particular individuals. This approach, which puts more emphasis on adapting hiring practices to an individual job applicant, attempts to maximize both job performance and job satisfaction. In the context of managing for diversity, such accommodations might respond to the special needs to working parents or other care givers, dual career marriage partners, handicapped workers, and others who could be attracted by an organization's special efforts to accommodate their needs. In addition to monetary incentives, flexible workplace or working conditions, day care, and other noncost incentives have been offered by government organizations.

Mobility. Mobility rules determine opportunities for career advancement in an organization. Opportunities for mobility within and between departments are important vehicles for improving the career horizons of employees and developing the capacity of incumbent employees. Rules define who is eligible for mobility opportunities and the criteria by which candidates will be assessed. Upward mobility programs within public agencies attempt to offset the extent to which personnel rules limit career advancement among those who have been socially or economically disadvantaged. The choice between educational and experiential criteria for placement, for example, has an impact on socially advantaged and disadvantaged groups differently as does the use of achievement and aptitude tests for hiring and promotion. Similarly, bridge jobs between career ladders provide alternative routes for mobility that extend employee career horizons. Some organizations are experimenting with different career tracks to allow workers to accommodate their personal and family obligations with their working life.

The tendency to require educational degrees and credentials limits access to professional positions and the upper rungs of career ladders. Where educational degrees are a formal requirement, the benefits of public employment fall to those who have the social advantage of advanced education. Variations exist among national civil service systems, however, in the extent to which they require high school or university undergraduate degrees for entry and advancement. West Germany has traditionally imposed relatively high educational requirements on its national civil servants, and historical data suggest that the trend has been toward higher credentials (Schmidt and Rose 1985, 148). Educational attainment is used not only as a criterion for job placement but also for eligibility for training opportunities. By law, across-the-board application of educational standards is prohibited in the United States. Selection tests must be job relevant and practical and, when degree standards are used, employers must be able to prove that they are valid job-related requirements.

The Japanese civil service selects employees on the basis of competitive exams, history of work performance, or on the evaluation of work skills. The examination process employs a general test as well as specialized tests and personality tests for work (Kim 1988). Many African countries link educational requirements to specific positions. Those patterned after the British system tend to measure degree attainment, while those modeled after the French system focus on years of schooling (Robinson 1990, 43–57).

Public sector organizations may have a strong influence on opportunities for upward mobility within a society and for the level of democracy and representativeness in a system (Bodiguel 1990; Wise 1990). Government employment has traditionally been a haven for those discriminated against by the competitive sector. Women and minority group members tend to occupy lower-ranking posts within an organization because formal and informal barriers to advancement restrict their movement within a civil service system. Col (1991), for example, reports that women in Thailand who represent more than 50 percent of the civil service are restricted from certain upper-management positions, and informal barriers in both hiring and advancement have restricted women's progress in the U.S. Civil Service (U.N. 1990). Rigid requirements or the absence of clearly defined careers paths for upward mobility in an organization thwart social mobility for these groups. Women's tendency to choose part-time positions is generally an impediment to their career progress, although many governments allow part-time employees to hold management positions. A study of women in the top ranks of the Swedish bureaucracy found that two percent of all national, six percent of county, and ten percent of local leadership posts were part-time positions (Wise 1991).

Cross-national research on opportunities for advancement within national civil service systems shows some variation among nations in opportunities for mobility. DiPrete's (1989, 9) summary of these studies indicates that earlier research showed little opportunity for advancement from one tier to another in Spain, Italy, or Denmark. French and British workers, however, had more opportunity for transfers between job ladders. The chances for Americans to move within the organization appeared higher, and lateral entry opportunities in the U.S. civil service also favored American public employees. Movement within a group of classes or job ladders is a characteristic of African civil service systems. Unlike the U.S. system, which restricts movement within a job category, for example clerical or technical work, African public servants working as technicians might be able to advance into the scientific class, especially if they have acquired additional education (Robinson 1990, 56–57).

Security. Job security is often considered a characteristic of public sector jobs, but substantial changes are under way. Government cutbacks in many countries over the last decade have been associated with reductions-in-force at all levels of government. In these cases, of interest are the criteria for establishing tenure rights and the tradeoff between individual employee's seniority and their perceived value in terms of performance rating scores or some other indicator of productivity. The reform movement of the late 1980s and early 1990s has been characterized by an increase in the number of noncareer public employees and greater reliance on temporary and contractual workers with no tenure rights. Patronage-based personnel systems do not promise lifetime employment and may encourage turnover among employees. Staff cutbacks in U.S. civil service systems are typically determined by a formal reduction-in-force policy (RIF). Unlike employees in countries where trade unions are strong, U.S. workers receive 60 days notice of pending discharge. In contrast, the Canadian Public Service, for example, provides a six-month placement period before implementing a staff reduction.

Compensation Systems

The perceived adequacy of compensation shapes the relationship between employees and management and affects government's ability to recruit and retain qualified workers. At the same time, the size of the public payroll and its rate of growth affect the competitiveness of a national economy.

Pay policy in the public-sector can be organized around three different dimensions: *market posture, social orientation,* and *organizational reward systems* of public organizations (Wise 1988). These three dimensions vary in importance over time in response to shifts in value structures or economic conditions. Market posture embraces both external and internal organizational purposes of pay policy. It involves the comparability of government's wage levels with the prevailing market rate. The principle of pay comparability between the public and private sectors has long been a standard for pay setting (Kessler 1983), but many countries, including the United States, have failed to achieve this standard in fact. Government studies estimate that on average federal civil service pay in the United States lags the market by about 25 percent (GAO 1990).

Both political and economic factors determine the market posture governments actually pursue. Political factors may drive pay levels down or may impose artificial ceilings on the earnings of public servants. Concerns about the rate of inflation or the size of the national debt may persuade governments to use their position as an employer to control the growth of wages. The common belief that public bureaucracies are inefficient because market principles do not operate in government fuels the claim that market parity is an inappropriate standard for determining public pay levels. Wise (1993) discusses this argument in the context of the Swedish case. Similarly, many contend that government offers compensating differentials, such as greater job security and better fringe benefits, offsetting differences between the sectors in pay levels. A recent Canadian study, however, concludes that a decline in job security as a result of government cutbacks has made public employees less willing to accept below-market wages (Treasury Board of Canada 1991, 70).

A second dimension of pay policy, social orientation, involves policies a government has regarding equality in the distribution of wealth and opportunity. Government jobs can be seen as a public good in this context and government payrolls a vehicle for redistribution of wealth (Rose 1985). Social values are expressed by the distance between the highest and lowest salaries allowed in a pay schedule. During the 1960s and 1970s many countries attempted to reduce the size of wage gaps between members of different social groups. Sweden's efforts to reduce the size of wage differentials and promote a policy of economic equality can be seen as an extreme example (Wise and Jonzon 1991; Wise 1993). Since the mid-1980s, however, the general global trend has been in the opposite direction as salary differentials have increased. This is largely because of the growing importance of the third dimension, individual reward structures, in pay setting. The construct of social orientation also includes the pay equity policy of equal pay for work of comparable value, also known as comparable worth. Although the U.S. federal sector has not adopted the philosophy of comparable worth, several U.S. state governments have, as have some national governments, including Canada. In other countries, including Sweden, study commissions are currently examining the issue of implementing a comparable worth policy.

The reward system pertains to the individual attributes and behaviors valued by public employers and contributes to the quality and efficiency of organizational productivity. Factors serving as determinants of entry-level pay advancement to higher-level jobs or opportunities for lateral pay increases represent qualities organizations value. Pay administration rules specify the factors that enable an individual to receive more money and advance in status. A trend toward more discretion in setting entry-level pay rates, and greater emphasis on individual performance as a basis for distributing organizational rewards, has begun to influence pay administration practices around the globe. Van der Hoek's (forthcoming) study of the Dutch civil service suggests that individual rewards have the effect of increasing wage differentials between advantaged and disadvantaged groups, and Zetterberg's (1992) study of wage differentials in Sweden's public sector comes to a similar conclusion, but the size of the differentials in the Swedish case are quite small.

Performance-Contingent Pay. Performance-contingent pay is one of several instruments that has been introduced or is under consideration to make pay rates more individualized in national, state, and local civil service systems. In addition to performance-contingent rewards, civil service systems have implemented market supplements, skill supplements, training premiums, and similar bonuses for workers in occupations with a high rate of attrition or who are highly valued in government. These new instruments of pay administration have the common effect of shifting public sector pay policies toward managerial discretion. The transition represents a shift toward a market model of public management likely to put greater emphasis on an upper-level civil servant's managerial role and less emphasis on his or her role in policy development (Peters, forthcoming). Pay-for-performance schemes can be seen as an attempt to increase intersectoral parity for those whose skills, training, or levels of productivity are highly valued in the labor market.

The Canadians are generally credited with having the oldest formal pay-for-performance merit award system for managers in the public service. A system first established in 1964 now gives deputy ministers full discretion in giving outstanding managers a maximum 10 percent increase in base pay or as a one-time bonus (Treasury Board of Canada 1991). The OECD (1991) studied the performance pay practices of industrialized countries based on different pay scheme characteristics. Countries appear to vary in the amount of payroll funds allocated for individual rewards and the maximum percent of salary an employee may receive, but, overall, very small amounts of payroll costs are set aside for special performance awards. In the United States, between 1.5 and 3.0 percent of payroll is allocated for performance. This undermines any potential positive motivational impact. As a percent of salary, American public managers may receive up to 20 percent as a one-time bonus or 10 percent as a salary increase. The average annual awards for mid-level managers, however, range around $1,000 (Wise, forthcoming).

A conclusion that can be drawn from the OECD study is that the majority of countries do not rely on performance factors for determining public managers' pay rates, and few countries require a formal linkage between pay and performance. Pay for performance may be more rhetoric than fact. A study of mid-level managers in the United States found that performance ratings were not reliable in accounting for differences in the size of individual bonuses and awards (Wise, forthcoming).

This transition in the status of the dimensions for setting public sector pay away from an emphasis on broad market parity and social equity toward individual rewards affects the way the incentive structure operates in both recruiting and retaining government employees. It implies that, in fact, different people will be attracted to public service than were recruited when other rewards were emphasized, for example, the opportunity for public service, the opportunity to participate in policy-making, and the desire to promote a social good.

CONCLUSIONS

Two distinct trends under way in public management are toward decentralization and greater flexibility on the one hand and greater demands for efficiency and accountability on the other. These broad trends have cultivated an environment in which greater integration of cultural groups and nationalities is emphasized in both North America and the European continent. The trend toward managing for diversity could not survive in the legalistic and structured public management environment of the past.

At the same time, shifts in the key components of personnel operations are also apparent in response to the new public management. Job evaluation systems can be assessed using the criteria or standards they employ for ranking employees and the way those standards have an impact on different groups of people. Staffing rules can be assessed by the way they provide opportunities for entrance and mobility in government organizations. Similarly, compensation policies represent a clear tension between efficiency and social values. The way performance and merit awards are administered to individuals may alter the apparent integrity of internal alignment among positions, particularly if bonuses are incorporated into base pay. Where individual awards are given as supplements over pay, the basic alignment among positions based on equal pay for equal work is less jeopardized. Although the introduction of pay-for-performance systems in the public sector may improve the competitiveness of the average pay offered workers relative to the rates paid by the private sector, it may impede efforts toward social equality in earnings and status in other ways and may alter the role of civil servants in policy-making.

People are an organization's most valuable resource. The development of policies that promote flexibility and efficiency without sacrificing fair treatment are the challenge of the 1990s. Public management organizations need to develop strategies to take advantage of a continent's rich human diversity. Although the question of whether these managerial reforms will take hold in the public sector as real as opposed to rhetorical or symbolic changes remains to be answered, they have already had an impact on the value structures of public personnel management creating an opportunity for change and revitalization.

REFERENCES

Bodiguel, J.-L. 1990 "Political and Administrative Traditions and the French Senior Civil Service." *International Journal of Public Administration* 13:707–740.

Boyle, R. 1991. "Civil Service Management Trends: Challenges for the 1990s." *Administration* 39:234–247.

Col, J. M. 1991. "Women in Bureaucracies: Equity Advancement, and Public Policy Strategies." In *Handbook of Comparative Development Public Administration*, ed. A. Farazmand. New York: Marcel Dekker.

DiPrete, T. 1989. *The Bureaucratic Labor Market: The Case of the Federal Civil Service*. New York: Plenum Books.

Hebe, A. 1991. "Trends in High Civil Services of Anglo-American Systems." *Governance* 4:489–510.

Kessler, S. 1983. "Comparability." In *Pay Policies for the Future*, ed. D. Robinson and K. Mayhew. New York: Oxford University Press.

Kim, P. S. 1988. *Japan's Civil Service System*. New York: Greenwood Press.

Krislov, S. 1989. "Evaluating Merit in Disbursing Social Positions: The New Affirmative Action." In *Equity in Public Employment Across Nations*, ed. K. Tummala. New York: University Press of America.

Leemans, A. F. 1987. "Recent Trends in the Career Service in European Countries." *International Review of Administrative Sciences* 53:63–88.

Mascarenhas, R. C. 1990. "Reform of the Public Service in Australia and New Zealand." *Governance* 3:75–95.

Newland, C. A. 1976. "Public Personnel Administration: Legalistic Reforms vs Effectiveness, Efficiency, and Economy." *Public Administration Review* 36:529–537.

Organization for Economic Co-Operation and Development (OECD). 1991. "First Report of the Panel on Performance-Related Pay Schemes for Public Sector Managers." Paris: OECD.

Orr, E. 1989. "Shaping Public Service Vision." *The Bureaucrat* Summer:17–23.

Peters, B. G. Forthcoming. "The Public Service, the Changing State, and Governance." In *Beyond the Bureaucratic Paradigm*, ed. P. Ingraham and B. Romzek. San Francisco: Jossey-Bass.

Robinson, D. 1990. *Civil Service Pay in Africa*. Geneva: International Labour Office.

Rose, R. 1985. "The Significance of Public Employment." In *Public Employment in Western Nations*, ed. R. Rose. Cambridge: Cambridge University Press.

Ruffing-Hilliard, K. "Merit Reform in Latin America: A Comparative Perspective." In *Handbook of Comparative Development Public Administration*, ed. A. Farazmand. New York: Marcel Dekker.

Sakamoto, M. 1991. "Public Administration in Japan." In *Handbook of Comparative Development Public Administration*, ed. A. Farazmand. New York: Marcel Dekker.

Sayre, W. 1948. "The Triumph of Techniques over Purpose." *Public Administration Review* 8:134–137.

Schmidt, K.-D., and R. Rose. 1985. "Germany: The Expansion of an Active State." In *Public Employment in Western Nations*, ed. R. Rose. Cambridge: Cambridge University Press.

Sedel, R. 1989. "Europe 1992: HR Implications of the European Unification." *Personnel* 66:19–24.

Stewart, J., and K. Walsh. 1992. "Change in the Management of Public Services." *Public Administration Quarterly* 70:499–518.

Treasury Board of Canada. 1991. "Performance Related Pay Schemes in the Public Service of Canada." Ottawa: Treasury Board of Canada.

United Nations General Assembly (U.N.). 1990. "Forward Looking Strategies for the Advancement of Women to the Year 2000," A/45/548. New York: United Nations General Assembly.

United States General Accounting Office (GAO). 1990. "The Public Service: Issues Affecting its Quality, Effectiveness, Integrity, and Leadership." Washington, D.C.: U.S. GAO.

U.S. Merit System Protection Board (USMSPB). 1992. "To Meet the Nation's Needs: Staffing the U.S. Civil Service and the Canadian Public Service." Washington, D.C.: USMSPB.

Van der Hoek, M. P. Forthcoming. "The Use of Labor Market Supplements by Central Government in the Netherlands." *Public Administration Quarterly*.

Wise, L. R. 1988. "Dimensions of Public Sector Pay Policy in the U.S. and Sweden." *Review of Public Personnel Administration* 8:61–83.

_____. 1990. "Social Equity in Civil Service Systems." *Public Administration Review* 50:567–575.

_____. 1991. "Women in the Swedish Government Bureaucracy." *Viewpoint Sweden* 8, New York: Swedish Information Service.

_____. 1993. "Whither Solidarity? Transitions in Swedish Public-Sector Pay Policy." *British Journal of Industrial Relations* 31:75–95.

_____. Forthcoming. "Factors Affecting the Size of Performance Awards for Mid-Level Managers in the United States." *Public Administration Quarterly*.

_____, and B. Jonzon. 1991. "The Swedish Civil Service: An Instrument for Achieving Social Equality." In *Handbook of Comparative Development Public Administration*, ed. A. Farazmand. New York: Marcel Dekker.

Zetterberg, J. 1992. "Effects of Changes Wage Setting Conditions on Male-Female Wage Differentials in the Swedish Public Sector." Working Paper no. 8, Department of Economics, Uppsala, Sweden: Uppsala University.

15

Environmental Policy and Management in the European Community and the United States: A Comparison

Mariëtte C. S. Glim

INTRODUCTION

The member-states of the European Community (EC) increasingly realize that on any subjects it is useful to cooperate. On the other hand, now that further steps have been initiated to "unite" Europe, the residents of the member-states seem to be more conscious than ever of their national identity. This is—in a nutshell—the core issue in the organization of the European (Economic) Community, or the European Union as it's now called. Part of national sovereignty has been relinquished to the EC, but the remaining power of the individual member-states should not be underestimated. It is precisely this complex linking of Community and national structures and processes that makes EC decision making interesting to discuss and compare.

More and more attention is given to a comparison of the EC with the United States. Some social scientists perceive great resemblances between the EC and the United States. Others conclude that "a comparison between the EC decision-making process and federal decision making in the United States is only of limited relevance" (van den Bos 1991, 18).

In this chapter a comparison is attempted with respect to the management of environmental affairs in the EC and the United States. In the next section a theoretical framework is presented that might guide the exploratory comparison. In the subsequent sections the three elements of this framework will be elaborated and applied to explore environmental management in the EC, using the United States as a comparative reference. In the final section an answer to the "comparativeness" of both experiences is attempted.

Theoretical Framework

A framework for comparative analysis is not readily available; it is needed to give structure and to provide an analysis that is more than just an accumulation of a variety of specific country-facts. A country- or Community-centric approach will not contribute to an understanding of why governmental organizations and policies function as they do (Peters 1988, 3).

In the classical doctrine of public administration, a distinction has been made between politics (making policy) and administration (the implementation of policy). This classical dichotomy was introduced by Woodrow Wilson and has influenced the classical thinking both in Europe and the United States. The central idea is that the implementation phase is a process of command and control based on rational views formulated in a policy-program. Implementation is analyzed by studying the discrepancies between an ideal-type of rationality and reality.

The "modern" approach to policy-analysis is more active; policy adapts constantly to changing circumstances. Implementation is seen as an evolutionary, and not a mechanical and passive, process initiated by a central policy. The implementing actors are both actually (by power and influence) and normative (by legitimacy) interdependent. On the one hand this can be seen as a problem of discretionary power. On the other, it is inevitable and desirable for processes with a diversity of actors, each with their own means, interests, opinion, and values. In this approach it is not the policy program that is the central theme, but, instead, the participants and their interactions (Toonen 1990, 338–339). In this perspective implementation is a collective enterprise that is difficult to manage. Interactions among the participants are games in which deliberation, conviction, and negotiation are important factors determining the success of the implementation (Bardach 1977). Effective implementation requires a creative dealing with this game of forces. The relationship between the central and local governments can be analyzed in terms of dependency and power relationships. Implementation is not the simple transmission of policy to a series of actions, but it is a process of negotiation while exchanging resources between the ones who want the policy to be implemented and the ones who are necessary for implementation (Rhodes 1979; Barret and Fudge 1981).

Still, the action approach is too general to explain the whole implementation process (Majone 1978). The theory is too focused on the operational side of the implementation process, neglecting institutional varieties in governmental organizations. The most important thing is not to find the "right" solution to solve a problem, but to judge as well as possible the main issue and the consequences that are accompanied by a choice of different institutional arrangements (Toonen 1990, 338–339). Jessop refers to the "state as idea" instead of the "idea of the state" that should guide policy studies (Jessop 1990, 48).

The state or *the* government does not exist. Speaking of the power of the state, one should speak of the variety of potential powers and possibilities of the state as an institutional ensemble. Neither simply the state nor the government is acting, but instead specific gatherings of politicians, administrators, and civil servants are activated in the network of the constitution of the state (Toonen 1990, 15).

An Exploratory Institutional Comparison

Following the concept of the "institutional ensemble," it is necessary to understand how the different parts of the network do relate. Analyzing the relationships among the activated governmental actors Kiser, Ostrom, and Wright identify "three worlds of action" (Kiser and Ostrom 1982, 197–222; Wright 1990, 168–178). Toonen used this idea to design a framework for institutional comparison (Toonen 1990, 39). The framework can be used to compare the governmental networks and the way they operate with respect to environmental policy in the United States and the EC. The governmental networks can be compared on three different levels:

1. The intergovernmental constitution (IGC), the constitutional, political, social-cultural, and economical conditions, rules, norms, and values, which are the context of the intergovernmental processes;
2. The intergovernmental relations (IGR), the system of legal, financial, political, and organizational relationships and the connections among the different governmental actors that can be identified;
3. The intergovernmental management (IGM) or administration, the whole of problem-solving activities, procedures, techniques, and administrative varieties that are used within the limitation of the constitutional and governmental framework by actors working on the edge of the different governmental organizations.

In the next sections these "three worlds of action" will be discussed, but just in an exploratory way. A comparison between the European Community (EC) and the United States is a comprehensive study. Only a "corner of the veil" can be lifted with an emphasis on IGC and IGR. The world of comparative IGM is still largely unexplored.

THE INTERGOVERNMENTAL CONSTITUTION OF THE EC AND THE UNITED STATES

In this section the "intergovernmental constitution" (IGC) of the EC and the United States will be compared. The comparison is limited though. The economic structure—for example, the political and cultural background, which is not of direct influence on the organizational structure—is very important for an international comparative understanding, but will not be considered in this analysis.

The European Community and Its Formal Structure

The Constitution of the EC is not recorded in a coherent document. The

Constitution is arranged by a collection of prescriptions and fundamental values that are binding. These norms are formulated in the treaties or in the EC decisions, but also find expression in regular habits.

There are three main treaties, but the Treaty of Rome is the most important constitutional document of the EC. In 1957 it was signed by Belgium, the Federal Republic of Germany (FRG), France, Italy, Luxembourg, and the Netherlands. Later, Denmark, Ireland, United Kingdom (1973), Greece (1981), Portugal, and Spain (1986) joined the EC. The essential part of the Treaty of Rome (the tasks and competences of the EC) is formulated in articles two and three. The means and the ways to reach the goals and objectives of the EC are written down in the remaining 245 articles. The EC environmental policy is partly based on article two. This article appoints the EC to improve the living and working circumstances of the citizens of the EC. Also, the countries of the EC together must pursue a harmonized development of the economical activities and an ongoing steady expansion. The Single European Act (SEA) of 1987 emphasizes that this is not possible without environmental management: "environmental protection requirements shall be a component of the EC's other policies" (articles 130R-S).

The Commission has since prepared five Environmental Action Programs (EAP) (1973, 1977, 1982, 1987, 1993) on which environmental policy could be based. In the fifth EAP, sustainable development is the central theme. The Commission feels that in the past years the making of rules and standards have been emphasized too much. In the new Action Program more attention will be paid to financial (fiscal and levying) measures to stimulate the actual implementation (application and enforcement) of EC legislation. This implies a change of direction, because, until now, attention has been restricted to the behavior of national member-states and the transposition of EC directives into national legislation.

The EC has a variety of governing bodies. The executing institution of the EC is the European Commission. The members of the Commission come from, but do not represent, the 12 member-states and have a term of office of four years (but can be reappointed by the joint national governments). The president and vice president are appointed for two years. The Commission is the guardian of the treaties, initiates new policy, and represents the interests of the EC in the Council of Ministers. The decisions of the Commission are taken by majority votes. The Commission is supported by a number of administrative units "Directorates-General" and "Services." DG XI is responsible for Environment, Consumer Protection, and Nuclear Safety. DG XI has about 140 civil servants. The overall EC-administration consists of approximately 12,000 civil servants.

The European Parliament (EP) has 518 members divided into nine political parties, who deliberate in nine different languages. In meetings the members are grouped according to their political color instead of their nationality. The EP has a controlling and advising function. With the exception of the EC budget, the EP has no real co-decision-making authority. The EP has 18 commissions that prepare the plenary meetings. One of them is the Commission on Environmental Management, Health, and Consumer Protection.

The Council of Ministers is the only institution in which the national governments are directly represented. Formally, only the ministers of foreign affairs are involved. Actually, it is a gathering of specialized councils, and according to the subject on the agenda the responsible ministers meet. The Council decides on propositions of the Commission.

The European Council or "Eurotop," which consists of the 12 heads of national governments, meets twice a year in the member-state that has the chair of the Council of Ministers. In this Council, the main political problems are discussed.

The Court of Justice has one judge from each member-state and a thirteenth from a main member-state (rotating). The Court makes decisions about cases of compliance with EC decisions, with the treaties, and about cases of a possible noncompliance of a decision of a member-state with EC regulation. Each member-state, organization, and person directly involved can apply to the Court. The decision of the Court (taken by majority vote) is binding; the member-states have to take care of the implementation of the decision.

The United States

The American political framework has a written constitutional document that confers and limits governmental powers and is characterized as federal in nature (Heady 1988, 396). The term federal has no clear, coherent, and concise meaning. James Madison, writing in Federalist Paper number 39, acknowledged that "the Constitution is, in strictness, neither a national nor a federal Constitution, but a composition of both." It was this revised, more nationalist framework that has subsequently, in the U.S. context, been called federalism. It includes the full range of institutional arrangements that disperse or fragment power within the U.S. political system. A further facet of this fragmented power framework is that it provided two types of incentives: (1) the stimulus to translate difficult political issues into legal cases for court determination; and (2) the tendency to give the U.S. Supreme Court the role of arbiter/umpire of national-state relationships. The Constitution then allocates powers to both the national (federal) and state governments. The national government possesses only delegated powers, with those powers not granted to the national government being reserved to the states by the Tenth Amendment. The Supreme Court functions as a last resort actor to resolve many of the most knotty problems of national-state conflicts (Wright 1990, 151–154). The responsibility for environmental policy and management in the United States is divided among three levels of government: federal, state, and local government. On the federal level, authority is divided among the two Houses of Congress and their respective committees; the White House and the Office of Management and Budget (OMB); the various administrative departments, agencies, and bureaus; and the courts (Rehbinder and Stewart 1985, 310).

IGC Compared

Article one of the U.S. Constitution strongly resembles article two of the Treaty of Rome. It allows the federal government to "regulate commerce with foreign nations, and among the several States." At the constitutional level some other elements of the U.S. and the EC constitutional basis are of comparative interest. The states in the United States are allowed to act in the absence of federal mandates on the condition that those actions are not in violation of the constitution. In the EC, it is the other way around. The EC identifies the areas in which it will develop policies. In areas that are not the subject of EC policy-making, the member-states are free to act. In the Treaty of Maastricht on the European Union (July 29, 1992, C 191, II, article 3B), it is stated that the EC will only take action according to the principle of subsidiarity. This means: "only if, and insofar as, these objectives can be better achieved by the Community than by the member-states acting separately, by reason of the scale or effects of the proposed action."

In the United States, state legislation, in addition to federal legislation, is only possible in the specified remaining areas of activity not already allocated to the federal government. This resembles EC directives, which allow member-states to adopt more stringent measures only. When state law is in conflict with federal regulation, just as in the EC, the matter has to be studied judicially.

In 1969, in drafting the National Environmental Policy Act (NEPA), Congress said that the U.S. government should "Use all practicable means . . . to create and maintain conditions in which man and nature can exist in productive harmony." NEPA was signed into law by President Nixon on January 1, 1970, and it established a framework for the government to assess the environmental impact of its major actions. The law established the Council on Environmental Quality to advise the president on national policies for improving environmental quality and to supervise the preparation of environmental impact statements by federal agencies whenever their actions significantly affect the quality of the human environment. The Environmental Protection Agency (EPA) has the responsibility for reviewing and commenting in writing on environmental impact statements that touch any aspect of its responsibilities (Ordway 1991, 678).

The federal government of the United States is able to rely upon its own administrative infrastructure at regional and local levels whenever it so chooses. The EC bodies do not have any authority that goes beyond Brussels, but are totally dependent on the individual member-states. These countries want to integrate to a certain extent, but the attraction is certainly not sufficient to persuade national governments to become a federal state along the line of the United States. The primacy of national control in the EC is reflected in the extremely limited authority of the EP even though it is elected directly, and also in the fact that the Commission as the executive body of the EC derives its authority from neither the EP nor from direct elections. Instead, the center of power has remained in the Council of Ministers, representing national governments, and in the periodic summit meetings of the European Council.

INTERGOVERNMENTAL RELATIONS: THE POLICY-PROCESS

The EC Policy-Process

Legislation is generally initiated by the Commission, which prepares and discusses a preliminary draft with government officials of member-states and other relevant bodies. If it then adopts the proposal, that must be published in the *Official Journal*. The continuation of the procedure depends on the treaty upon which the proposal is based. Since the SEA was adopted, two procedures relating to EP involvement can be identified: the "consulting procedure," and an increase in the powers of the EP by the "cooperation procedure." When, and if, the Treaty of Maastricht is adopted, there will be a third procedure: the "Co-decision procedure." Following the "consulting procedure," the Council of Ministers seeks the opinion of the European Parliament and the Economic and Social Committee (ECOSOC). Both opinions are published in the *Official Journal*. The draft then returns to the Commission, which may amend the proposal if appropriate, and may refer the revised proposal to the European Parliament and ECOSOC. The Commission then sends the amended proposal back to the Council, which refers it to one of its working parties to discuss the text and comment on it. Then it goes to the Committee of Permanent Representatives (COREPER), which prepares it and sends it back to the Council, which under the traditional consultation procedure either rejects or adopts it and again publishes it in the *Official Journal* (Roney 1990, 20). In the "cooperation procedure," the proposal of the Commission is discussed in a report by one of the Members of Parliament. This means that if necessary the proposal can be amended. Then the Council adopts a "common position," and the proposal goes back to the EP for a second reading. The EP can approve the common position, amend it, or reject it by an absolute majority. The Commission can then adapt the proposal, and the Council can approve it with a qualified majority. If the Council wants to change the proposal or to adopt an amendment that had not been adopted by the Commission, it has to be unanimous. Introducing the "co-decision procedure," the Treaty of Maastricht increases the influence of the EP. When the EP has amended or rejected a proposal in the second reading, a special committee—which consists of members of the Council and members of the EP—has to bring the Council into agreement with the EP. If an agreement has been reached both the Council and the EP have to approve. When they do not, the committee has to start deliberations again. In case no agreement can be reached, the EP is allowed to reject the proposal by unanimity of votes.

The Commission has the solemn right of initiative of legislation, but there are many actors inviting the Commission to come with a proposal concerning a certain subject. These actors are, for example, Members of the EP, member-states, interest groups, and the COREPER. The EP has different ways to move the Commission to make a certain proposal. For example by their reports in the first reading, asking the Commission to come with a new proposal; or individual Members of Parliament or parties can present a draft resolution, in which the Commission is invited to write a proposal. When the Commission wants to initiate a proposal on a new policy in a certain sector, broad discussions are organized with political parties and different business groups. If more practical measures are to be prepared, all kinds of experts are invited including civil servants of national governments. Research shows that the working-group level and the Council of Ministers level are the negotiating levels in Brussels where important substantive decisions are made that largely shape the final agreement (van den Bos 1991, 232).

The EC environmental policy is very extensive; there is currently a body of 200 items of EC legislation (Haigh 1991, 62–63). EC environmental policy is, according to article 189 of the Treaty of Rome, embodied in directives, regulations, and decisions, but most of all in directives. Directives are addressed to the national governments. A directive prescribes the goal to be achieved, not the way this goal has to be reached. A directive is not directly applicable; however, the European Court of Justice (ECJ) has developed the doctrine of "direct effect," by which national courts can apply a directive, lacking national implementing legislation, if its requirements are sufficiently clear (Haigh 1990, 63). Usually the directive will give the national governments two years to comply (adopt the necessary legislation) and to take the administrative measures needed. Each directive deals with a narrow subject. A directive deals with the subject in depth, setting numerical standards and limits, and requirements. Some directives have set environmental quality standards combined with implementation plans or monitoring systems. The systems allow the member-states more latitude in setting controls on actual emissions by individual polluters while meeting overall goals set by the Community (Glim 1990, 16).

Twice a year a progress report on the implementation of directives in the member-states is submitted to the Commission. The Commission has to monitor two phases of implementation: (1) the formal compliance, the harmonization of national law with the provisions of the directive, and (2) the practical compliance, what is done in reality to achieve the goals set in the directive. The first phase can take a long time when the directive has to go through the normal national legislation process as it has to in most member-states. It is very difficult for the Commission to monitor on the second phase of implementation. The Commission cannot have an inspectorate to see that practical results have been achieved. It is dependent on the information of the member-states and of individual citizens or nongovernmental organizations (NGOs) to inform the Commission when a directive is not properly applied.

The Policy-Process in the United States and IGR Compared

In the United States, federal environmental regulation was introduced after the national product markets were already well established and before any extensive state regulation had been adopted. This has been different in the EC. In the EC environmental legislation was introduced before a common market was established.

Also, some member-states already had adopted quite extensive environmental legislation. For those member-states it is very difficult to comply formally with EC legislation. It has been found that it is much easier to formally comply when a country does not have any legislation on the subject concerned. Member-states that already have national laws generally covering the same subject have to adapt this variety of laws to formally comply with a directive (Glim 1990).

In U.S. policy-making, the Congress plays a major role. In Europe laws are formulated by the national governments; but in Washington and in the states, laws are initiated by members of the legislature.

The decentralized committee structure of Congress permits and encourages politically ambitious members to enhance their power and reputation by sponsoring, obtaining passage, and overseeing the implementation of new legislation, the so called: "Congressional entrepreneurship." There are fewer political rewards for careful and constructive legislative oversight and correction of ongoing administrative implementation and enforcement than there are for initiating new legislation. (Rehbinder and Stewart 1985, 307)

The U.S. environmental policy is very issue-oriented. The federal government is primarily engaged in environmental legislation related to nationally sold products (cars for example). Also, at the federal level norms are set for industrial processes and toxic waste dumps, but in these areas implementation and management is delegated to the state-level. Regulation concerning land-use, raw materials, water, sewage systems, and waste management is the authority of the state and local governments, stimulated by federal directives and financial incentives (Rehbinder and Stewart 1985, 288). Some environmentally minded states did adopt strong regulatory programs of their own, although they were often prosperous states, like California, with relatively large internal markets and obvious pollution problems (Rehbinder and Stewart 1985, 289). In the EC environmental legislation is often initiated by individual member-states. When the EC is not yet ready for it, those member-states adopt such legislation themselves. This collides more and more with industry interest groups, who want to wait for Community legislation.

In the United States a distinction can be made between state implementation of federal standards and federal encouragement of state regulation. This distinction is not a clear one though. On the one hand "federal financial assistance, provision of information, and the threat of more intrusive federal measures are also present in programs involving state implementation of federal standards." On the other hand "the federal standards governing the eligibility of state regulatory programs for financial assistance are often quite detailed, allowing federal administrators to exert considerable authority over state programs." Direct enforcement is possible in the case of state implementation of federal standards, which proves to be insufficient (Rehbinder and Stewart 1985, 290). EC laws always have to be implemented by the member-states and especially the regional and local governments. Until now, just the national governments were answerable to the Commission for ensuring that directives are applied. If the Commission is not satisfied, it is the national government that will be taken to the Court. The national government therefore has to satisfy itself that local governments or other subnational units that may be responsible for practical implementation do indeed ensure that the desired practical results are achieved. This is very difficult and does not seem to work very well. So, the Commission has the strong intention to delegate to the regions directly the responsibility to see that the goals set by the directive are achieved. The possibilities to fine the responsible authority that did not comply are still being discussed.

The U.S. policy process is very open and has a nearly unlimited obligation to inform. In contrast to the EC, the United States has many professionalized environmental pressure groups. The U.S. system of participation and judicial judgment overemphasizes the procedural aspects that have caused an enormous accumulation of cases in the courts and a prolongation of the policy-making process. This improves the role of the courts that, in turn, undermines the system of political responsibility. The United States is an example of the conflict model, which is based on the conflict of interests among different actors and on sanctions against polluters. In Europe the political culture is more consensus-oriented (Tuininga 1990, 534).

Environmental Management

The fact that an EC directive is formally complied with does not mean that it will be actually applied and enforced in the national context too. Just as in the United States, there is a big implementation gap. In the United States, programs of direct federal regulation and federal programs relying on the states or on encouragement of state regulation are badly applied and enforced. In the EC this may have various reasons. The EC is especially dependent on the local and regional actors to get policy implemented. These lower-level governments have most experience in implementing environmental policy, but are not invited to join the EC policy-making process. This often results in unrealistic legislation and laws that are difficult to apply. Vaguely defined EC policy seems to be a necessary condition to reach consensus and to leave some space for adaptation to local and changing circumstances. When the regional and local governments are not involved and informed, and yet expected to be the implementors of just national legislation, it is very difficult to implement a directive according to its goals, and it will be impossible to achieve some consistency of application throughout the Community. The passage "best practical means," when used in a directive, may be interpreted by the national government in a mechanical sense, with neither clear technical standards nor explicit technical goals. This presents problems for the regional and local governments that have not been involved in the preparation of the Community legislation.

In some areas a generalizing division can be made between the northern and the southern European member-states. In general the southern European member-states have serious problems with the actual implementation (though often these member-states formally implement very well). One of the main reasons is that they are industrializing countries, which means that greater attention is given to the development of industry. In the United States the same can be observed, there is a correlation between the leverage of industry over state and local decision makers and the amount of money to be spent on environmental policy-implementation (Rehbinder and Stewart 1985, 301). Except for the industrial lobby at the national level, there is also a difference in environmental problems in the—crudely generalized—northern and southern European member-states. The legislation initiated by the northern member-states does not always correspond with the environmental issues in the southern European countries (for example in Spain there is hardly any acid precipitation problem).

In the United States, in most cases solutions have been sought in a top-down approach, such as more stringent and more detailed executing measurements, that has not worked (Rehbinder and Stewart 1985, 301). Until recently the EC was also very much focused on central legislation and formal compliance issues. Now, tendencies can be observed to attention for the regions. This manifests itself in stimulation of regional trans-frontier cooperation (money), and an improved participation of the regional and local governments in the environmental policy-making process.

The question remains whether it is of any use to compare the EC with the United States? Probably, when the EC should be compared with anything, it should be with the trade agreement among the United States, Canada, and Mexico, a kind of budding EC. It is, of course, useful to learn from each other in a broad sense. Especially on the IGR and IGM level, the United States and the EC could mutually learn something from each other's experiences about how relations among the legislative body and the individual "states" and the executing organizations work. The EC has become increasingly integrated, perhaps, but—as appears from all three levels—the EC cannot be considered a federal union. The EC could learn from the United States, though, with respect to the discretionary space in legislation. This has already been initiated in the Treaty of Maastricht and the Fifth Environmental Action Program: the EC should create no new specific environmental legislation, but only framework regulation, leaving member-states to adapt the laws to regional and local circumstances. But both the Treaty of Maastricht and the Fifth EAP are still to be adopted and/or to be implemented.

REFERENCES

Bandach, E. 1977. *The Implementation Game: What Happens After a Bill Becomes a Law.* Cambridge: The MIT Press.

Barret, S. and C. Fudge, eds. 1981. *Policy and Action.* London: Methuen.

Bos, Jan M. M. van den. 1991. *Dutch EC Policy Making.* Thesis Amsterdam.

Conservation Foundation. 1990. *Environmental Policy in a Federal System: The United States and the European Community.* The Hague: Ministerie van V. R. O. M. Publikatiereeks milieubeheer nr. 1990–1993.

Glim, C. M. S. 1990. *European Environmental Legislation: What Does it Really Mean?*
    Delft: Eburon.
Haigh, N. 1991. "EEC." *European Environmental Yearbook 1991.* DocTer, Institute for
    Environmental Studies, Milan. U.K./London: DocTer International.
Heady, F. 1988. "The United States." In *Public Administration in Developed Democracies,*
    ed. D. C. Rowat. New York and Basel: Marcel Dekker, Inc.
Jessop, B. 1990. "Putting States in their Places: State Systems and State Theory." In *New
    Developments in Political Science: An International Review of Achievements and
    Prospects,* ed. A. Leftwich. Aldershot: England.
Kiser, L. and E. Ostrom, 1982. "The Three Words of Action: A Metatheoretical Synthesis of
    Institutional Approaches." In *Strategies of Political Inquiry,* ed. E. Ostrom. Beverly
    Hills: Sage Publications.
Majone, G. and A. Wildavsky, 1978. "Implementation as Evolution." In *Policy Studies
    Review Annual,* ed. H. E. Freeman. London: Sage.
Metcalfe, L. 1978. "Policy Making in Turbulent Environments." In *Interorganizational
    Policy Making: Limits to Coordination and Central Control,* ed. K. Hanf and F. W.
    Scharpf. London and Beverly Hills, Cal.: Sage Publications.
Neunreiter, K. 1991. *The Fundamental Choice for the European Community: Federation,
    Confederation or Subsidiary System?* Research Committee on European Unification.
    15th World Congress of the International Political Science Association, Buenos Aires.
Ordway, G. L. 1991. "USA." *European Environmental Yearbook 1991.* DocTer, Institute for
    Environmental Studies Milan. U.K./London: DocTer International.
Peters, B. G. 1988. *Comparing Public Bureaucracies.* Birmingham: University of Alabama
    Press.
Rehbinder, E., and R. Stewart. 1985. *Environmental Protection Policy.* New York: Walter
    de Gruyter.
Rhodes, R. A. W. 1979. "Research into Central-Local Government Relations in Britain: A
    Framework for Analysis." In *Central-Local Government Relationships,* ed. R. A. W.
    Rhodes. London: SSRC.
Roest, N. F., K. J. M. Mortelmans, A. P. Oele, and J. H. Boone, eds. 1991. *Europa binnen
    het bestuur.* Raad voor het Binnenlands Beestuur. The Hague: SDU Uitgeverij.
Roney, A. 1990. *The European Community Fact Book.* London: Chambers.
Scharpf, F. W. 1978. "Interorganizational Policy Studies: Issues, Concepts and Perspectives."
    In *Interorganizational Policy Making: Limits to Coordination and Central Control,* ed.
    K. Hanf and F. W. Scharpf. London and Beverly Hills, Cal.: Sage Publications.
_____, B. Reissert, and F. Schnabel. 1978. "Policy Effectiveness and Conflict Avoidance in
    Intergovernmental Policy Formation." In *Interorganizational Policy Making: Limits to
    Coordination and Central Control,* ed. K. Hanf and F. W. Scharpf. London and Beverly
    Hills, Cal.: Sage Publications.
Sharpe, L. J. 1987. "The Western European State: The Territorial Dimension." In *Tensions
    in the Territorial Politics of Western Europe,* ed. R. A. W. Rhodes and V. Wright.
    London: Frank Cass.
Siedentopf, H., and J. Ziller. 1988. *Making European Policies Work, Vol. I, Comparative
    Syntheses.* European Institute of Public Administration, Brussels and London: Sage
    Publications.
Toonen, Th. A. J. 1990. *Internationalisering en het openbaar bestuur als institutioneel
    ensemble.* The Hague: Vuga.

Tuininga, E. J. 1990. "Een wereld van verschil: lange-termijnmilieubeleid in de Verenigde Staten van Amerika." In *Het milieu: denkbeelden voor de 21ste eeuw*. Commissie Lange Termijn Milieubeleid.

Vig, N., and M. Kraft. 1990. *Environmental Policy in the 1990s*. Washington: Congressional Quarterly Press.

Wright, D. S. 1990. "Conclusion: Federalism, Intergovernmental Relations and Inter-govermental Management—Conceptual Reflections, Comparisons and Interpretations." In *Strategies for Managing Intergovernmental Policies and Networks*, ed. R. W. Gage and M. P. Mandell. New York: Praeger.

16

Information Resource Management: A Framework for Comparison

Rolland Hurtubise

INFORMATION OR TECHNOLOGY?

The present-day public organization produces, consumes, and distributes information at phenomenal rates. It is important, therefore, that information be considered as a major resource essential to all decision making that takes place at all management and operational levels within an organization. In addition, information must be managed in a forthright manner.

Fortunately, concepts and methodologies for integrating information and organization are taking hold, notably in the public sector. This chapter's goal is to furnish a sufficiently elaborate basis of knowledge to permit comparisons among various facets of the ever-evolving information resource management (IRM) field. To compare meaningfully public sector efforts in managing information and technology, it is essential that a clear distinction be made between a number of popular abbreviations, such as IRM, MIS, DSS, IT, DP, and OA.

Every government organization has one or more information systems for its various functions, departments, divisions, services, and levels. These systems have always existed. They retrieve daily operational data that can then be processed and used to prepare reports. There is no doubt that the public manager has always been interested in information systems. However, it would seem to many that the traditional approach to controlling public information has been to drown management under an unremitting flow of paper. In recent years, managers and analysts have realized that a more efficacious approach entails supplying each decision maker with information specific to each decision-making situation (Vroom and Jago 1988). This realization suggests that an evolutionary system should be designed so that specific data will be transformed into information for operational and control purposes and be further refined to serve top management planning. The management information system (MIS) is this evolutionary design. With it, the various organizational units use a system that exploits information technology (IT)—automatic/electronic data processing (DP), office automation (OA), and telecommunications—and makes full use of available resources. In converting data into information, information into decisions, and decisions into significant actions, an MIS becomes a decision support system (DSS). Viewed from its most elementary state, the MIS is a process that transforms data into information; it is DP or OA. Viewed from its most evolved state, it is a process that allows informed decision: it is a DSS (Hurtubise 1984).

The introduction of central computing or DP technology in organizations as a management tool dates back 40 years. Its introduction was done gradually. More recently, the combined effect of lower hardware and software costs, and ever-increasing computing power, has made IT more accessible. Therefore, a question that a public manager must address is the following: If the ultimate aim of MIS is decision, what must I manage—information or technology? The answer emerges from the fact that decision making is the motor of any organization, the culmination of all managerial effort, and, admittedly, information is what the decision maker needs in order to decide (Simon 1977). However tempting, public management must not be lured by IT, its hardware, its software. It must manage every element of the decision-information-technology continuum.

A FRAMEWORK FOR COMPARISON

If IRM is achieved by means of the MIS concept and IT is its technological provider, what is the basis for comparison among nations, levels of government, agencies, institutions, departments, etc.? From a comparative management standpoint, what can be compared and how? Of course, everything can be compared and answers to the following questions are not only possible, but very revealing: Do IRM plans exist and if so, is management involved? How evolved is the use of IT (DP, OA, and telecommunications)? Are databases made available? Are MIS design methods used? To what extent is IRM different from IT? Is artificial intelligence (AI) present? So many simple questions, yet most require complex answers.

The proposed framework is a practical comparative model intended to provide and structure answers to numerous similar questions. It is inspired by the logic and procedure advocated for the design, development, and eventual installation of an MIS (Blumenthal 1969; Bowman, Davis, and Wetherbe 1981) and is composed of three overlapping phases: IRM plan, MIS design, and MIS development, exploitation, and management.

IRM AND MIS DESIGN LOGIC

Phase I—IRM Plan

Strategic Planning. At the beginning of the IRM effort, a basic premise must be followed: decision makers are responsible for managing information and its technologies. Consequently, it is important that top management be involved from the very outset (Lederer and Mendelow 1988). As a result, a strategic plan must be defined that will comprehensively integrate information resource planning with the organization's overall planning process. This integration can be achieved by first illustrating the relations between organizational objectives, strategies, and strategic attributes on the one hand and the MIS objectives, constraints, and design considerations on the other (King 1978); and, subsequently, by establishing periodic planning mechanisms (whereby IRM plans are submitted for approval, for instance). In this way, the plan becomes a guide, thereby constraining the behavior of that portion of the organization responsible for the design of the proposed MIS. Furthermore, it will determine a reasonable sequence of development in terms of payoff potential, probability of success, and allocation and conservation of resources. In avoiding unnecessary duplication of major systems across organizational lines, and in reducing the number of small, isolated systems to be developed, operated, and maintained, the plan also looks to the future. In laying a foundation for coordinated development of consistent and comprehensive, organization-wide and inter-organizational information systems, the plan provides for adaptability of systems to change and growth without periodic major overhaul. As a result, the plan may well establish guidelines for and directions to continuing studies and projects on a short-, medium-, and long-term basis. A plan may also refer to a number of specific management related topics: the sectors involved in the MIS effort, including project boundaries and limits; the mandate and composition of the design team; the creation of a unit responsible for information management and its relationship with other units; the position and functions of the information resource manager; memberships in MIS steering and design committees; MIS design method selection, system evaluation, and cost-benefit analysis; and project management considerations such as calendar, cost, and training.

Over the past 15 years, a number of nations have been involved with IRM issues and planning at both government (federal, state, local) and agency levels. In 1980 the United States—the undisputed leader in this field—promulgated the federal government's Paperwork Reduction Act, which establishes a mechanism to manage governmental information resources. The objectives of this act include minimizing the federal paperwork burden imposed upon the public and the cost of collecting, maintaining, using, and disseminating information, while maximizing the usefulness of federal information (Office of Management and Budget 1992). Another objective was to ensure that IT was acquired and used by the federal government in a manner to improve service delivery and program management, increase productivity, and reduce waste, fraud, and the information processing burden (Horton and Marchand 1982). The U.S. Congress strengthened these goals in 1986, notably, by clarifying the control aspect of federal agency information collection activities and by expanding the public's role for comment. No doubt other paperwork reduction and federal information resources management acts will appear in the future to amend existing acts. Not only will they minimize the paperwork burden for taxpayers, small businesses, and state and local governments, they will also maximize the usefulness and public access to federal government information. Their purposes will be directly related to effective and efficient IRM and IT. They will serve to coordinate, to integrate, and to make uniform federal information policies and practices, as well as to guarantee that government information activities are conducted in such a way as to improve the quality of decision making.

In Canada, federal government institutions have developed plans for information technology and systems since the mid-1970s. The recent Management of Information Technology policy, which refers to "Information Management Plans," continues this requirement with the added emphasis on the establishment of government-wide directions. The policy stipulates that federal institutions must apply IT to reduce the burden on respondents from whom information is collected (from small businesses, for example), make information more easily accessible, complete transactions more quickly and accurately, support employees, and thus reduce costs for all parties. Moreover, it ensures that IT allows services to be provided to the public in both of Canada's official languages. Accompanying this policy is the Management of Government Information Holdings policy, related to the cost-effective and coordinated management of federal government information holdings (Treasury Board of Canada 1991). In Quebec, MIS development policies, some dating back to 1976, and IRM programs have been in effect for a number of years (Treasury Board of Quebec 1988). A noteworthy example of IRM planning at the local government level in the province of Quebec is Montreal's Strategic OA Plan (Montreal 1989). As a rule, interest in IRM planning exists in public organizations in a number of nations (Avgerou 1991; Willcocks 1991). For example, in the Commonwealth of Independent States (CIS), the former USSR, "efforts have been made to strengthen both the production of information technology and its successful use in all aspects of economic and social life" (Chereshkin 1991, 107).

IRM stages. The manner and precision with which an organization conducts IRM can be measured in terms of its informational and technological maturity. The more mature organization is IRM-conscious. It is aware of the importance of defining user needs, establishing its IT orientations, and managing information. Such concerns are often neglected by younger, computer-mesmerized organizations. Nolan (1985) has proposed a useful model consisting of a number of evolutionary growth stages, identifying where an organization and its units are located in terms of IRM evolution. This descriptive framework, which considers such variables as management, budget, users, analysts, and applications, may help plan a more harmonious and efficient transition from one stage to the next.

The following variation of the Nolan model describes five IRM stages or categories:

1. Initiation is the introductory DP and/or OA computer-acquisition stage, when basic data and transaction-processing takes place, possibly accompanied by application-sharing by means of networking. At this stage, user involvement is minimal and control and planning functions are decentralized and often left to analysts.
2. Expansion of computer systems is the second category. It is characterized by the proliferation of applications developed by segregated analyst-user teams. Basic and simple applications become more complex and sometimes integrated. Little control and planning take place.
3. Control is the attempt to consolidate and rationalize the expansion process. At this third stage, performance measures are imposed, both on users and analysts. Furthermore, financial techniques, such as charging for computer services, are used to manage systems. As a result, problems may arise as to data and systems ownership.
4. Appropriation sees the users take control of the MIS design and development phase. This may be a time of turmoil, when technological, administrative, and budgetary distinctions are sought and made between central and local applications.
5. Maturity, the final stage to this model, involves the attributes discussed in this chapter, not the least of which is the integration of IRM planning to the organization's strategic plan.

It can be argued that the deployment of microcomputers in American and Canadian agencies (federal, state, and local) during the past decade have influenced public organizations in such a way that most have left the third or control stage by the end of the 1980s, and are presently at the fourth or appropriation level. A similar situation may well exist for agencies in certain European nations such as France and the United Kingdom.

A survey conducted in the United States in mid-1988 that polled high-level public managers in federal, state, and county agencies shed some light on IRM stages in the public sector. For this study, a four-level model was developed. The stages used were initiation, expansion, formalization, and integration (this last category encompassed the appropriation and maturity stages of the model just described). In the total sample, 47 percent of the responses were in the integration stage, 28 percent were in the formalization stage, 21 percent were in the expansion stage, and 5 percent were in the initiation stage (Caudle, Gorr, and Newcomer 1991).

Phase II—MIS Design

MIS Methodologies. The second phase of IRM and MIS design logic can summarily be referred to as the analysis and determination of information needs and the resulting identification and development of specific applications. This hase involves one or more methods (techniques)—steps to follow and rules to abide by— for planning, designing, developing, and documenting information systems, their applications (hardware, software, and telecommunication components), accompanying databases, operational and administrative procedures, etc. Although methods and techniques may be created by in-house systems groups, many are commercially available from consulting firms and hardware and/or software manufacturers. Some of these methods include planning topics belonging to Phase I, the IRM plan.

MIS design methods and techniques have been developed in a number of nations. For instance, the notion of "structured programming" originated in the Netherlands (Dijkstra 1965). As a rule, data and information flow diagrams, system and program flowcharts, data dictionaries, and decision tables and trees are used throughout the world. The United States has seen the creation of many design tools: Hierarchy Plus Input, Process, Output (HIPO) (Katzan 1976) and Business Systems Planning (BSP) from IBM, Bachman's Data Structure Diagrams (Bachman 1969), Data Flow Diagrams (DeMarco 1979), Structured Analysis and Design Technique (SADT) (Ross and Schoman 1977), Problem Statement Language and Analyzer (PSL/PSA) (Teichroew and Hershey 1977), Structured Systems Analysis (Gane and Sarson 1979), Yourdon Structured Design and Programming Method (Yourdon 1989), James Martin Methodology (Martin 1984), Critical Success Factors (Rockart 1982), and Entity-Relationship Diagramming method for database design (Chen 1977). A popular design technique originating in the United Kingdom is known as Jackson's Data Structure Diagrams (Jackson 1975). In France, The Warnier-Orr method for structured program design (Warnier 1976; Orr 1977) and design methods such as MERISE (Matheron 1987), RACINES (Ministry of Research and Industry 1982), and CERVOISE (Gassani 1988) were created. Finally, in Canada, a popular systems design method is Productivity Plus, developed by the consulting firm of Ducros, Meilleur and Roy (DMR 1990).

CASE. MIS design logic suggests the use of CASE Computer-Aided Systems (or Software) Engineering tools. CASE implies sophisticated software to design, develop, manage, and maintain other software. Such a tool is a software manufacturing plant made up of a front- and a back-end: the "front-end" is a powerful planning and analysis instrument enabling the creation of relations between various decision levels and information structures, whereas the "back-end" offers a set of automated tools to create, update and document the software (computer programs) making up the MIS (Burch and Grudnitski 1989). By the mid-1990s, many MIS will be designed using CASE tools.

A noted announcement was made in 1989 when IBM introduced its application development (AD)/cycle, a "strategy" whereby standardized design specifications allow CASE tools to communicate with each other. Most CASE instruments have been developed in the United States. It is estimated that approximately one-third of CASE users are from the public sector (Eastwood 1992).

Information Technology. There is little doubt that the effective use of IT, ranging from centralized DP (mainframe computing and telecommunications) to decentralized OA (microcomputers and local area networks), is part of the solution to the IRM and MIS challenge in public organizations (Levinson 1991). For this reason, an important product of the MIS design phase is the system schema or configuration which illustrates an MIS' technological modules, both hardware and software.

Most member countries of the Organization for Economic Cooperation and Development (OECD) have developed national IT programs intended to promote domestic research and development by encouraging collaboration between industry and research institutions. In Canada, for instance, the *Innovation* program aims at improving access to IT knowledge developed in research centers. Many programs such as VHSIC (Very High-Speed Integrated Circuit), SEMATECH (Semiconductor Manufacturing Technology), and STARS (Software Technology for Adaptable, Reliable Systems) were initiated in the United States (OECD 1992).

The public sector is looking more and more to technology as a means of increasing its productivity (Office of Management and Budget 1991). Because of the phenomenal growth of OA and individual processing systems, public organizations have seen their annual IT expenditures during the past decade increase at phenomenal rates, to the order of 15 to 20 percent for certain agencies. One significant observation: in many American and Canadian agencies, the combined computing power of microcomputers exceeds that of mini and central computers (Hurtubise and Pastinelli 1987).

The Canadian government is estimated to have had approximately 80,000 computers in its possession in 1990. Another estimate predicts that within the next decade, nearly 80 percent of all public sector information in Canada will be computerized (Information Commissioner of Canada 1991). That is far from the case for nations of the CIS where the lack of computer hardware and software, and the underdevelopment of telecommunications, serve to illustrate how very slowly IT has progressed in centrally planned economies (Faulhaber 1991).

Artificial Intelligence. In the next century—the next millennium!—extraordinary technologies will assist the decision maker: super-performing computers the size of books and artificial intelligence (AI) or, more accurately, knowledge-based systems (KBS) (Applegate, Cash, and Quinn Mills 1988).

National AI programs exist. They have been much publicized and are not to be confused with national IRM acts and policies. In 1981, Japan's Ministry for International Trade and Industry (MITI) announced plans to develop powerful intelligent "fifth-generation" computers that would have the intelligence to converse in natural spoken language and would have human-like decision-making capabilities. A year later, Japan's Institute for New Generation Computer Technology (ICOT), a corporate consortium formed to meet some of the goals of the fifth-generation computer project, began active development with funding of $1 billion (half from MITI, half from Japanese industry) over ten years. A few months after ICOT began development, 21 leading United States computer and electronics companies formed the Microelectronics and Computer Technology Corporation (MCC), with a $65 million yearly budget aimed at a wide variety of AI problems. In 1983, the Defense Advanced Research Projects Agency (DARPA) unveiled the Strategic Computing Initiative (SCI), a $100 million per year program for research in microelectronics, computer architectures, and AI. The following year, the European Economic Community (EEC) created the European Strategic Program for Research in Information Technology (ESPRIT), a $1.5 billion program to fund all areas of computer technology, including intelligent computers (Kurzweil 1990).

One particular class of KBS is referred to as expert systems (ES), intelligent programs that use knowledge and procedures belonging to experts. By all evidence, ES can be used to solve many kinds of public management problems (Snellen 1991). The design of such systems is straightforward: once the goal has been determined, a design team, usually made up of a knowledge engineer, one or more experts, and users set about acquiring, representing, and, eventually, inserting knowledge into a software known as an ES shell. After testing and prototyping, the system is ready for use. Basically, there are four types of ES, classified according to both cognitive and technological complexity (Meyer and Foley Curley 1991):

1. Personal productivity systems, the least complex ES, assist the individual decision maker and supports his or her personal productivity.
2. Power decision systems, the cognitively complex ES, may be used by an entire organizational unit, thereby increasing its decision-making capacity.
3. Integrated production systems, the technologically complex ES, involve an organization's computer resources and are intended for integrated operational-level decision making.
4. Finally, strategic impact systems, the most complex ES, deal with decision making at the highest management levels.

In 1985, Harmon and King foresaw two major waves of ES applications. First-wave applications are medium-sized and designed to solve specific problems, whereas second-wave applications—foreseen for the 1990s—are more impressive: not only do they reproduce human reasoning, they compete with human beings.

Approximately 2,200 ES applications had been developed in the United States by 1988. The U.S. share of the world market in KBS (50 percent) is estimated at $812 million in 1991, $1.063 billion in 1992, and $2.383 billion in 1995. In Europe, France is the leader with an estimated $132 million spent on KBS development and services in 1991. In 1995, the French internal market for KBS is expected to grow to $389 million (Janiaux 1991). In 1991, no fewer than 148 ES applications were identified in the French public sector (CIIBA 1991). These applications are far-ranging, from aids to writing formal administrative documents to financial analysis and control. Noteworthy applications include financing projects in developing nations, counseling students, establishing air traffic control procedures, assisting police inquiries, and managing hostage-taking situations. Finally, in Quebec, 87 ES projects have been undertaken by 28 public and private sector organizations (Théoret and Gadbois 1991).

Another class of KBS is known as neural networks (NN). These are systems which simulate the brain's neurons and distribute knowledge in an associative memory composed of many processing elements or artificial neurons. An NN is not programmed in a traditional manner; rather, it "learns" by means of examples. It is expected that this type of KBS will be preferred over ES in circumstances when rules or object descriptions are too difficult or impossible to establish. As is the case with ES, software shells are commercially available for building neural networks (Caudill and Butler 1990).

Phase III—MIS Development, Exploitation, and Management

The IRM Organization. The final phase of IRM and MIS design logic refers to the information organization that will not only design and develop the MIS but will materialize the basic concepts and principal guidelines outlined in the IRM plan (be it of strategic level or otherwise). Therefore, Phase III may refer to many things, including the information manager, system performance, charge-back techniques, and cost-benefit analysis.

A number of means are available for managing the informational and technological resource in the public sector: integration of information and technology expenses within an agency's programs and activities; billing mechanisms for the use of information and technology; creation of information centers for end-user training and computing; sharing and transfer of technology by cooperative arrangements; establishment of an investment fund for priority project development, etc. As the modern-day MIS is a subset of the more global IRM concept, a definite MIS development cycle needs to be undertaken and managed. To this end, MIS project selection, including problem definition and evaluation, solution feasibility, and project extent are a follow through to any IRM plan devised during Phase I. An organization must not only design and install its MIS, it must undertake acceptance evaluation and complete its cost-benefit study. The degree of exploitation (operation), maintenance, and updating of an MIS depends upon its management, and more precisely, the management of the information resource which, in turn, depends upon control and change. Such topics as application and database design, software development, mainframe and microcomputer acquisition are but part of the issue. Most importantly, a uniform and consistent information management policy must be established.

In the United States, the Paperwork Reduction Act of 1980 established an Office of Information and Regulatory Affairs (OIRA) in the Office of Management and Budget (OMB) with the responsibility for developing and implementing uniform and consistent IRM policies, overseeing the development of IRM principles, standards, and guidelines, and monitoring agency activities related to the acquisition and use of IT. Two areas of OMB involvement are the Program for Priority Systems (focusing senior management attention on important MIS design, development, and acquisition projects) and the Federal Information Locator System (intended to be an authoritative register of federal information). Other topics of concern are Electronic Data Interchange between public and private sector computers, Privacy Act issues, computer security, and federal statistical needs. Since the Paperwork Reduction Act amendments of 1986, OIRA's tasks include reviewing agency requests for approval of information collections and ensuring active public involvement in their development. This office must also produce an annual IRM Plan that comprises the Information Collection Budget through which OMB and federal agencies plan for, measure, and control the cost of federal information collection activities (Office of Management and Budget 1992). Naturally, federal agencies are themselves responsible for carrying out IRM activities: aside from designating a senior "IRM official," an agency must develop and annually revise its IRM plan.

An additional U.S. agency involved with IRM oversight is the General Services Administration (GSA). One of its units, the Information Resources Management Service (IRMS), is responsible for coordinating and directing a federal government-wide program for the management, inventorying, procurement, and utilization of IT and telecommunications equipment and services, as well as for planning and directing programs for improving federal records and information management practices. In addition to providing technical and contracting assistance in software, hardware, data communications, and OA, this service offers information planning assistance and assists agencies in establishing strategic, tactical, and operational IRM planning programs. The IRMS is further responsible for coordinating policy-making activities related to information functions and authorities. Yet another U.S. IRM-oriented organization is the Information Resources College, created as a full college of the National Defense University. Although most of its courses and programs are primarily for Department of Defense military and civilian personnel, the college has courses open to other federal, state, and local government employees (Office of the Federal Register 1990).

In Canada, the Treasury Board, through its Secretariat (Information Management Division, Administrative Policy Branch), is responsible for the leadership and coordination and the establishment of overall directions for IRM on a federal government-wide basis. Federal institutions participate in the setting of these directions by informing the Secretariat of their plans and long-term strategies. Not only must an institution designate a senior official as its representative, it must develop a plan for the transition to full conformance with approved strategic directions, including standardization, and implement approved government IT standards in accordance with Treasury Board criteria. As well, it must adopt a business-case approach that relates IRM strategies and plans to program priorities and to measurable improvements in program performance. Canadian federal government institutions develop annual information management plans, tailored to their needs, that support their missions and operational plans. Also, Treasury Board approval is required for IT investments exceeding certain amounts (Treasury Board of Canada 1991). Finally, the National Archives are responsible for auditing the application by government institutions of Treasury Board records management policies (National Archives of Canada 1990).

The Treasury Board of Quebec has similar responsibilities: whenever operational costs exceed a certain amount and a number of agencies are involved, its Secretariat must approve MIS "administrative designs," comprising elements from both Phases I and II of the IRM and MIS design logic. Since 1988, agencies must develop annual IT Strategic and Operational Development Plans that are linked to their annual organizational priorities. The agency plans, submitted to the Treasury Board, as well as to the Department of Communications, the Department of Supply and Services, the Department of Industry, Commerce and Technology, and to the controller general, not only provide a global IT view, but favor technology transfers and acquisition strategies. In Quebec, the Department of Communications is responsible for research and coordination related to government-wide IT planning (Treasury Board of Quebec 1988).

Finally, in France, the "Inter-Ministerial Committee on Data Processing and Office Automation," chaired by the prime minister, is responsible for instigating and coordinating IRM in government agencies (Bottin Edition 1991).

Accessibility and Protection. The advent of the new technology has made public sector information more accessible. For this reason, the subject of data protection—integrity and security—is very popular (Loch, Carr, and Warkentin 1992). While integrity is related to data, information, processing, hardware, and software quality, accuracy, and timeliness adequacy, security is concerned with appropriate protocol and data and information access controls. Providing quality assurance of data contained in databases and diagnosing and protecting against computer viruses are matters of importance to all organizations. However, on the topic of accessibility and protection, public organizations must maintain a much broader view.

Most government agencies in a number of nations come under the jurisdiction of two acts: the Freedom of Information Act and the Privacy Act. The first act provides a right of access to information in records under the control of an agency, in accordance with the principles that government information should be available to the public. The second act provides individuals with access to their personal information held by governments and, as well, protects an individual's privacy by limiting those who may see his or her information. (It also controls collection, use, and disclosure of personal information.) To comply with these acts, a government organization must make provision, within the scope of its IRM plan and its MIS design, to respond to information requests and to protect against personal information abuses. For public organizations (federal, state, and local), where management information identifies and describes individuals, compliance with Freedom of Information and Privacy acts may involve important expenditures and oblige MIS users to balance their information needs with legislative requirements.

Freedom of Information and Privacy acts exist at the federal and state levels in the United States (Guidebook to the Freedom of Information and Privacy Acts 1986-1994). Nearly identical acts are to be found for Canada and Quebec (Information Commissioner of Canada 1991; Privacy Commissioner of Canada 1991; Publications du Québec 1991).

At the Canadian federal level, the Access to Information Act makes government institutions accountable for the information they control and for providing access to it (except in limited circumstances), whereas the Privacy Act protects the privacy of individuals with respect to personal information about themselves held by a government institution and provides individuals with a right of access to such information. Moreover, the Canadian Human Rights Act requires controls over and the inventorying of all personal information used for administrative purposes, regardless of its form or medium. Access rights were further extended in 1988 by the Canadian Government Communications Policy that requires institutions to make information from databases available for purchase wherever there is significant demand.

In France, the management of public information acts is undertaken by two government organizations: the "National Commission on Data Processing and Liberties" and the "Access to Administrative Documents Commission." One control feature of the first commission is that it be informed of any processing involving personal information (Dreyfus and d'Arcy 1989). Furthermore, the "Inter-Ministerial Delegation for Information Systems Security," under the authority of the General Secretariat for National Defense, oversees the uniformity of agency MIS security procedures.

Although American and Canadian information policies and these nations endorsement of information protection principles offer legal protection against information abuses in the public sector, there are no controls over the private sector, notwithstanding the proliferation of on-line databases: in 1980, their number worldwide was 400; at the end of 1990, there were 4,615. Sellers of on-line services have grown from 59 to 654 during the same period. The total electronic information revenues in North America alone were over $6 billion in 1988 and are forecast to reach $19 billion by 1994 (Information Commissioner of Canada 1991). Commercial trafficking in personal information is estimated at $3 billion annually in the United States (presumably, $300 million in Canada) (Privacy Commissioner of Canada 1991). European nations seem to have been more aware of such situations, for most members of the EEC have imposed data protection controls over both the public and the private sectors (Privacy Commissioner of Canada 1991).

BASIS FOR FUTURE COMPARISON

IT expenditures in the public sector compose much of total organizational development and operational costs. Nevertheless, technology management, often acting as a catalyst, must remain a subset of information management.

In this chapter, it has been argued that MIS, the concept by which IRM is achieved, is modeled on an organization's structure and is built by progressively integrating many components into a well-coordinated set which accounts for the organizational functions. Again, the mission is decision. To this end, an effective MIS must be selective and pertinent. In addition, if IT is to represent a synthesis of each manager's changing information needs and take into account his or her decision-making responsibilities, IT must be flexible. It must evolve!

The comparative framework presented in this chapter will also have to evolve, just as the MIS concept and the IRM ambition will evolve. For this reason, a look to the future is warranted.

In terms of human resources, tasks will have to be redefined and personnel reclassified if IRM, MIS, IT, and AI are to be introduced into public organizations in an harmonious manner. The development of mainframe and microcomputer applications to respond to individual user needs and the substitution of technology for trained personnel are all issues that will have to be addressed in time.

As regards decision making, there is no doubt that the development of local applications will facilitate the direct control and exploitation of data and information by public managers themselves. Such practices should do much to help shift the informational-decisional outlook in many public organizations from transaction and operation-oriented processing to management control and planning.

Also, the MIS design phase will become more encompassing. Not only will it span the entire scope of the design logic, from data acquisition to decision making, it will directly consider individual communication and information presentation preferences and incorporate the analysis of decisional methods and styles. Thoroughly integrated IRM and MIS design and development software will be available. Fundamentally based on knowledge, they will relate to all phases, from IRM planning, through MIS design, to MIS development, exploitation, and management.

Truly, the basis for future comparison of Information Resource Management in the public sector will be the level of integration of the decision-information-technology continuum to the organization.

FREQUENTLY USED ABBREVIATIONS

AI   Artificial Intelligence
CASE Computer-Aided Systems/Software Engineering
CIS   Commonwealth of Independent States
DP   (Automatic/Electronic) Data Processing

DSS   Decision Support System
EEC   European Economic Community
ES   Expert System
IRM   Information Resource Management
IRMS   Information Resources Management Service
IT   Information Technology
KBS   Knowledge-Based System
MIS   Management Information System
NN   Neural Network
OA   Office Automation
OIRA   Office of Information and Regulatory Affairs
OMB   Office of Management and Budget

REFERENCES

Applegate, L. M., J. I. Cash, Jr., and D. Quinn Mills. 1988. "Information Technology and Tomorrow's Manager." *Harvard Business Review* 66 (2):128–136.

Avgerou, C. 1991. "Information Systems Planning in Social Administration." *Informatization and the Public Sector* 1 (1):59–73.

Bachman, C. W. 1969. "Data Structure Diagrams." *Data Base: The Quarterly Newsletter of the Special Interest Group on Business Data Processing of the ACM* 1 (2):4–10.

Blumenthal, S. C. 1969. *Management Information Systems: A Framework for Planning and Development*. Englewood Cliffs, N.J.: Prentice-Hall.

Bottin Edition. 1991. *Bottin administratif 1992*. Paris: Bottin S.A.

Bowman, B., G. Davis, and J. Wetherbe. 1981. "Modeling for MIS." *Datamation* 27 (7):155–164.

Burch, J., and G. Grudnitski. 1989. *Information Systems: Theory and Practice*, 5th ed. New York: John Wiley & Sons.

Caudill, M., and C. Butler. 1990. *Naturally Intelligent Systems*. Cambridge, Mass.: The MIT Press.

Caudle, S. L., W. L. Gorr, and K. E. Newcomer. 1991. "Key Information Systems Management Issues for the Public Sector." *MIS Quarterly* 15 (2):170–188.

Chen, P. 1977. *The Entity-Relationship Approach to Logical Database Design*. Wellesley, Mass.: Q.E.D. Information Sciences.

Chereshkin, D. 1991. "National IT Policy in the New Socioeconomic Environment in the USSR." *Informatization and the Public Sector* 1 (2):107–115.

CIIBA. 1991. *Liste des systèmes-experts dans l'administration*. Paris: Comité Interministériel de l'informatique et de la bureautique dans l'administration.

DeMarco, T. 1979. *Structured Analysis and System Specification*. New York: Yourdon Press.

Dijkstra, E. 1965. "Programming Considered as a Human Activity." In *Proceedings of the 1965 IFIP Congress*. Amsterdam: North-Holland Publishing, 213–217.

DMR. 1990. *System Development Guide*, 4th ed. Montreal: Ducros, Meilleur, and Roy.

Dreyfus, F., and F. d'Arcy. 1989. *Les institutions politiques et administratives de la France*, 3d ed. Paris: Economica.

Eastwood, A. 1992. "CASE Study Bad News for Vendors." *Computing Canada* 18 (2):20–21.

Faulhaber, G. R. 1991. "Informatization of Soviet Society: American Observations." *Informatization and the Public Sector* 1 (2):95–101.

Gane, C., and T. Sarson. 1979. *Structured Systems Analysis: Tools and Techniques.* Englewood Cliffs, N.J.: Prentice-Hall.

Gassani, R. 1988. *La méthode Cervoise: Comment élaborer, représenter et valider l'organisation des informations d'un système d'entreprise.* Paris: Editions d'Organisation.

Guidebook to the Freedom of Information and Privacy Acts, 1986–1994, 2d ed. New York: Clark Boardman.

Harmon, P., and D. King. 1985. *Expert Systems: Artificial Intelligence in Business.* New York: Wiley & Sons.

Horton, F. W., and D. A. Marchand. 1982. *Information Management in Public Administration.* Arlington, Va.: Information Resources Press.

Hurtubise, R. 1984. *Managing Information Systems: Concepts and Tools.* West Hartford, Conn.: Kumarian Press.

_____, and J.-P. Pastinelli. 1987. *L'information et les technologies dans l'organisation: L'implication de la haute direction.* Montreal: Agence d'ARC.

Information Commissioner of Canada. 1991. *Annual Report Information Commissioner 1990–1991.* Ottawa: Minister of Supply and Services Canada.

Jackson, M. A. 1975. *Principles of Program Design.* London: Academic Press.

Janiaux, P. 1991. "L'intelligence artificielle: des marchés bien réels." *01 Informatique supplement (Les promesses de l'informatique)* 1166 (14):31–33.

Katzan, H., Jr. 1976. *Systems Design and Documentation: An Introduction to the HIPO Method.* New York: Van Nostrand Reinhold.

King, W. R. 1978. "Strategic Planning for Management Information Systems." *MIS Quarterly* 2 (1):27–37.

Kurzweil, R. 1990. *The Age of Intelligent Machines.* Cambridge, Mass.: The MIT Press.

Lederer, A. L., and A. L. Mendelow. 1988. "Convincing Top Management of the Strategic Potential of Information Systems." *MIS Quarterly* 12 (4):524–534.

Levinson, E. 1991. "Using Information Technology Effectively in Government Organizations." *Informatization and the Public Sector* 1 (2):143–254.

Loch, K. D., H. H. Carr, and M. E. Warkentin. 1992. "Threats to Information Systems: Today's Reality, Yesterday's Understanding." *MIS Quarterly* 16 (2):173–186.

Martin, J. 1984. *An Information System Manifesto.* Englewood Cliffs, N.J.: Prentice-Hall.

Matheron, J.-P. 1987. *Approfondir MERISE*, vol. 1, Paris: Eyrolles.

Meyer, M. H., and K. Foley Curley. 1991. "Putting Expert Systems Technology to Work." *Sloan Management Review* 32 (2):21–31.

Ministry of Research and Industry. 1982. *RACINES: schéma directeur de l'informatique*, 2d ed. Paris: La documentation française.

Montreal. 1989. *Plan stratégique bureautique.* Service de l'approvisionnement et des immeubles, Ville de Montréal.

National Archives of Canada. 1990. *Annual Report 1989–1990.* Ottawa: Minister of Supply and Services Canada.

Nolan, R. L. 1985. "A Model for Peaceful Coexistence." *PC World* 3 (9):202–204.

OECD. 1992. *Information Technology Outlook 1992.* Paris: Organization for Economic Cooperation and Development.

Office of the Federal Register. 1990. *The United States Government Manual 1990/91.* Washington, D.C.: National Archives and Records Administration.

Office of Management and Budget. 1991. *Current Information Technology Resource Requirements of the Federal Government: Fiscal Year 1992.* Washington, D.C.: Superintendent of Documents, U.S. Government Printing Office.

———. 1992. *Managing Federal Information Resources. Ninth Annual Report Under the Paperwork Reduction Act of 1980.* Washington, D.C.: U.S. Government Printing Office.

Orr, K. T. 1977. *Structured Systems Development.* New York: Yourdon Press.

Privacy Commissioner of Canada. 1991. *Privacy Commissioner Annual Report 1990–1991.* Ottawa: Minister of Supply and Services Canada.

Publications du Québec. 1991. *Commission d'accès à l'information. Rapport annuel 1990–1991.* Quebec.

Rockart, J. F. 1982. "The Changing Role of the Information Systems Executive: A Critical Success Factors Perspective." *Sloan Management Review* 24 (1):3–13.

Ross, D. T., and K. E. Schoman, Jr. 1977. "Structured Analysis for Requirements Definition." *IEEE Transactions on Software Engineering* SE-3 (1):6–15.

Simon, H. A. 1977. *The New Science of Management Decision,* 3d ed. Englewood Cliffs, N.J.: Prentice-Hall.

Snellen, I. Th. M. 1991. "Expert Systems in Public Administration." *Informatization and the Public Sector* 1 (1):75–81.

Teichroew, D., and E. A. Hershey. 1977. "PSL/PSA: A Computer-Aided Technique for Structured Documentation and Analysis of Information Processing Systems." *IEEE Transactions on Software Engineering* SE-3 (1):41–48.

Théoret, A., and S. Gadbois. 1991. "Bilan des systèmes experts au Québec." *ICO Québec* 3 (2):13–18.

Treasury Board of Canada. 1991. "Information Management." In *Information and Administrative Management.* Ottawa: Minister of Supply and Services Canada.

Treasury Board of Quebec. 1988. "Concernant certaines modalités d'application de la politique concernant le developpement des systèmes informatisés de gestion." In *Répertoire des politiques administratives.* Quebec.

Vroom, V. H., and A. G. Jago. 1988. *The New Leadership. Managing Participation in Organizations.* Englewood Cliffs, N.J.: Prentice-Hall.

Warnier, J.-D. 1976. *Logical Construction of Programs,* 3d ed. New York: Van Nostrand Reinhold.

Willcocks, L. 1991. "Informatization in Public Administration and Services in the United Kingdom: Toward a Management Era?" *Informatization and the Public Sector* 1 (3):189–211.

Yourdon, E. 1989. *Modern Structured Analysis.* Englewood Cliffs, N.J.: Prentice-Hall.

17

Comparative Industrial Policy

Roy W. Shin

In response to severe budget deficits and declining competitiveness of industries in many parts of the world, a heated debate has raged over what role, if any, governments should play in improving the international competitiveness of their nation's industries. The development and implementation of sound industrial polices by government and business should enable industries to improve their competitiveness in world markets, markets that are growing as the global economy continues to open up. In studying industrial policy, it is important to look at the policies as they occur within countries and the effect the policies have across national boundaries. Within a country, industrial policies can affect all aspects of business and industry, in both positive and negative ways. Because the global economy is becoming more interdependent across national boundaries, policy strategies adopted in one country often have important impacts on policy-making in other countries. Comparing different ways of coping with similar problems can give guidance on what to do and what not to do (Heidenheimer et al. 1990, 2).

Presidents Clinton, Bush, and Reagan in the United States and Prime Ministers Major and Thatcher in the United Kingdom have tried different approaches to their respective economic and industrial problems but have enjoyed very little success in changing the tide. Germany, Japan, and Korea, on the other hand, have been much more successful in competing in the global economy. The industrial policies adopted by an individual country have greatly influenced the success or failure of the country's industries in the worldwide marketplace.

In order to understand how government decisions such as industrial policy are developed, the interactions between the government and its bureaucracies and business interest groups must be examined. The structure and operation of the interactions are culture-bound and are tied to the country's institutions and history. Thus, the resulting industrial policy developed by a nation is also related to its institutional and cultural setting. Japan, as a more traditional and closed society with a close working relationship between government and industry, has developed organized industrial policies that strongly benefit business. The United States, conversely, has a more open society with looser ties between government and industry and has less cohesive industrial policies. It is important to realize that the success of a policy is dependent on the context in which it was developed. The culture of a specific country with its own political and institutional regimes can determine the outcomes of interactions between government and industry.

The success of an industrial policy is less dependent on the political structure of a nation than it is on the overall institutional and sociocultural makeup of the country. Countries with the same political arrangement may not have similar approaches to and resolution of public policy problems. For example, Germany and the United States are both federal states, but Germany has well-directed and planned industrial policies while the United States does not. As is the case with Japan and the United States discussed above, the political structure of the country is less important than the interactions between government and industry and the institutional and sociocultural setting in which the policy decisions are made.

We will illustrate the presence of policy networks between government, industry, and institutions in the making of industrial policy.

Even though the policies that a nation implements are culture-bound, certain policy features and problems are common across national boundaries. While this study focuses on a comparative analysis of the development and operation of industrial policy in the United States and Sweden, we will also look at ways in which some of the world's industrial countries have coped with problems of industrial economic development and will identify common features of successful industrial transformation.

THE POLICY NETWORK SETTING

We often cite France, Germany, Japan, and Korea as examples of countries in which close business-government relations have enabled a number of their industries to improve and successfully compete in the global economy. The United States and Sweden have also pursued industrial policies to improve international competitiveness. The key factor for any nation in improving economic competitiveness for the global marketplace might be how to combine various policy measures into a concerted program for building an industrial structure that enables the country to compete internationally.

The United States

What makes America distinctive is not so much the effect of its public policies on business as the way in which they are made. There are a number of characteristics. First, the range of policy instruments available to the American government to shape the structure of the American economy is different from those in other capitalist polities. The pattern of government assistance to industry in the United States is often characterized as an irrational array of subsidies, tax policies, price-support programs, and loan guarantees, bearing no relationship to any coherent set of objectives. These measures are isolated, makeshift devices to deal with microeconomic problems and are not part of a comprehensive government plan or a unified course of action. Second, it can be argued that the business community, like all other interest groups in American society, remains politically fragmented. The dynamics of a pluralistic society are such that the number and configuration of participants change from time to time. Therefore, it is rather difficult to identify permanent power centers within configurations in the United States that are similar to the iron triangles (government, unions, and industrial associations) found in Sweden that have considerable influence on the agenda of political choice and the conduct of policy making (Heclo and Madsen 1987, 44).

A textbook case of American industrial policy and the close relationship between business and government in the United States is agriculture. For some time agriculture has been America's largest and most successful industry in terms of assets, productivity, and export values. Yet only 50 years ago farming was a highly fragmented industry that kept most farmers at a subsistence income (Lawrence and Dyer 1983, 119). The role played by the American government in this transformation was a decisive one.

In concert with the major thrust of the New Deal's agricultural policy, the U.S. government established an elaborate system of price supports and output controls for agricultural products. By shielding farmers from the instability of fluctuating prices, the government made it possible for them to invest in expensive farm machinery, fertilizers, and pesticides and to benefit from the scientific knowledge disseminated by the state-supported land grant institutions (Vogel 1987, 98). These efforts were expanded during the 1950s, when the Foreign Agricultural Service was established within the Department of Agriculture to help domestic producers respond to overseas market opportunities (Lawrence and Dyer 1983, 119). Moreover, the American government established a special set of financial institutions, for example, the Federal Farm Board, Farm Credit Administration, and Commodity Credit Corporation, that were empowered to assist cooperatives and farmers monetarily. With this type of action, the federal government demonstrated its ability to redirect the flow of capital to a needy industry.

The most important focus of sectoral intervention by the American government can be observed in the area of defense and space. The federal government has played a critical role in developing the aerospace, computer, and semiconductor industries as well as communication satellite technology. The most obvious impact of this example of America's concerted industrial strategy is evident in record sales of $140 billion in 1991 for the U.S. aerospace industry. As always, aerospace substantially boosted the U.S. trade account with a projected surplus of $30 billion in 1991 *(National Journal* 12/21/91, 3083). The government's current initiatives in industrial policy are not exclusively limited to defense and space-related industries.

The United States has also been able to respond to emerging industries, now beginning to become commercially viable, through its biotechnology programs.

But what of the capacity of the American government to resist the demands of declining or noncompetitive sectors for assistance? Direct government subsidy to sunset industries is less common in the United States than in European countries. But the positive relationships between the U.S. government and the successful agriculture and defense industries suggest that the development of strategies designed to improve the competitiveness of other sectors is not beyond the capacity of the American political system (Vogel 1987, 103–104).

Sweden

The political logic of Sweden stands in contrast to the decentralized, dispersed power centers and largely adversarial pluralism of the United States. The Swedish system arranges things in such a manner that results can be achieved only if participants play their clearly established roles in group settings (Heclo and Madsen 1987, 21). What distinguishes the Swedish system is the extent to which interest groups and professional associations are generally regarded as the necessary and sufficient building blocks for national policy-making. The world of Swedish policy-making is a cozy realm where structured consultation takes place (Wilson 1985, 104–105). Within the system, there is encouragement for cooperation between participants rather than confrontation.

Extremely well-organized labor and business groups engage in ongoing negotiations to hammer out important public policy issues. Schmitter and Lehmbruch (1980) point out that the Parliament in Sweden more or less acts to ratify the "tripartite" accord between government, labor, and business regarding the main contours of economic and social policy. The Swedish government encourages integrated participation in public policy-making for it is believed that the corporatist representation will give workers, businessmen, and entrepreneurs enough power not to be exploited by dominating producers (Wilson 1985, 107). The corporatist policy-making model is predicated on the assumptions that the market structure emphasizes the power of producers over that of workers, and thus, the "structured consultation" framework is necessary to enable industry-labor negotiations (Anheier and Seibel 1990, 88). However, there is essentially a two-actor struggle in Sweden— between labor and their political allies in the electoral/parliamentary arenas on one side and business employers/industrialists on the other. In this context of the "neocorporatist" policy-making process, industrial policy is nothing more than an instrument in a government's buying of votes and of politically viable compromises. The dynamics of Swedish politics are such that each policy initiative underscores the biased nature of corporatist thinking (Heclo and Madsen 1987, 318). For example, wage earner funds and work place codetermination policies were insti-tuted despite the sustained opposition of employer groups (Heclo and Madsen 1987, 315).

Social policy constructed on the corporatist policy-making model tends to create and maintain privilege and benefit. These entitlements are particularly hard to combat because the participants strive to protect and defend the bargains they negotiated among themselves. They have also spawned an excessive bureaucracy for administration. Costs in the Swedish public sector, including transfer payments, are about two thirds of the country's GNP. Sweden produces about as much as it did in 1974 but consumes much more (Ekman 1982, 20). Yet readjustments are difficult to accomplish because Swedish polity permits interest-group collusion under the aegis of the state. The challenge of industrial policy for Sweden is how to bring about structural industrial change based on rational economic efficiency, without alienating the political coalition.

THE PROBLEM OF INDUSTRIAL ADJUSTMENTS

All countries today follow various industrial policies, with differing degrees of success. One policy that has been established by most countries is in the area of industrial adjustments. France, Germany, Japan, and Korea have been skilled in the industrial policy of supporting and rescuing outmoded, collapsing companies and industries, technologies that are not competitive. The United States and Sweden, on the other hand, have not had as much success in assisting struggling companies to compete domestically and globally (Ekman 1982, 14).

Sweden

Sweden has long had a relatively small, open economy highly dependent on foreign trade and its economic growth to underwrite the high levels of employment and egalitarian social welfare programs in the country. Herein lay the rationale for Sweden's economic policy consensus. The industrial policy that encouraged structural mobility in the Swedish economy was "promobility" policies which were designed to cushion the effects of industrial rationalization. Notable among them was an active labor market policy with a set of programs to retrain workers and to establish incentives for people to migrate from less developed northern areas to more industrialized regions of the country.

Throughout the postwar period, a social democratic vision of Sweden was consistent with rapid economic growth. Beginning in the 1970s the country's comparative advantage started to erode. As a nation dependent on foreign trade and imported oil, Sweden could not escape the deteriorating international economic situation. The spillover effects of the global economic condition further deteriorated the domestic economic circumstances with budget deficits, thus resulting in foreign borrowing during much of the 1970s and 1980s (Heclo and Madsen 1987). Both the Social Democratic party and nonsocialist governments of the 1970s mounted an industry program targeting "sunrise" industries with heavy R&D subsidies. A state-owned bank was created to provide more venture capital for the nascent "high-tech" industries that would keep Sweden competitive in the future global marketplace. In light of a growing decentralization trend within the country, Sweden's attempt to implement an industrial policy to nurture future industries has met with mixed results (Krauss and Pierre 1992).

The problem of the automotive industry is a good example, with many built-in conflicts. The automotive industry represents one of Sweden's most important export earners. This industry's growth has been predicated on the home market being a cornerstone for both Volvo and Saab (Ekman 1982, 19). During the oil crisis in the mid-1970s car exports equaled oil imports in value. High quality, durability, safety and comfort, as well as environmentally acceptable engines, were guiding features for the Swedish car manufacturers. All of these benefits, though, cost more, and the effect of the higher production costs makes a striking example of the conflict between corporate strategy and state intervention. Marketplace logic dictates that within the company, strategy and structure must be shaped and adapted to competitive conditions. For example, Volvo as a group has to have a structure and business mix that spreads risks, that can tolerate fluctuation in the world economy, and that can effectively compete for capital and talents to maintain its growth.

The United States

The United States has an arsenal of microeconomic policies. These consist of various protectionist measures (i.e., tariffs and quotas); tax policies; price support programs and subsidies; and financial assistance in the forms of loan guarantees, low interest loans, export financing, and total bailouts of failing companies. These measures are isolated, makeshift devices to deal with microeconomic problems, but they are not substitutes for a comprehensive policy and a coherent course of action. Without a unified set of nationwide strategies, lose-lose situations arise.

An anti-dumping case in 1991 illustrates the nature of the interdependent economy in America and how no-win situations can come about. A computer screen maker called Planar System Inc. lodged a complaint against Japanese screen imports under the anti-dumping law. When the alleged complaint was sustained, Japanese imports were curbed with a tough anti-dumping measure of 62 percent import duties. However, what was good for Planar System has hurt other American computer giants like IBM and Apple as the source of their inexpensive supply was hit, and the supply shortage of screens interrupted their production schedule. Apple Computer Inc. has now set up a screen production plant in Ireland in order to meet its needs. This represents a classical case of a "lose-lose" situation.

The American government has yielded to the demands of a number of noncompetitive sectors for protection from foreign producers in such industries as steel, textiles, shoes, semiconductors, and automobiles. For the most part, the intervention of the American government has been limited to restricting imports and manipulating tax codes. While these policies have raised prices for American consumers, both employment and investment in domestic steel, textiles, and automobile production have continued to decline (Vogel 1987, 105).

The significance of U.S. policy responses to various industry interest groups must be placed in perspective, as some of the policy measures have not succeeded. The steel and automotive industries illustrate how the policy of protectionism has failed to benefit U.S. businesses. Under the guise of anti-dumping and trigger-price mechanisms, the United States has protected the American steel industry. When the industry failed to innovate and reduce its costs, markets naturally went to more efficient producers abroad. In the case of the U.S. auto industry, the American automakers lived off the largesse of the 1980s. More than a trillion dollars went into mergers and acquisitions during that decade—money that could have been better invested in equipment and people, as was done in Germany and Japan. The U.S. auto industry went for short-term interests, rather than long-run. Short-term concern for profits, jobs, and living standards is the enemy of long-term social and economic security. In contrast, Germany and Japan have instituted programs of worker adjustment assistance. Both governments provides programs of loans and subsidies that are designed to induce the least competitive firms to exit from the declining industry and to shift resources into growing industries. Japan provides workers with adjustment assistance for job training when they become unemployed due to the industrial dislocation. Germany has a similar program that provides displaced workers with vouchers than can be cased by firms that agree to employ them (Reich 1982, 864).

Are imports the cause or merely the manifestation of a structural malaise in some U.S. industries? Regardless of the different perspectives on the question, it should be obvious that there is a need to promote a structural transformation of industry where necessary. The policies of the federal government toward the declining basic steel industry and the Planar System episode exemplify the costs of responding to crisis with no coherent plan. The implication of this piecemeal, uncoordinated approach well demonstrates both the weakness of the American government and the strength of a pluralistic society.

What is needed in the United States is a comprehensive industrial policy which encompasses a coherent, long-run national strategy. The American government can borrow ideas and strategies from its successful "industrial" policies for agriculture, defense, and aerospace and extend them to other, equally important, industrial sectors.

INDUSTRIAL STRATEGIES: A COMPARATIVE PERSPECTIVE

The question central to the industrial policy debate in the United States and Sweden is what to do about lagging basic and manufacturing industries, and how to reverse their loss of international competitiveness. To deal with this problem, some would argue that these industries should be protected from unfair trade practices and injurious imports. Furthermore, an industrial policy would provide guidance and support to the lagging business sectors in order to modernize and make them competitive.

Japan and other Asian countries have clearly advanced their industrial interests by adopting a coherent plan and pursuing a national strategy in which government acts in concert with business to promote certain industries (Lodge 1990, 5). It is debatable whether or not the U.S. government can forge such a national strategy for industrial change. First, the political ideology that believes in limited government holds that power should be dispersed and its authority should be checked. Out of this American tradition grew values encouraging individualism and refusal to bow before the government (Kelman 1981, 119). Second, dispersed power centers (e.g., decentralization and separation of powers) fragment policy-making. The combination of these forces makes the American government vulnerable to interest group pressure and makes the adoption of a coherent and consistent set of policies toward industry difficult. Lodge (1987, 126) argues that by focusing on long-term goals, the nation could better identify those issues that could be best addressed on local or regional levels and those that require a federal approach.

As for Sweden, Kelman (1981, 119) suggests that dominant values in Sweden encourage individuals to defer to the wishes of government and encourage leaders to be self-confident in charting a course of governance. In light of this, the principal policy question should be how to change the course or agenda. The "managed pluralism" approach to policy-making provides stability by allowing built-in structured consultation, but stability is obtained ultimately at the expense of Swedish productive sectors. So-called "managed pluralism" seems to suffer from a theoretical flaw based on the precepts of what Theodore Lowi 1979) calls "interest-group liberalism"—the belief that the public interest will be best served when the power to make policy is parceled out to organized interest groups. It presumes bargaining and consultation between the iron triangle—the government (the Social Democratic party or nonsocialists), LO (the blue-collar union federation) and TCO (the white-collar federation), and SAF (Swedish Employers Federation)—will not only define society's best collective interest but also safeguard the general interest of a nation.

The Swedish model suggests, however, that power coalesces rather than countervails. The problem is that the Swedish model of corporatism entails a status quo orientation that does not account for the strategic calculations of the country (Heclo and Madsen 1987, 316). As the blueprint for industrial policy, Sweden must place a high priority on substantive policies designed to strengthen the productive/supply capabilities of the economy, rather than on distributive and redistributive policies. It will require bold leadership and a new compact between the tripartite relationships.

THE ROLE OF OTHER NATIONS

As a result of the economic problems of the last decade in some industrialized countries, the strategic issues of industrial policy have become salient. They have centered around two basic propositions. One is concern over the question of deindustrialization. The other is that some countries such as Germany, Japan, and Korea, have developed governmental policies that effectively promote industrial growth (Schultze 1985). These two propositions are the explicit premises on which advocates of industrial policy rest their case.

There are also two implicit premises. The first is that the government has the capability to determine what industrial structure is appropriate and can pick potential winners and losers. The second is that any government can make such critical choices on the basis of economic criteria rather than political pressure.

Despite the fact that many nations have pursued an industrial policy of one sort or another, the relative degree of state intervention has varied from "strong" for such countries as Japan, Korea, France, and Germany to "weak" for Great Britain and the United States. In contrast with the relatively poor performance of Britain, France, and the United States in their respective economies, Germany, Japan, and Korea have achieved economic success.

The difference between "weak" and "strong" countries can be seen in Great Britain and France. Great Britain has a centralized bureaucracy and considerable resources which can be deployed in pursuit of a particular strategy, as Prime Minister Thatcher's experience in her privatization drive demonstrated. On the other hand, some European countries like France, where large sectors of the economy are publicly owned, have given large subsidies and financial assistance to business. In an attempt to infuse more money into the financially strapped Thomson (MNC) Consumer Electronics Division of Thomson of France, the French government has recently restructured a new high-technology group consisting of four Thomson companies with the French government being the primary shareholder (*The Wall Street Journal* 11/16/91). With combined revenues of $17 billion, the new group, dubbed Thomson CEA Industries, will provide a long-term and durable financial structure that can support R&D programs in emerging technologies.

What are we to make of all this? The strategies of industrial policy can be properly assessed only in a political/economic context, considering the dynamics of a labor-industry-government complex and institutional linkages to successful implementation of the policy. In "success" countries, industrial policy identifies national goals and resources. There also is interplay and exchange of information among government, industry, and financial institutions. Three key features characterize "success" countries. First, there appears to be a commitment to action in the national interest which transcends the interests of individuals or particular groups. The government seems to enjoy a greater capability to deal with problems of industrial transformation or adjustment through a pattern of elite collaboration between the state, industry, labor, and financial communities. The importance of this orientation is that it allows the state to facilitate action which promotes the achievement of long-term, national goals.

Second, there is a tight relationship between government, business, and financial organizations, and this relationship is used to promote industrial policies. Through financial intermediaries in Japan and Korea where government can intervene in credit allocation, the state has pursued the objectives of industrial policy by channeling the flow of investment toward targeted firms and industries. In Germany, government industries such as Deutsche Bundesbahn and Deutsche Bundespost have been utilized as vehicles for public purchasing policies which have served the interest of German firms. Moreover, when the German government has intervened, it has been to support reorganization strategies, rather than to underwrite a bailout of policies that have failed (Streeck 1984, 64–65).

At the industry level, the role of banks becomes much clearer. Close ties between banks and firms are seen as essential to the successful working of the economic strategy. The most important elements of this relationship are that banks maintain substantial shareholdings in major industrial firms, particularly through the mechanism of proxy shareholdings, and the presence of bank representatives on the governing boards of firms (Grant et al. 1987, 40). The Korean government has generally used its quite extensive shareholdings in "specialized" banks (e.g., agricultural, development, and industrial) to influence their policies since its majority shareholdings have given it an important source of leverage over capital allocation. The commercial banks and industry are also enmeshed with one another in Germany, and on occasion, the banks have mounted rescue operations. For example, in 1979 the banks pumped 930 million DM into the ailing electrical giant, AEG Telefunken, and rescheduled its debts (Grant et al. 1987, 40).

Third, there is a uniqueness to industrial relations in the "success" countries. Labor unions, business, and professional associations function as "efficient agents of interest aggregation" that have supported export expansion. They seem to assume the functions of private governments regulating their constituents on behalf and in lieu of the state in pursuit of the country's economic growth (Katzenstein 1978, 202).

It may be observed that all countries' institutions carry the imprint of their historical past and reflect political ideologies of their own. Policies and policy-making networks in the industrial sector seem most successful in those countries in which business and labor have departed from the familiar role of special interest group and instead have cooperated on policy formulation and execution. In essence, industrial policy must be conceived from a long-range macro perspective based on a society's desire to control and adjust the conditions of commerce and industry in the best interests of its citizenry at large.

REFERENCES

Anheier, H. K., and W. Seibel, eds. 1990. *The Third Sector: Comparative Studies of Nonprofit Organizations*. Berlin: Walter de Gruyter & Co.

Donges, J. 1980. "Industrial Policies in West Germany's Not So Market-Oriented Economy." *World Economy* 3:185–202.

Ekman, B. 1982. *Thoughts on Industrial Policy and Corporate Strategy: The Swedish Case*. New York: Aspen Institute.

Grant, W., W. Paterson, and C. Whitston. 1987. "Government-Industry Relations in the Chemical Industry: An Anglo-German Comparison." In *Comparative Government-Industry Relations*. Oxford: Clarendon Press.

Heclo, H., and H. Madsen. 1987. *Policy and Politics in Sweden*. Philadelphia: Temple University Press.

Heidenheimer, A. J., H. Heclo, and C. T. Adams. 1990. *Comparative Public Policy*. New York: St. Martin Press.

Katzenstein, P. J., ed. 1978. *Between Power and Plenty: Foreign Economic Policies of Advanced Industrial States*. Cambridge, Mass.: Harvard University Press.

Kelman, S. 1981. *Regulating American, Regulating Sweden: A Comparative Study of Occupational Safety and Health Policy*. Cambridge, Mass.: MIT Press.

Krauss, E. S., and J. Pierre. 1992. "Targeting Resources for Industrial Change." In *Do Institutions Matter: Comparing Capabilities in the U.S. and Abroad*, ed. B. A. Rockman and R. K. Weaver. Washington, D.C.: The Brookings Institution.

Lawrence, P., and D. Dyer. 1983. *Renewing American Industry*. New York: The Free Press.

Lodge, G.C. 1990. *Comparative Business-Government Relations*. Englewood Cliffs, N.J.: Prentice Hall.

Lodge, G. C., and Z. F. Vogel, eds. 1987. *Ideology and National Competitiveness*. Boston: Harvard Business School Press.

Lowi, T. J. 1979. *The End of Liberalism*. New York: W. W. Norton.

National Journal, 12/21/91.

Reich, R. 1982. "Making Industrial Policy." *Foreign Affairs* 62:852–881.

Schmitter, P. C., and G. Lehmbruch, eds. 1980. *Trends Toward Corporatist Intermediation*. Beverly Hills, Cal.: Sage.

Schultze, C. L. 1985. "Industrial Policy: A Dissent." *Policy Studies Review* Annual 7:143–162.

Streeck, W. R. 1984. *Industrial Relations in West Germany*. London: Heinemann.

Vogel, D. 1987. "Government-Industry Relations in the United States: An Overview." In *Comparative Government-Industry Relations*, ed. S. Wilks and M. Wright. Oxford: Clarendon Press.

The Wall Street Journal, 11/16/91.

Wilks, S., and M. Wright, eds. 1987. *Comparative Government-Industry Relations*. Oxford: Clarendon Press.

Wilson, G. K. 1985. *Business and Politics*. Chatham, N.J.: Chatham House.

18

Privatization: A Comparative Focus

Donald E. Fuller

PRIVATIZATION AND PUBLIC CHOICE

Privatization has descended upon the United States and other societies in answer to a number of ills. In the United States, collective bargaining, weighty pension requirements, and declining revenues prompt continuing review of privatization opportunities. Abroad, particularly in Eastern Europe and the People's Republic of China (PRC), privatization possesses "religions" qualities, becoming the current orthodoxy. Economic tribulations notwithstanding, it is important to examine theoretical premises on which privatization is, or might be, based. Second, privatization results suggest differing outcomes. Attributing unrestrained optimism toward privatization seems misplaced without examining comparative outcomes. Pressure may develop for revisionist or even reactionary public policies should privatization outcomes not match expectations.

The ascendancy of economic theory applied to public policy emerged significantly in the "public choice" literature. Public choice applies economic analysis to the political market. It postulates that individuals are the basic decision-making units acting through governments, parties, and legislatures, and that individuals are guided by self-interest (Johnson 1991, 12). Operationally, public choice seeks to examine to what extent "public" functions may be arranged with substantial private responsibility or retained by public bodies. Within this mix, activities may be competitive or noncompetitive (electricity, perhaps), regulated or nonregulated (utilities, in general), profit or nonprofit (a public defenders' group, for example), partially private and partially public (many of the European airlines), and totally or partially civilianized (police often use civilians as dispatchers and in other nonsworn functions).

The following figure shows the dimensions of financing and delivery for both the public and private sectors (Donahue 1989, 7):

	Collective Payment	*Individual Payment*
Public Sector Delivery		
Private Sector Delivery		

The sectors may be identified as follows:

Private Sector Delivery/Individual Payment: private economy in which government enforces contracts and otherwise regulates, monitors, and certifies private exchange;

Public Sector Delivery/Private Financing: sale of services such as the U.S. Post Office; admission fees at national parks;

Private Sector Delivery/Collective Payment: U.S. defense weapons, police patrol cars, consultants, other government procurement;

Public Sector Delivery/Collective Payment: traditional public functions such as police, fire, and military forces.

Public choice examines factors such as transaction costs, economies of scale, and marginal utilities in assessing the appropriate arrangement for "public functions" (Johnson 1991, 26–31). It may find an appropriate medium for both private and public institutions as in U.S. higher education. The United States permits public and private educational institutions utilizing competition among both sectors to control costs while balancing the state's interest in providing affordable public education. Thus, educational institutions compete, to some extent, not only to control costs but to reduce the monopolistic tendency of public institutions possessing a comparative financing advantage. Governments control expenses in public educational institutions and limit enrollments, thus regulating or controlling the comparative advantage. With declining public revenues, governments may need to increase costs (tuition to students) or reduce inputs (Ferris 1991, 93–108).

Governments employ regulation to reduce monopolistic practices in the public sector while fostering competition in the private sector. Regulatory strategies seek to increase efficiency among both public and private institutions. This comparison may be observed in the following figures:

	Regulated	*Deregulated*
Public		
Private		

	Competitive	*Noncompetitive*
Public		
Private		

A public utility might well be regulated and noncompetitive since a monopoly in gas and electricity may seem desirable for engineering purposes and to prevent multiple transmission lines disfiguring the landscape. To the contrary, U.S. telephone service now utilizes multiple transmission lines and sharing of lines in the interest of spurring competition and presumed efficiency and effectiveness.

Deregulated airlines may foster competition in ways similar to dual national airlines although most countries do not permit their *public* airlines to compete on the same routes. More likely, a country such as Australia might permit a public and private airline to compete, on different routes, to test the hypothesis that one is more efficient than the other, assuming some equality of routes. Other comparisons among private and public activities might include trash collection, defense support services, transportation, railroads, water and power utilities, and electricity (Donahue 1989, 58–77).

Various options exist for financing such operations, which might include direct public funding, private contracting, private franchising, and private competition (Donahue 1989, 62). Donahue provides this comparison utilizing a study by Savas (1977). Savas found that the private contract yielded the lowest cost per ton among the four alternatives.

Policy objectives of privatization may be examined in Domberger and Piggott (1986, 155).

BALANCING EFFICIENCY AND EFFECTIVENESS

Economic calculations may or may not totally determine final arrangement of public functions. Political factors may predominate (governmental tobacco monopoly in France); organizational resistance may obstruct the choice (law enforcement is often reluctant to yield positions to civilians since fewer positions would remain for assignment of injured, "burned out," or other sworn officers unable or unwilling to patrol the streets). Temptation may exist for contracting public functions out in order to relieve public pension systems and/or union intransigence. Unions typically oppose such contracting out.

Governments pursue goals with strategies that address public policies (providing access to education, providing safe streets, producing electricity and gas, providing air travel and others). Governments seek to balance the provision of a legitimate state interest against the opportunity to shift the cost of such services to users, thereby reducing net costs, which in turn permits allocation of revenues to other public purposes. Governments employ mechanisms such as competition and regulations to produce maximum return on such expenditures while maintaining desired levels of quality or effectiveness.

Relationships between the government (the principal) and those who carry out its tasks (the agent) require different arrangements for different public functions (Donahue 1989, 38). While public servants provide services for an agreed upon wage, others, seeking profit, deliver a product for a price. While nonproductive public servants may be "corrected" by their superiors, profit seekers have varying degrees of specificity guiding their behavior. Contracts may be contingent, all-encompassing, or vague. Unforeseen contingencies create problems (Donahue 1989, 43–45).

Comparing efficiency and effectiveness of public servants and private, profit seekers may create measurement problems. It is often assumed that the profit seeker who provides the same service at a lower cost than the public servant must be more productive. It may or may not be. Costs may ultimately be incurred by the government should it be determined that a privatized function may create partial governmental accountability.

Public functions often create perplexing questions of *accountability*. Traditionally, assumptions have placed police, fire, and military within *public* accountability. Despite civilianizing certain police functions, few have suggested that sworn officers, who may restrict one's liberty and, in special circumstances, may be forced to take a citizen's life, should be privatized (private security officers are, of course, increasing, yet they basically must make citizen arrests within narrow circumstances).

"Private" prisons raise questions of ultimate public accountability. Should an inmate escape and engage in murder and mayhem is the government ultimately accountable? Are private employees in private prisons barred from seeking benefits and working conditions as well as employment rights comparable to public employees? Should employees in public versus private hospitals be treated differently?

LABOR MARKET FLEXIBILITY

Salaries or compensation for public and private employees differ around the world. To some extent private employees often have higher wages. The PRC has tended to pay higher wages to those working in public enterprises since they are capable of generating profits resulting in revenues to the government. This is not unheard of in public corporations in Pakistan, Saudi Arabia, and elsewhere.

In the United States, public salaries are usually linked to average salaries in the private sector ("equal pay for equal work"). Presumably this reduces inherent salary differences at the margin. Naturally, certain individuals within various professions may exceed the average, for example in law and medicine.

Workers who are paid in excess of the minimum needed to keep them on the job are called "rent seekers" (Donahue 1989, 52). Such rent seeking may exist in noncompetitive labor markets. Postal employees working in a tight labor market might find difficulty in locating alternative work at the same wage level (thus, collecting rent above their utility elsewhere in the market).

Market economies, public or private, depend partially on labor market flexibility. This assumes (a) that workers are mobile and will respond to employment opportunities, and (b) that workers have the requisite skills to compete for employment opportunities. Unlike market economies, command economies have been driven by the political policy of full employment (as the Chinese say, the "iron rice bowl").

Privatization in market economies, to some extent, draws upon labor market flexibility to perform those tasks already extant in the private sector. While such skills as garbage collection, food service, custodial services, clerical services, data processing, and numerous other skills exist in private markets, astronauts, armies, police officers, and firemen must be trained by the government. Naturally, in time, certain of these personnel may obtain employment with other public agencies.

As command economies shift toward markets, the requisite skills may or may not exist. A television or computer facility located in a socialist economy may be unable to compete with Western competitors without additional training or education. Venture capitalists, particularly from the west, may employ capital intensive strategies, thus creating redundancy among workers except for the few highly skilled technicians.

Government response to labor market flexibility or rigidity creates a dichotomy between worker rights and presumed gains in efficiency achieved through privatization. As Rosenberg comments (1989, 13):

Restrictive macroeconomic policies causing high levels of unemployment undermine labor's bargaining strength and thus increase the relative bargaining power of employers. . . . Providing generous unemployment benefits and mandating high minimum wages advances labor's interests, by lessening the economic pain of unemployment and raising the floor of the wage structure.

EXAMINING EFFICIENCY FINDINGS

In examining the efficiency of public enterprises, Domberger and Piggott present a comparison of activities in which public service provision appears to be more efficient (electric utilities, hospitals, refuse collection) versus additional studies concluding that no difference existed in efficiency (railroads, insurance sales and servicing and *refuse collection*, contrary to the findings of the former studies) (Domberger and Piggott 1986, 151).

Domberger and Piggott and Donahue report a comparison of a public Australian airline (Trans Australian Airlines) and a private airline (Ansett Australian National Airways). Donahue reports an analysis by Davies (1971; 1977). Davies concludes that "the private firm, operating under the rules and customs associated with exchangeable private property rights, is more productive than the public enterprise" (Davies 1977, 226). Domberger and Piggott add findings from 12 studies of the two major domestic airlines (including Davies) and concluded, "First, both airlines are much less efficient than 'similar' North American operations. Second, the private enterprise is somewhat more efficient than the public enterprise" (1986, 153). Domberger and Piggott assert in a footnote that the lesser performance of the two airlines is "consistent with the international literature on the effects of regulation on performance" (1986, 152, n.19).

Donahue examines the literature regarding analyses of refuse collection, Pentagon support services, office cleaning, fire fighting services, transportation (the two Australian airlines and additionally, railroads in Canada and buses in the United States), and water and power utilities (1989, 58–78), then concludes:

1. The profit seeking firm is *potentially* a far superior institution for efficient production;
2. Productive potential can be tapped only under certain circumstances. *Public versus private* matters, but *competitive versus noncompetitive* usually matters more;
3. When a well-specified contract in a competitive context can enforce *accountability* (emphasis added), the presumption of superior private efficiency in delivering public services holds true;
4. Half of a market system-profit drive without meaningful specifications or competitive discipline, can be worse than none. (Donahue 1989, 78)

THE EASTERN EUROPE EXPERIMENT

As Western literature concerns itself with public choice, allocative efficiency, accountability, liability, and performance measures, policymakers in Eastern Europe have proceeded into privatization at breakneck speed. While the details may differ—Czechoslovakia may use the voucher system while the Hungarians may emphasize joint stock companies and employee stock ownership—a laboratory exists for observing substantial attempts at privatization.

If the prior analyses lend credence that competition, deregulation, and accountability are important variables and that labor market flexibility is an intervening variable, a prism may exist through which to examine Eastern Europe. Eastern Europeans appear to have calculated the benefits of privatization rather fundamentally: a one-time windfall profit to the government; the potential to attract Western investors and Western currency; and the assumption that privatizing would lead to increased efficiency.

Unlike Western democracies, Eastern enterprises were organized vertically, that is, lacking bankruptcy and anti-trust laws, publicly financed enterprises tended to produce their products without competition as a cog within COMECON, the Eastern European trading bloc. Economy of scale suggested to Socialist planners that total output would be enhanced by such vertical specialization. One anomaly was that specific parts of electronic equipment or mechanical equipment might be manufactured in one location and nowhere else. A computer, for example, might consist of various parts manufactured in various locations. With the transition to a market economy, enterprises are not experienced in integrating these components nor in integrating the use of suppliers. This is partially true since East European enterprises, now demanding Western currency, may turn toward Western suppliers or even manufacturers such as Volkswagen, to be assembled in Eastern Europe until such time as local components may be substituted (except perhaps for the engine).

Thus, Eastern European enterprises are not used to competing and may well resist the advent of competition. One model existing in Eastern Europe appears to consist of privatizing a public enterprise through a joint stock company (management and government are separated) and the prior Socialist bosses purchase the stock thus reaping the profits in a noncompetitive market or sell the stock at inflated levels.

The new "Designer Capitalism" (Stark 1992) takes many forms, described by Stark as the *Treuhandanstalt*, a strong, all-encompassing public agency that may dispose of public entities or maintain them much as in bankruptcy until such time as they may be divested; voucher schemes (Czechoslovakia); certificates (Poland); and cross-ownership (found in Hungary and involving cross-ownership by other limited liability companies, joint public enterprises, owned by the state) (Stark 1992, 3).

As is sometimes the case during periods of change, societies seek the instruments of systems without understanding the systemic force fields nor the values driving such systems. In the PRC, for example, reformers seek to establish (some day) a civil service system driven by merit. Values that drive merit systems tend to include such components as equity, equality, fairness, efficiency and effectiveness. Processes must be established to monitor progress around these values. Such talk fails to impress Chinese reformers seeking to incorporate scientific instruments which will lead to the "one best way."

Public and private markets (public, in the sense that public agencies may have to compete with others such as a city contracting with a sheriff's department to perform law enforcement services rather than create its own police department) send numerous signals to suppliers, consumers, and investors. Such signals tend to be interrelated, having evolved over time as the result of public-private trade offs, political interference, and regulatory practice. Eastern Europe may encounter serious disruptions, having inaugurated privatization in a public-private milieu characterized by labor market inflexibility, inflation, unemployment, social, political, and economic change, historical legacy of central planning, and entrenched bureaucracy (nomenklatura), a nonconvertible currency, disruptive trading relationships (e.g., the demise of Comecon and shift toward Western Europe), a paucity of local investors, and a history of authoritarian, nonrational (non-Weberian) organizations.

The Dynamics of Movement from Public to Private Provision of Services

The following factors have been identified as influencing the private-public mix:

- labor market flexibility
- accountability
- potential windfall profit to the government (or, perhaps, continuing profits as in operating an international airline)
- reducing the governmental subsidy to nonprofitable activities
- moral and political doctrine (as in the choice of *public* police, fire, and national defense).

In examining nations that are leaping toward privatization, one is struck by the significant difference between private versus public output, or contribution to GNP, shown in the market economies versus those command economies now "transforming" themselves in the market mode. Public functions are distributed unevenly across nations. Ninety-seven percent of value added in Czechoslovakia during the mid-1980s occurred in the public sector; in contrast, the following figures characterized Western Europe and the United States: France, 17 percent; Italy, 14 percent; West Germany, 11 percent; U.K., 11 percent; and the United States, 1 percent ("Business in Eastern Europe" 1991).

While the remainder of Eastern Europe resembles Czechoslovakia, the PRC has changed its mix of public and private output rather dramatically. Both Prybla (1992) and Gottschang (1992) observe that the private, nonstate, entrepreneurial segment of the PRC is rapidly expanding. Prybla observes:

In 1990, 70 percent of the country's industrial growth stemmed from private, cooperative, and foreign invested ventures, and half of China's exports were made outside the state plan. In 1978, the non-state sector accounted for 20% of China's output of manufactured goods; in 1991, it produced 50%, and this year the figure is expected to exceed that level for the first time since the early 1950's. (Prybla 1992, 264)

Markets in the west have been characterized by rather modest levels of public production with the possible exception of nationalization periods in the U.K. Consequently, the public-private relationship has emphasized private production of goods and services, operating within varying degrees of regulated or deregulated controls, influenced by laws of private property, bankruptcy, patents and copyrights, subject to anti-trust laws and varying degrees of administrative or judicial enforcement. Attempts at privatizing public functions have tended to be at the margin (again with the exception of U.K. nationalization) in which the trade-off between cost and additional revenue received has persuaded public bodies to privatize to avoid costs, whether economic or political, and in which the market produced a supplier whose proposed price cleared the transaction presumably at an acceptable public price.

In Western market-oriented nations, both labor flexibility and management innovation existed in the two sectors: public and private. The act of employees leaving government and joining the private sector, and the reverse, presumably raised the level of expertise of both while salaries remained at least mildly competitive in both sectors except for top management levels (many of whom seemed able to switch back and forth without severe economic adversity).

It is possible that Eastern Europe will not achieve singular success in privatizing, at least initially, regardless of the logic (whether public choice or windfall profits), since it lacks complex markets, a system of laws (patents, property, contracts, bankruptcy, and anti-trust), and capital, which must be invested not only at the margin (which makes contracting feasible) but for purposes of profit (if, for example, unregulated as is the current case with U.S. airlines).

The PRC represents a departure from Eastern Europe and resembles, partially, the experience of South Korea, Taiwan, Singapore, and Hong Kong. These "tigers" all benefited from massive investment from outside, open export markets (e.g., the United States), and singular political purpose bordering on "state capitalism." The PRC, benefiting from massive investment in South China through its Special Economic Zones, proximity to Hong Kong, freedom to export, and abiding overseas enthusiasm for Chinese as well as Japanese goods, represents a society attempting to achieve an economic miracle through a dominant political party (as, it would seem, the "tigers" have done), while attempting to avoid political change particularly in spheres other than commerce and trade.

At the present time, the PRC's entrepreneurial and business expertise, while not facing perhaps full market competition (because of low labor costs) has not shown any inclination toward sharing its "expertise" with state enterprises or public managers. As it continues on its present course, however, its privatization, or more accurately, its nonstate activities (permitted to remain private by the PRC government) seems likely to eschew Eastern European interest in pluralistic democracy and concentrate on the economic fruits of "bourgeois capitalism."

REFERENCES

Borensztein, Eduardo, and Peter Montiel. 1992. "When Will Eastern Europe Catch Up with the West?" *Finance and Development* 29 (3):21–29.

"Business in Eastern Europe Survey." 1991. *The Economist.* September 21–27. 1–30.

Davies, David G. 1971. "The Efficiency of Public versus Private Firms: The Case of Australia's Two Airlines." *Journal of Law and Economics* 14:149–165.

_____. 1977. "Property Rights and Economic Efficiency—The Australian Airlines Revisited." *Journal of Law and Economics* 20:223–236.

Domberger, Simon, and John Piggot. 1986. "Privatization and Public Enterprise: A Survey." *Economic Record* 177:145–162.

Donahue, John D. 1989. *The Privatization Decision.* New York: Basic Books, Inc.

Ferris, James M. 1991. "Competition and Regulation in Higher Education: A Comparison of the Netherlands and the United States." *Higher Education* 22:93–108.

Gabrisch, Hubert, and Kazimierz Laski. 1991. In *Dismantling the Command Economy in Eastern Europe*, ed. Peter Havlik. Boulder, Colo.: Westview Press.

Gottschang, Thomas R. 1992. "The Economy's Continued Growth." *Current History* September:268–272.

Johnson, David B. 1991. *Public Choice: An Introduction to the New Political Economy*. Mountain View, Cal.: Mayfield Publishing Company.

Kovacs, Janos Matyas. 1991. "From Reformation to Transformation: Limits to Liberalism in Hungarian Economic Thought." *East European Politics and Societies* 5 (1):41–72.

Ostrom, Vincent, Robert Bish, and Elinor Ostrom. 1988. *Local Government in the United States*. San Francisco: Institute for Contemporary Studies.

Prybla, Jan. 1992. "China's Economic Dynamos." *Current History* September:262–267.

Rosenberg, Samuel, ed. 1989. *The State and the Labor Market*. New York: Plenum Press.

Savas, E. S. 1977. "Policy Analysis for Local Government: Public vs. Private Refuse Collection." *Policy Analysis* 3:66, table 6.

Stark, David. 1992. "Can Designer Capitalism Work in Central and Eastern Europe?" *Transition: The Newsletter about Reforming Economies*. The World Bank 3 (5).

Thayer, Frederick C. 1991. "Privatization: Carnage, Chaos, and Corruption." In *Public Management: The Essential Readings*, ed. Steven J. Ott, Albert C. Hyde, and Jay M. Shafritz. Chicago: Lyceum Books.

Index

Contributors

ROBERT AGRANOFF is professor of public and environmental affairs at Indiana University, Bloomington, and director of the joint Ph.D. program in public policy. He specializes in intergovernmental relations and management and human services management. In 1990 he was a Fulbright lecturer in intergovernmental relations at the Fondación Ortega y Gasset in Madrid, where he continues to be associated as a lecturer and researcher. Currently he is co-editing a book in Spanish on federalism in Spain.

STEVEN H. ARNOLD is on the faculty of the School of International Service at the American University, and has served as the director of its International Development Program since 1975. He has co-authored studies for the World Bank, the Inter-American Development Bank, and the Agency for International Development. Most recently he has served as a consultant to the World Bank on the use of training to improve the performance of its operational managers.

RANDALL BAKER is a graduate of the University of Wales and holds his doctorate from the University of London. He is now professor at Indiana University's School of Public and Environmental Affairs and director of that school's international programs. He has spent long periods in Africa, the Middle East, and the Pacific. Most recently he has helped to design new public administration programs in Bolivia and in Bulgaria, where he was a Fulbright scholar in 1992.

GERALD E. CAIDEN is a native of London, England, and a graduate of the London School of Economics and Political Science. He has served on the faculties of London University, Carleton University, The Australian National University, Hebrew University, UC Berkeley, Haifa University, and currently, the University of Southern California. The author of more than 25 books and monographs, and editorial consultant to several leading journals, he has also served as a consultant to the World Bank and various branches of the United Nations.

NAOMI CAIDEN is chair and professor in the Department of Public Administration at California State University, San Bernardino. She is editor of *Public Budgeting and Finance* and has written extensively on comparative and historical aspects of public budgeting. She is co-author, with Aaron Wildavsky, of *Planning and Budgeting in Poor Countries.*

WOLFGANG DEICHSEL was born in Bonn, and holds a master's degree in law and sociology from the University of Munich and a Ph.D in law from the same institution. He is currently a defense lawyer in Munich and an assistant professor at the *Aufbau- und Kontaktstudium Kriminologie* at the University of Hamburg.

DONALD E. FULLER is director of the International Public Administration Center and Judicial Administration Program at the School of Public Administration, University of Southern California. His current research focuses on an analysis of personnel administration in the People's Republic of China, South Korea, and the Republic of China.

MARIËTTE C. S. GLIM is a graduate of Erasmus University, Rotterdam, and is now director of the Bureau voor Contract Research BV in Rotterdam. She does research on different environmental topics for a variety of organizations such as the Commission of the European Community, governmental organizations (ministries, regional and local governments, inspectorates), industry, organizations of employers, and advisory boards.

ROLLAND HURTUBISE is professor at the École Nationale d'Administration Publique at the University of Quebec. Born in Ottawa, he is a graduate of the University of Ottawa, of Laval University, and of the Canadian Navy's Fleet School in Halifax. He was formerly secretary of the Defense Research Board of Canada, is the author of over 20 books and monographs on various aspects of IRM, and is a holder of the Quebec government's Communication Prize.

EUGENE B. McGREGOR, JR., is professor of public and environmental affairs at Indiana University, Bloomington. He received an A.B. in government from Dartmouth College in 1964 and a Ph.D. in political science from the Maxwell School, Syracuse University, in 1969. McGregor is the author of 1991 book, *Strategic Management of Human Knowledge, Skills, and Abilities: Workforce Decision Making in the Post-Industrial Era.* In 1990 he was a visiting professor in the Netherlands in the Department of Public Administration, Erasmus Universiteit Rotterdam and Rijkuniversiteit Leiden. He is currently conducting research on the role of information technology in public sector organization design and management and on the connection between education and economic development.

E. PHILIP MORGAN, a veteran faculty member in the School of Public and Environmental Affairs at Indiana University, has special interests in public sector management. His research and consulting have focused on public organizational performance and institutional development in developing countries, especially in Africa where these subjects are closely interactive with development assistance. He is a former director of the university's International Development Institute. Most recently Morgan has been a co-principal investigator of a multidimensional World Bank study on Indigenous Institutions and Management Practices in Africa.

B. GUY PETERS is the Maurice Falk Professor of American Government and chair of the Department of Political Science at the University of Pittsburgh. He taught previously at Emory University in Georgia and at Tulane and Delaware Universities. He has held visiting positions in the United Kingdom, Sweden, the Netherlands, Norway, and Switzerland. He was the founding co-editor of *Governance* and has written a number of seminal texts.

FRED W. RIGGS is professor emeritus at the University of Hawaii. He was born in China and took his doctorate from Columbia University. He was later the Arthur Bentley Professor of Political Science at Indiana University. During the 1960s he chaired the Comparative Administration Group of the American Society for Public Administration. He is the author of more than a dozen books and is currently the comparative specialist on the editorial board of the *Public Administration Review*.

RICHARD W. RYAN is a professor and the coordinator of the MPA program at the Imperial Valley campus of San Diego State University. Teaching near the U.S.-Mexico border has led to his research on the increasingly internationalized role of local government administrators. He is the author of *Teaching Comparative-Development Administration at U.S. Universities*.

LARRY SCHROEDER is professor of public administration and economics in the Maxwell School, Syracuse University, and is also Senior Research Associate in its Metropolitan Studies Program. He holds a doctorate in economics from the University of Wisconsin. His research interests focus on public finance and financial management, and he has worked as a consultant for the World Bank and others principally in Asia. He is the co-author, with Elinor Ostrom, of a book on institutional incentives and sustainable development.

ROY W. SHIN is professor at the School of Public and Environmental Affairs, Indiana University, Bloomington. His fields of specialization include comparative public policy and management. His current research interests focus on the transboundary industrial location decisions of multinational corporations and the broader field of comparative industrial policy.

PAUL SOLANO is a political economist and associate professor in the College of Urban Affairs and Public Policy at the University of Delaware. He holds a Ph.D. from the University of Maryland and specializes in the areas of government revenue and expenditure policies, benefit-cost analysis, municipal bonds and public budgeting.

CURTIS VENTRISS, at the time of writing, is a visiting fellow at Oxford University, England. At Oxford he is lecturing and conducting research on the European Community and the changes that will be posed by unification, especially in regard to regional policy. Professor Ventriss is the author of several books. His permanent base is at the Department of Public Administration of the University of Vermont in Burlington.

LOIS R. WISE is an associate professor at the School of Public and Environmental Affairs, Indiana University, Bloomington. Her research and teaching interests center on a broad area of employment policies with a special focus on the public sector. She has conducted specialized research into the Swedish civil service over a number of years and has written extensively on the subject.